THE PARSON IN ENGLISH LITERATURE

Edited by

F.E. CHRISTMAS

ALAN SUTTON
1983

Alan Sutton Publishing Limited
17a Brunswick Road
Gloucester GL1 1HG

Copyright © 1950 F.E. Christmas

First published in 1950 by Hodder & Stoughton
This edition first published 1983

ISBN 0-86299-107-2

Cover picture: detail from A Village Choir *by Thomas Webster. Victoria and Albert Museum, London*

Printed and bound in Great Britain
by Redwood Burn Limited, Trowbridge, Wiltshire

THE PARSON IN
ENGLISH LITERATURE

Dull though important, peevish tho' devout,
With wit disgusting, and despised without,
Saints in design, in execution men,
Peace in their looks and vengeance in their pen.

CRABBE.

And he was kind, and loved to sit
   In the low hut or garnished cottage,
And praise the farmer's homely wit,
   And share the widower's homelier pottage:
At his approach complaint grew mild
   And when his hand unbarred the shutter,
The clammy lips of fever smiled
   The welcome which they could not utter.

PRAED.

ACKNOWLEDGMENTS

THE publishers and the compiler tender their sincere thanks for permission to include copyright material to: the Literary Executors and Constable & Co. Ltd. for *The Egoist*, by George Meredith; Hodder & Stoughton Ltd. for *The Autobiography of Mark Rutherford*; Methuen & Co. Ltd. for *Old Country Life*, by S. Baring Gould; The Literary Executors of Samuel Butler and Jonathan Cape Ltd. for *The Way of All Flesh*; Miss Nancy McIntosh and Macmillan & Co. Ltd. for *The Reverend Simon Magus*, by Sir W. S. Gilbert; William Heinemann Ltd. for Sir Edmund Gosse's *Father and Son*; J. M. Dent & Sons Ltd. for Augustine Birrell's *Miscellanies* and W. H. Hudson's *Afoot in England*; Mr. Vyvyan Holland for *A Woman of No Importance* by Oscar Wilde; Mr. Bernard Shaw for *Candida*; the Literary Executors of Sir William Watson for *To a Literary Critic*; the Executors of Sir Arthur Conan Doyle and John Murray for *Through the Magic Door*; Hodder and Stoughton Ltd. for Sir James Barrie's *Auld Licht Idylls*; Mrs. G. P. Wells for *Tono Bungay* and *The Soul of a Bishop*, by H. G. Wells; Mr. Laurence Housman and Jonathan Cape Ltd. for *Victoria Regina*; Miss Collins and Hutchinson & Co. Ltd. for G. K. Chesterton's *Autobiography*; the Society of Authors, as Literary Representatives of Dr. John Masefield, O.M., for *The Everlasting Mercy*; the Literary Executors of Mary Webb and Jonathan Cape Ltd. for *Gone to Earth*; the Literary Executors of Sir Hugh Walpole for *The Cathedral*, published by Macmillan & Co. Ltd.; Chatto and Windus for *Eminent Victorians* by Lytton Strachey, and *Crome Yellow* by Aldous Huxley; Routledge and Kegan Paul Ltd., for Dr. Esme Wingfield Stratford's *Victorian Tragedy*; the Trustees of the James Joyce Estate and Jonathan Cape Ltd. for *The Dubliners*; Jonathan Cape Ltd. for *Elmer Gantry* by Sinclair Lewis; Cassell & Co. Ltd. for Ernest Raymond's *Through Literature to Life*; Mr. Howard Spring and W. Collins

Sons & Co. Ltd. for *Hard Facts*; Mr. Cedric Belfrage for *The Promised Land*; George Allen and Unwin Ltd. and Mr. Frank Ernest Hill for his *Rendering for Modern Readers of the Canterbury Tales*; Sheen and Ward Ltd. and Mr. Henry Wells for his *Modernised Version of The Vision of Piers Plowman*; St. Hugh's Press for *Close of Play* by Alan Miller; Miss Vera Brittain for *Eutychus*, by Winifred Holtby; Mr. Tyrone Guthrie for *The Flowers are not for You to Pick*; Mr. Evelyn Waugh and Chapman and Hall Ltd. for *A Handful of Dust*; Sir Osbert Sitwell for *Ultimate Judgment*, from his *Collected Poems and Satires*, published by MacMillan & Co. Ltd.

INTRODUCTION

THE large space devoted to the parson in the works of imaginative writers, particularly novelists, has no doubt been chiefly due to the fact that the parson has been socially much in evidence. Of the members of the learned professions he alone came into continuous association with the man in the street, even when the man in the street was only fitfully and reluctantly the man in the pew. People who could afford to send for the doctor only at the last gasp turned naturally to the parson in every kind of trouble. To multitudes he was a friend; and when he was regarded as an enemy the quarrel was usually of a personal kind, and not concerned with his office as such. Many people have wanted the clergy in England to be reformed. Comparatively few have wanted them to be abolished. By finding a target in the papacy, long regarded as the foremost enemy of the nation, anti-clericalism in England has heightened the social importance and sometimes the popularity of the indigenous cleric.

To-day the position has greatly changed. The physician has to a large extent supplanted the minister of religion as a trusted confident. Advice bureaux and wireless speakers offer counsel on practical matters about which in the past ministers were usually consulted. Marriages in ever-increasing numbers are celebrated at registrars' offices instead of in church, and parents are more concerned that their children should be vaccinated than christened. Like the doctor of yesterday, the cleric is now most frequently associated with the rites of death.

None the less, people continue to be interested in the parson, not least when they write to the papers explaining why the Church has ceased to interest them. For the parson stands for a qualitative interpretation of life that marks him out from other men. Lord Chesterfield would not have told his son that parsons "are very

9

like other men, and neither better nor worse for wearing a black gown" unless they were expected to be different; and the expectation has had a marked effect upon the way in which they are received, and not infrequently upon the way in which they behave in public. Sydney Smith expressed the matter wittily when he said that there are three sexes—men, women and parsons. It is the fact that the parson is a man apart, almost as much as the fact that he has been socially so much in evidence, that has fascinated imaginative writers and led them to pay him so much attention, flattering or otherwise. To trace the reaction of English writers to this figure since the days of Chaucer, when the human interest was substituted for the divine judgment of character, is to discover matter of infinite jest and most pleasing fancy, not without its serious import.

In gathering together some passages on the theme my object has not been to offer a conspectus of what every English writer has said about clerics (a purpose for which no single volume known to publishers would suffice), but to make an anthology that can be read with enjoyment. The book is the result of discursive reading, not systematic research, and makes no pretence to scholarly completeness; but it should perhaps be said that a great accumulation of material has been discarded, and the absence of some well-known study of clerical life (*Robert Elsemere* for example, or J. D. Beresford's *A Candidate for Truth*) does not necessarily mean that its claims have been ignored. A glaring omission, if an effort were being made to interrogate every great English writer about clerics, would be Shakespeare himself. But his cardinals and archbishops, his friars and parsons cannot be conveniently lifted from their context in the whole play; and Shakespeare is in this respect typical of many dramatists. Invaluable to the social historian, they are of little value to the anthologist, who must give jealous consideration to the question of space. Hence the Venerable Archdeacon Daubeny in *A Woman of No Importance* is legitimately brought in, while countless more serious and important dramatic studies of the cleric (including Wilde's own study of Canon Chasuble) have been left out. Daubeny is a very minor character, but he is brilliantly sketched, and to lift him from the context of the play in no way diminishes a crescendo of delightful extravagance, very far from being merely frivolous.

While I have been primarily concerned with literary qualities I have also been influenced in selection by a consideration of a different kind. When the material is so abundant, any choice must be bold to the point of recklessness, and nothing would be easier than to caricature what English literature has to say about the moral nature of clerics. It is only necessary to compare Goldsmith's romantic picture of the eighteenth-century village parson with Crabbe's biting etching of the same figure, or to contrast in the nineteenth century the clergymen of George Eliot and Thackeray, to know the false impression that could be given by biased selection. Casting my net fairly widely, therefore, I have tried to pull in, not only an entertaining variety, but a representative selection, and plenty of queer fish, amusing enough in themselves, have been thrown out because they would have disturbed the ethical balance. The result is totally inadequate if the reader is looking for a comprehensive range of literary specimens, but by no means unsatisfactory as an assortment of clerical types.

Literature, like history, has a way of repeating itself, although always (like history) with a difference. Sinclair Lewis's hot-gospeller, eyeing the girls and pawing his secretary, is Langland's wenching pardoner in twentieth-century American dress; just as the pardoner is the recrudescence in the twelfth century of "those who having the form of godliness creep into houses and take captive silly women," of whom the writer of the *Second Epistle to Timothy* writes. Cedric Belfrage's amusing Hollywood preacher is the Charles Honeyman of to-day, and even the Rev. Anthony Anderson in *The Devil's Disciple* is prefigured by the Rector of Briarfield in *Shirley*. In short, human types recur, and literature repeats itself because the living models of writers in every century from the first to the twentieth have a family likeness, no less than because writers, consciously or unconsciously, echo the work of their predecessors. It is not impossible, therefore, to convey a just impression of what imaginative writers have said about clerical types within the limits of a single anthology.

I use the term "imaginative writers" somewhat loosely to denote dramatists, novelist and essayists whose work is a transcript of their fantasies and ideals, as distinct from the historian and biographer whose imaginations must work within the limits imposed by actual events. It is scarcely necessary to remark that the historian and biographer require very considerable imaginative powers, and a few excerpts from both have been included, partly as a reminder that fiction is based on fact. The Calvinistic fanaticism of Scott's Hezekiah Mucklewrath had by the time of Barrie become the quaint and endearing solemnity that condemned Paper Watts. Both writers seem to be indulging in flights of the imagination, and both were keeping very close to earth. Scott was reconstructing history while Barrie was recalling his childhood. Stiggins, to take another example, is usually regarded as a wild caricature, and has even been denounced as a libel on the Nonconformist minister. He was, in fact, one of many unordained and squalidly ignorant pastors of independent Bethels that flourished in London when *The Pickwick Papers* was being written, and, except for a few rollicking touches, Dickens might have been drawing from life. Browning's *Christmas Eve and Easter Day* portrays exactly the same type; but Browning gives us a savage theological cartoon where Dickens gives us a comic and human sketch.

Where an explanation of the passages seemed necessary, I have ventured a few introductory words. But I have kept them decently brief and have resisted the temptation to offer critical judgments.

At the end of the book I have tried to assess what literature has to say about the qualities that are liked least and admired most in parsons. Generalisations upon such a theme are bound to be influenced by personal tastes, but I have been as objective as I could, carrying the discussion beyond the material in the book itself. Involving as it must ethical judgments, the subject is highly controversial, but it is not less entertaining on that account, and some readers at least may find it interesting to compare impressions.

CONTENTS

14

CHARITY HAS TURNED CHAPMAN

Piers Plowman *is valued for the information it gives about life in the*
fourteenth century, and as a satire on clerical abuses. It is primarily
a religious poem, men and women being viewed in the light of the
Divine righteousness.

PILGRIMS and palmers were plighted together
To seek Saint James and saints in Rome.
They went on their way with many wise stories,
And had leave to lie for a lifetime after.
I saw some who said that they sought for relics;
In each tale that they told their tongue would always
Speak more than was so, it seemed to my thinking.

A host of hermits with hocked staves
Went to Walsingham with their wenches behind them.
These great lubbers and long, who were loath to labour,
Clothed themselves in copes to be distinguished from others,
And robed themselves as hermits to roam at their leisure.
There I found friars of all the four orders,
Who preached to the people for the profit of their bellies,
And glossed the gospel to their own good pleasure;
They coveted their copes, and construed it to their liking.
Many master-brothers may clothe themselves to their fancy,
For their money and their merchandise multiply together.
Since charity has turned chapman to shrive lords and ladies,
Strange sights have been seen in a few short years.
Unless they and Holy Church hold closer together
The worst misery of man will mount up quickly.

There a pardoner preached as priest of the parish,
And brought out a bull with a bishop's signet,

Said that he himself might assoil all men
Of all falsehood in fasting and vows that were broken.
Common folk confided in him and liked his preaching,
And crept up on cowed knees and kissed his pardons.
He abused them with brevets and blinded their eyesight;
His devil's devices drew rings and brooches.
They gave their gold to keep gluttons,
And believed in liars and lovers of lechery.
If the bishop were blessed and worth both his ears
His seal would not be sent to deceive the people.
But the power of the bishop is not this preacher's licence,
For the parish priest and the pardoner share the profits together
Which the poor of the parish would have if these were honest.

Because parishes were poor since the pestilence season,
Parsons and parish priests petitioned the bishops
For a licence to leave and live in London
And sing there for simony, for silver is sweet.

Bishops and bachelors, both masters and doctors,
Who have cures under Christ and are crowned with the tonsure,
In sign of their service to shrive the parish,
To pray and preach and give the poor nourishment,
Lodge in London in Lent and the long year after,
Some are counting coins in the king's chamber,
Or in exchequer and chancery challenging his debts
From wards and wardmotes, waifs and strays.
Some serve as servants to lords and ladies
And sit in the seats of steward and butler.
They hear mass and matins and many of their hours
Are done without devotion. There is danger that at last
Christ in his consistory will curse many.

I pondered on the power which Peter was given
To bind and to unbind as the Book tells us.
He left it with love at our Lord's commandment
And in care of four virtues, which are fairest of all virtues,

These are called cardinal, or hinges to the gateway
Where Christ is in his kingdom; they close it to many
And open it to many others and show them heaven's glory.
Yet I dare not deny that the dignity of Peter
Is in cardinals at court who command this title
And presume on its power in the pontiff's election.
The election belongs to love and to learning.
I might but I must not speak more of their college.

> *From* THE VISION OF PIERS PLOWMAN,
> by William Langland (*c.* 1322–1400).
> (Modernised version by Henry Wells.)

2

MONK AND FRIAR

*The worldliness of prelates in the fourteenth century, when feudalism
was losing its vigour, is glaringly apparent in the pages of Chaucer.*

A MONK there was, as fair as ever was born,
An out-rider, that loved the hounds and horn,
A manly man, to be an abbot able.
Full many a blooded horse he had in stable,
And when he rode ye might his bridle hear
Jingle upon the whistling wind as clear
And loud as ever the chapel bell could ring
Where this same monk and lord was governing.
The rules of Maurice and of Benedict,
These being ancient now, and rather strict,
This monk ignored, and let them go their ways,
And laid a course by rules of newer days.
He held that text worth less than a plucked hen
Which said that hunters were not holy men,
Or that a monk who follows not the rule
Is like a fish when it is out of pool—

That is to say, a monk out of his cloister.
Indeed, he held that text not worth an oyster;
And his opinion here was good, I say.
For why go mad with studying all day,
Poring over a book in some dark cell,
And with one's hands go labouring as well,
As Austin bids? How shall the world be served?
Let Austin's work for Austin be reserved!
Therefore he hunted hard and with delight;
Greyhounds he had as swift as birds in flight;
To gallop with the hounds and hunt the hare
He made his joy, and no expense would spare.
I saw his sleeves trimmed just above the hand
With soft grey fur, the finest in the land;
And fastening his hood beneath his chin,
Wrought out of gold, he wore a curious pin—
A love-knot at the larger end there was!
His head was wholly bald and shone like glass,
As did his face, as though with ointment greased;
He was full fat and sleek, this lordly priest.
His fierce bright eyes that in his head were turning
Like flames beneath a copper cauldron burning,
His supple boots, the trappings of his steed,
Showed him a prelate fine and fair indeed!
He was not pale like some tormented ghost.
He loved a fat swan best of any roast.
His palfrey was as brown as is a berry.

There was a Friar, a wanton and a merry,
Licensed to beg—a gay, important fellow.
In all four orders no man was so mellow
With talk and dalliance. He had brought to pass
The marrying of many a buxom lass,
Paying himself the priest and the recorder:
He was a noble pillar to his order!
He was familiar too and well-beloved
By all the franklins everywhere he moved

And by good women of the town withal,
For he had special powers confessional
As he himself would let folk understand:
He had been licensed by the Pope's own hand!
Full sweetly would he listen to confession,
And very pleasantly absolved transgression;
He could give easy penance if he knew
There would be recompense in revenue;
For he that to some humble order hath given—
Is he not by that token all but shriven?
For if he gave, then of a certain, said he,
He knew the man was penitent already!
For many a man may be so hard of heart
He can not weep, though sore may be his smart;
Therefore his case no tears and prayers requires:
Let him give silver to the needy friars!
Always he kept his tippet stuffed with knives
And pins, that he could give to comely wives.
By patent and by full commission too.
For his renown and for the law he knew
He won good fees, and fine robes many a one.
Conveyancer to match him was there none:
All turned fee simple underneath his hand;
No work of his but what was made to stand.
No busier person could ye find than he,
Yet busier than he was he seemed to be;
He knew the judgments and the cases down
From the first day King William wore his crown;
And he could write, and pen a deed in law
So in his writing none could pick a flaw,
And every statute could he say by rote.
He wore a simple, vari-coloured coat,
Girt with a fine-striped sash of silken stuff:
This, as to his array, will be enough.

From THE PROLOGUE TO THE CANTERBURY TALES,
by Geoffrey Chaucer (*c.* 1340–1400). (A Rendering for Modern Readers by Frank Ernest Hill.)

3

THE FRIAR'S DREAM OF HELL

The Friar's Tale shows the corruption that had overtaken the ecclesiastical courts, which at the time of Chaucer dealt with the sins, particularly those of a sexual nature, outside the civil jurisdiction. Penances were generally commuted for cash payments, and from that, as Trevelyan says, "the step was short to blackmail of sinners in their own homes by officers of the Bishop's Court, particularly the 'summoner,' who had a most evil reputation."

The Friar's Tale reflects the contempt in which summoners were held:

> *"Art thou a bailiff? Yes quoth he.*
> *He durst not for very filth and shame*
> *Say he was a summoner, for a name."*

The Summoner, before telling his own tale, generously repays the Friar's abuse.

THE Summoner in his stirrups rises high,
Such rage and madness glittering in his eye
That like an aspen leaf he shakes for ire.
"Lordings, one thing alone do I desire;
I ask you as a courtesy," he cries,
"That since this Friar has filled you with his lies,
Ye let me tell the tale that I shall tell.
This friar hath boasted that he knoweth hell;
And God knows too that it is little wonder;
Your friars and fiends are not so far asunder.
For often times, by God, have ye heard tell
How once a friar was snatched away to hell
In spirit as he dreamed. An angel there
Led him about, and showed him everywhere
The torments that were wrought in smoke and fire.
And yet in all the place he saw no friar,
Although enough of other suffering men.
Unto this angel spoke the friar then.

"Now, sir," he asked, "have friars so large a grace
That none of them are coming to this place?"
"Yes, many a million come," said he, replying,
And led him down where Sathanas was lying.
"Satan," he told him, "hath a tail as large
As any sail that flies upon a barge.
Hold up thy tail, thou Sathanas!" said he;
"Show us thine arse, so that the friar may see
Where all the friars are nesting in this place!"
Before a man could walk a furlong's space,
As from a hive a swarm of bees comes pouring,
Out of the devil's arse there tumbled roaring
Some twenty thousand friars in a crowd,
And up and down through hell went swarming loud,
And, hurrying back as fast as they could run,
Into his arse went creeping every one.
Then down he clapped his tail, and lay there still.
This friar, when he had looked, and seen his fill
Of all the torments in that hellish hole—
God in his grace again restored his soul
Back to his body, and so he woke at last.
And yet for fear he lay and shook, aghast—
The devil's arse forever in his mind,
The natural heritage of all his kind.
God save you all now, save this curséd friar;
No more of prologue doth my tale require.

From A Rendering for Modern Readers by
Frank Ernest Hill of THE CANTERBURY TALES,
by Geoffrey Chaucer (*c.* 1340–1400).

4

JOHN BALL'S PREACHING

In the mid-fourteenth century scarcity of labour, due to the Black Death, led to a demand for higher wages by the surviving and newly emancipated villeins. Attempts by the landowners to re-establish serfdom, and a series of oppressive government measures, including fine and imprisonment for those who refused to accept the old rates of pay, started John Ball preaching social equality, and led to the peasant's revolt.

OF this imagination was a foolish priest in the County of Kent called John Ball, for the which foolish words he had been three times in the Bishop of Canterbury's prison. For this priest would often times on Sundays, after mass, when the people were going out of the minster, to go into the cloister and preach, and made the people assemble about him; and would say thus: "Ye good people, matters go not well to pass in England, nor shall not do till everything be common, and that there be no villeins nor gentlemen, but that we may be all joined together, and that the lords be no greater masters than we be. What have we deserved, or why should we be kept thus in bondage? We be all come from one father and one mother, Adam and Eve. Whereby can they say or show that they be greater lords than we be, saving that they cause us to win and labour for that they spend? They are clothed in velvet and we be vestured with poor clothes: they have their wines and spices and good bread, and we have the drawings out of chaff and drink water. They dwell in fair houses, and we have the pain and travail, rain and wind in the fields. And by that, that cometh of our labour, they keep and maintain their estates. We be called their bondmen, and without we do them service readily, we be beaten. And we have no sovereign to whom we may complain, nor that will hear us, nor do us right. Let us go to the King, he is young; and show him what servitude we be in: and show him how we will have it otherwise, or else we will provide us of some remedy. And if we go together, all manner of people that be now in any bondage will follow us, to the intent to be made free. And when the King seeth us, we shall have some remedy, either by fairness or otherwise."

Thus John Ball said on Sundays, when the people moved out of the churches in the villages. Wherefore many of the mean people loved him, and such as intended to no goodness, said how he said truth; and so they would murmur one with another in the field and in the ways as they went together: affirming how John Ball said Truth.

From FROISSART'S CHRONICLES, translated by John Bouchier, Lord Berners (1467–1532).

5

MOST DILIGENT PRELATE

THERE is one that . . . is the most diligent prelate in all England. And will ye know who it is? I will tell you! It is the Devil! Among all the pack of them that have cure, the Devil shall go for my money, for he appliest his business. Therefore, ye imprecating prelates, learn of the Devil to be diligent in your office. If ye will not learn of God, for shame learn of the Devil.

From A SERMON AT ST. PAUL'S CROSS, by Hugh Latimer (*c.* 1485–1556).

6

SIR JOHN THE PRIEST

"The Merry Play between Johan Johan the Husband, Tyb his Wife, and Sir John the Priest" *is attributed to John Heywood, a friend of Sir Thomas More, and, like More, a Catholic. He became the producer of entertainments at the Court of Henry VIII through the good offices of his friend. The Play describes the mortification of a husband whose shrewish wife is engaged in an intrigue with the priest. More than a little suspicious, the husband is momentarily reassured when the priest refuses an invitation to supper on the ground that Johan's wife dislikes him.*

SIR JOHN PRIEST: I shall tell thee now the matter plain:
She is angry with me and hath me in disdain
Because that I do her oft entice
To do some penance after mine advice,
Because she will never leave her squalling,
But alway with thee she is chiding and brawling,
And therefore I know she hateth my presence.

JOHAN: Nay in good faith saving your Reverence——

SIR JOHN: I know very well she hath me in hate.

JOHAN: Nay, I dare swear for her Master Curate.
(But was I not a very knave!
I thought surely, so God me save,
That he had loved my wife for to deceive me
And now he quitteth himself and here I see
He doth as much as he may for his life
To stint the debate between me and my wife.)

SIR JOHN: If ever she did or thought me any ill
Now I forgive her with my free will.
Therefore Johan Johan now get thee home,
And thank thy wife, and say I will not come.

JOHAN: Yet let me know now good Sir John
Where you will go to supper then.

SIR JOHN: I care not greatly and I tell thee.
On Saturday last I and two or three
Of my friends made an appointment
And against this night we did assent
That in a place we would sup together.
And one of them said he would bring thither
Ale and bread; and for my part I
Said that I would give them a pie,
And there I gave them money for the making
And another said she would pay for the baking,
And so we purpose to make good cheer
For to drive away care and thought.

JOHAN: Then I pray you, sir, tell me here
Whither should all this gear be brought.

SIR JOHN: By my faith and I should not lie
It should be delivered to thy wife, the pie.

JOHAN: By God! it is at my house standing by the fire.

SIR JOHN: Who bespake that pie I thee require?

JOHAN: By my faith I shall not lie
It was my wife and her gossip Margery,
And your good worship called Sir John,
And my neighbour's youngest daughter Ann.
Your worship paid for the stuff and making
And Margery she paid for the baking.

SIR JOHN: If thou wilt have me now in faith I will go.

JOHAN: Yea, Mary, I beseech your worship do so;
My wife tarrieth for none but us twain;
She thinketh long or I come again.

SIR JOHN: Well now if she chide me in your presence
I will be content and take in patience.

JOHAN: By God's soul! and she once chide
Or frown or lour or look aside,
I shall bring you a staff as much as I may have,
Then beat her and spare not. I give you good leave
To chastise her for her shrewish tongue.

TYB: The devil take thee for thy long tarrying:
Here is not a whit of water, by my gown,
To wash our hands that we might sit down;
Go and hie thee as fast as a snail
And with fair water fill me this pail.

JOHAN: I thank our Lord of his good grace
That I can not rest long in a place!

TYB: Go fetch water I say at a word,
For it is time the pie were on the board,
And go with a vengeance and say thou art prayed.

SIR JOHN: Aye, good gossip, is that well said!

TYB: Welcome mine own sweet heart,
We shall make some cheer or we depart.

JOHAN: God's soul: look how he approacheth near
Unto my wife. This abateth my cheer.

SIR JOHN: By God! I would ye had heard the trifles,
The toys, he mocks the fables and the tales
That I made thy husband to believe and think.
Thou mightest well into the earth sink
As thou couldest forbear laughing any while.

TYB: I pray thee let me hear part of that wile.

SIR JOHN: Mary, I shall tell thee as fast as I can;
But peace! No more! Yonder cometh thy good man.

JOHAN: God's soul, what have we here!
As far as I saw he drew very near
Unto my wife.

TYB: What! Art thou come so soon.
Give us some water to wash now.
Have done.   [*Then he bringeth the empty pail.*]

JOHAN: By God's soul it was even now full to the brink
But it was out again or I could think.
Whereof I marvelled by God almight.
And then I looked between me and the light
As I spied a cleft both large and wide:
Lo wife here it is on the one side.

TYB: Why dost not stop it?

JOHAN: Why how shall I do it?

TYB: Take a little wax.

JOHAN: How shall I come by it?

SIR JOHN: Mary, here be two wax candles I say
Which my gossip Margery gave me yesterday.

TYB: Tush! let him alone for by the rood
It is a pity to help him or do him good.

SIR JOHN: What, Johan Johan, canst thou make no shift?
Take this wax and stop therewith the cleft.

JOHAN: This wax is as hard as any wire.

TYB: Thou must chafe it a little at the fire.

JOHAN: She that brought these wax candles twain
She is a good companion certain.

TYB: What, was it not my gossip Margery?

SIR JOHN: Yea, she is a blessed woman surely.

TYB: Now would God I was as good as she,
For she is virtuous and full of charity.

JOHAN: Now so God help me and by my holydome
She is the erranst bawd between this and Rome.

TYB: What sayest?

JOHAN: Mary, I chafe the wax,
And I chafe so hard that my fingers break.
But take up this pie that I here turn;
And it stand long it will certainly burn.

TYB: Yea, but thou must chafe the wax I say.

JOHAN: Bid him sit down I thee pray:
Sit down, good Sir Johan I you require.

TYB: Go, I say, and chafe the wax by the fire
While that we sup Sir Johan and I.

JOHAN: And how now, what will ye do with the pie;
Shall I not eat thereof a morsel?

TYB: Go and chafe the wax while thou art well
And let us have no more prating thus.

SIR JOHN: Benedicte.

JOHAN: Dominus.

TYB: Now go chafe the wax with a mischief.

JOHAN: What, I come to bless the board, sweet wife.
It is my custom now and then.
Much good may it do you Master Sir Johan.

TYB: Go chafe the wax and here no longer tarry.

JOHAN: And is not this a very purgatory
To see folks eat and may not eat a bite?
By God's soul! I am a very woodcock.
This pail here now, a vengeance take it.
Now my wife giveth me a proud mock.

TYB: What dost?

JOHAN: Mary, I chafe the wax here
And I imagine to make you good cheer:
That a vengeance take ye both as ye sit,
For I know well I shall not eat a bit,
But yet in faith if I might eat one morsel
I would think the matter went very well.

SIR JOHN: Gossip Johan Johan, now much good do it you:
What cheer make you there by the fire?

JOHAN: Master Parson I thank you now,
I fare well now after mine own desire.

SIR JOHN: What dost Johan Johan I thee require?

JOHAN: I chafe wax here by the fire.

TYB: Here is good drink and here is good pie.

SIR JOHN: We fare very well, thanked be our Lady.

TYB: Look how the cuckold chafeth the wax that is hard
And for his life dareth not look hitherward.

SIR JOHN: What doth my gossip?

30

JOHAN: I chafe the wax.
And I chafe it so hard that my fingers crack,
And eke the smoke putteth out my eyes two.
I burn my face and soil my clothes also,
And yet I dare not say one word,
And they sit laughing yonder at the board.

TYB: Now by my troth it is a pretty jape
For a wife to make her husband her ape.
Look at Johan Johan which maketh hard shift
To chafe the wax to stop therewith the cleft.

JOHAN: Yea that a vengeance take ye two both,
Both him and thee and thee and him also;
And that ye make choke with the same meat
At the first morsel that ye do eat.

TYB: Of what thing now doth thou chatter?
Johan Johan, on whereof doth thou patter?

JOHAN: I chafe the wax and make hard shift
To stop herewith of the pail the rift.

SIR JOHN: So must he do, Johan Johan, by my father's kin,
That is bound of wedlock in the yoke.

JOHAN: Look how the pie the priest crammeth in,
That would to God he might therewith choke.

TYB: Now Master Parson pleaseth your goodness
To tell us some tale of mirth or sadness
For our pastime in way of communication.

SIR JOHN: I am content to do it for our recreation,
And of three miracles I shall to you say.

JOHAN: What, must I chafe the wax all day
And stand here roasting by the fire?

SIR JOHN: Thou must do somewhat at thy wife's desire.
I know a man which wedded had a wife—
As fair a woman as ever bear life—
And within a sennight after, right soon
He went beyond sea and left her alone,

31

And tarried there about a seven year:
And as he came homeward he had a heavy cheer
For it was told him that she was in heaven;
But when that he come home again was,
He found his wife and with her children seven
Which she had had in the meanspace.
Yet she had not had so many by three
If she had not had the help of me.
Is not this a miracle if ever were any,
That this good wife should have children so many
Here in this town while her husband should be
Beyond the sea in a far country?

JOHAN: Now in good sooth this is a wondrous miracle,
But for your labour I would that your tackle
Were in scalding water well sod!

TYB: Peace I say, thou hinderest the word of God.

SIR JOHN: Another miracle eke I shall you say,
Of a woman which that many a day
Had been wedded and in all that season
She had no child neither daughter nor son;
Wherefore to Saint Modwin she went on pilgrimage
And offered there a live pig as is the usage
Of the wives that in London dwell.
And through the virtue thereof, truly to tell,
Within a month after, right shortly
She was delivered of a child as much as I.
How say you, is not this miracle wonderous?

JOHAN: Yea in good sooth sir, it is marvellous;
But surely after mine opinion
That child was neither daughter nor son,
For certainly, and I be not beguiled,
She was delivered of a Knave child.

TYB: Peace, I say, for Goddes passion!
Thou hinderest Sir Johan's communication.

SIR JOHN: The third miracle also is this:
I knew another woman likewise

32

Which was wedded and within four months after
She was delivered of a fair daughter
As well formed in every member and joint,
And as perfect in every point,
As though she had gone nine months full to the end.
Lo here is five months of advantage.

JOHAN: A wondrous miracle so God me mend.
I would each wife that is bound in marriage
And that is wedded here within this place
Might have as quick speed in every such case.

TYB: Forsooth Sir John, yet for all that
I have seen the day when puss my cat
Hath had in a year kittens eighteen.

JOHAN: Yea, Tyb my wife, and that have I seen.
But how say you Sir John, was it good your pie?
The devil the morsel that thereof eat I.
By the God Lord, this is a piteous work!
But now I see well the old proverb is true,
The parish priest forgetteth that ever he was clerk.
But Sir Johan, doth not remember you,
How I was your clerk and helped you mass to sing
And held the basin alway at offering?
You never had half so good a clerk as I,
But notwithstanding all this now our pie
Is eaten up, there is not left a bit,
And you two together there do sit
Eating and drinking at your own desire,
And I am Johan Johan which must stay by the fire
Chafing the wax and dare none otherwise do.

SIR JOHN: And shall we always sit here still we two.
It were too much.

TYB: Then rise we out of this place.

SIR JOHN: And kiss me then instead of grace,
And farewell leman[1] and my love so dear.

[1] Leman = lover.

33

JOHAN: God's body, this wax it waxeth cold again here,
But what, shall I anon go to bed
And eat nothing, neither meat nor bread?
I have not been wont to have such fare.

TYB: Why were ye not served there as ye are
Chafing the wax standing by the fire?

JOHAN: Why, what meat gave ye me I you require?

SIR JOHN: Wast thou not served I pray thee heartily
Both with the bread, the ale and the pie?

JOHAN: No sir, I had none of that fare.

TYB: Why were ye not served there as ye are
Standing by the fire chafing the wax?

JOHAN: Lo here be many trifles and tricks:
By God's soul they think I am either drunk or mad.

TYB: And had ye no meat, Johan Johan, no bad?

JOHAN: No Tyb my wife, I had not a whit.

TYB: What, not a morsel?

JOHAN: No, not one bit:
For hunger now I shall fall in a swoun.

SIR JOHN: O that were a pity I swear by my crown.

TYB: But is it true?

JOHAN: Yea for sure.

TYB: Dost thou lie?

JOHAN: No, so mote I the

TYB: Hast thou had nothing?

JOHAN: No, not a bit.

TYB: Hast thou not drunk?

JOHAN: No, not a whit.

TYB: Where was thou?

JOHAN: By the fire I did stand.

TYB: What didst?

JOHAN: I chafed this wax in my hand,
Where as I knew of wedded men the pain
That they have and yet dare not complain,
For the smoke put out my eyes two,
I burned my face and spoilt my clothes also,
Mending the pail which is so rotten and old
That it will not scant together hold;
And since it is so, and since that you twain
Would give me no meat for my sufferance,
By God's soul, I will take no longer pain:
Ye shall do all yourself with a vengeance
For me and take thee there thy pail now,
And if thou canst mend it let me see how.

TYB: A horson knave hast thou broke my pail.
Thou shalt repent by God's lovely nail!
Reach me my distaff or my clipping shears,
I shall make the blood run about his ears.

JOHAN: Nay, stand still, drab, I say, and come not near,
For by God's blood if thou come here
Or if thou once stir toward this place
I shall throw this shovelfull of coals in thy face.

TYB: Ye horson devil, get thee out of my door.

JOHAN: Nay, get out of my house, thou priest's whore.

SIR JOHN: Thou hest horson cuckold even to thy face.

JOHAN: And thou hest bald priest with an evil grace.

TYB: And you hest.

JOHAN: And you hest Sir.

TYB: And you hest again.

JOHAN: By God's soul, horson priest thou shalt be slain.
Thou hast eat our pie and give me naught.
By God's blood! it shall be full dearly bought.

TYB: At him, Sir John, or else God give thee sorrow.

JOHAN: And have at your whore and there Saint George to borrow.

> [*Here they fight by the ears a while and then the priest
> and wife go out of the place.*]

JOHAN: Aye Sirs, I have paid some of them even as I list
They have borne many a blow with my fist.
I thank God I have shaken them well,
And driven them hence. Yet can ye tell
Whither they be gone? for by God I fear me
That they have gone together he and she
Unto his chamber, and perhaps she will
Spite of my courage tarry there still:
And peradventure there he and she
Will make me cuckold ever to anger me,
And then had I a pig in the worse basket.
Therefore by God I will hie me thither
To see if they do me any villany.
And thus farewell this noble company.

7

CRANMER AT THE STAKE

First issued under the title of The Acts and Monuments of These
Latter and Perilous Days, *John Foxe's* Book of Martyrs, *as it was
afterwards called, profoundly influenced Protestant sentiment in England
for three centuries. Its author's boundless interest in the mechanics of
torture might to-day make him a subject for psycho-pathological inquiry,
but his gift for vivid narrative is beyond question.*

BUT when he came to the place where the holy bishops and martyrs
of God, Hugh Latimer and Nicholas Ridley, were burnt before
him for the confession of the truth, kneeling down, he prayed to
God; and not long tarrying in his prayers, putting off his garments
to his shirt, he prepared himself to death. His shirt was made
long, down to his feet. His feet were bare; likewise his head, when
both his caps were off, was so bare, that one hair could not be
seen upon it. His beard was long and thick, covering his face with
marvellous gravity. Such a countenance of gravity moved the hearts
both of his friends and of his enemies.

Then the Spanish friars, John and Richard, of whom mention was made before, began to exhort him, and play their parts with him afresh, but with vain and lost labour. Cranmer, with steadfast purpose abiding in the profession of his doctrine, gave his hand to certain old men, and others that stood by, bidding them farewell. . . .

Then was an iron chain tied about Cranmer, whom when they perceived to be more steadfast than that he could be moved from his sentence, they commanded the fire to be set unto him.

And when the wood was kindled, and the fire began to burn near him, stretching out his arm, he put his right hand into the flame, which he held so steadfast and immovable (saving that once with the same hand he wiped his face), that all men might see his hand burned before his body was touched. His body did so abide the burning of the flame with such constancy and steadfastness, that standing always in one place without moving his body, he seemed to move no more than the stake to which he was bound; his eyes were lifted up into heaven, and oftentimes he repeated "his unworthy right hand," so long as his voice would suffer him; and using often the words of Stephen "Lord Jesus, receive my spirit," in the greatness of the flame he gave up the ghost.

From THE BOOK OF MARTYRS,
by John Foxe (1516–87).

8

THEIR END IS TO ENRICH THEMSELVES

The author of The Anatomy of Melancholy *was a learned and entertaining Anglican priest who suffered from moods of depression. His book got Dr. Johnson out of bed two hours before he wanted to rise—the only book, said Johnson, to do so.*

WHAT power of Prince, or pœnal law, be it never so strict, could enforce men to do that which for conscience sake they will voluntarily undergo? As to fast from all flesh, abstain from marriage, rise to their prayers at midnight, whip themselves, with stupend fasting and pennance, abandon the world, wilfull poverty, perform canonical and blind obedience, to prostrate their goods, fortunes, bodies, lives, and offer up themselves at their superior's feet, at his command? What so powerful an engine as superstition? which they right well perceiving, are of no religion at all themselves: . . . "The worst Christians of Italy are the Romans, of the Romans the Priests are the wildest, the lewdest Priests are proferred to be Cardinals, and the baddest man amongst the Cardinals is chosen to be Pope," that is an Epicure, as most part the Popes are, Infidels and Lucianists, for so they think and believe; and what is said of Christ to be fables and impostures, of heaven and hell, day of judgment, paradise, immortality of the soul, are all

> "Rumores vacui, verbaque inania,
> Et par sollicito fabula somnio."

Dreams, toys, and old wives' tales. Yet as so many whetstones to make other tools cut, but cut not themselves, though they be of no religion at all, they will make others most devout and superstitious, by promises and threats, compel, enforce from, and lead them by the nose like so many bears in a line; When as their end is not to propagate the Church, advance God's Kingdom, seek his glory or common good, but to enrich themselves, to enlarge their territories, to domineer and compel them to stand in awe, to live in subjection to the See of Rome. For what otherwise care they?

From THE ANATOMY OF MELANCHOLY,
by Robert Burton (1577–1640).

CHARACTER OF JOHN DONNE

HE was of stature moderately tall; of a straight and equally proportioned body, to which all his words and actions gave an unexpressible addition of comeliness.

The melancholy and pleasant humour were in him so contempered, that each gave advantage to the other, and made his company one of the delights of Mankind.

His fancy was inimitably high, equalled only by his great wit; both being made useful by a commanding judgement.

His aspect was chearful, and such as gave a silent testimony of a clear knowing soul, and of a Conscience at peace with itself.

His melting eye showed that he had a soft heart, full of noble compassion; of too brave a soul to offer injuries, and too much a *Christian* not to pardon them in others.

He did much contemplate (especially after he entered into his Sacred Calling) the mercies of Almighty God, the immortality of the Soul, and the joys of heaven; and would often say in a kind of sacred ecstasy, "Blessed be God that he is God, only and divinely like Himself."

He was by nature highly passionate, but more apt to reluct at the excesses of it. A great lover of the offices of humanity, and of so merciful a spirit, that he never beheld the miseries of Mankind without pity and relief.

He was earnest and unwearied in the search of knowledge, with which his vigorous soul is now satisfied, and employed in a continual praise of that God that first breathed it into his active body; that body, which once was a Temple of the Holy Ghost and is now become a small quantity of Christian dust:—But I shall see it reanimated.

From THE LIFE OF JOHN DONNE,
by Isaak Walton (1593–1682).

A RAW YOUNG PREACHER
AND A GRAVE DIVINE

In his earlier days, John Earle, a seventeenth-century Bishop of Salisbury, wrote a series of character sketches of inconspicuous types, "the plain country fellow," "a modest man" and the like. The sketches mark a stage in the development of the essay, and are lively enough to retain their interest for the general reader.

A RAW YOUNG PREACHER

Is a bird not yet fledged, that hath hopped out of his nest to be chirping on a hedge, and will be straggling abroad at what peril soever. His backwardness in the university hath set him thus forward; for had he not truanted there, he had not been so hasty a divine. His small standing, and time, hath made him a proficient only in boldness, out of which, and his table-book, he is furnished for a preacher. His collections of study are the notes of sermons, which, taken up at St. Mary's, he utters in the country: and if he write brachigraphy,[1] his stock is so much the better. His writing is more than his reading, for he reads only what he gets without book. Thus accomplished he comes down to his friends, and his first salutation is grace and peace out of the pulpit. His prayer is conceited, and no man remembers his college more at large. The pace of his sermon is a full career, and he runs wildly over hill and dale, till the clock stop him. The labour of it is chiefly in his lungs; and the only thing he has made *in* it himself, is the faces. He takes on against the pope without mercy, and has a jest still in lavender for Bellarmine: yet he preaches heresy, if it comes in his way, though with a mind, I must needs say, very orthodox. His action is all passion and his speech interjections. He has an excellent faculty in bemoaning the people, and spits with a very good grace. [His style is compounded of twenty several men's, only his body imitates some one extraordinary.] He will not draw his handkercher out of his place, nor blow his nose without

---

[1] Shorthand.

discretion. His commendation is, that he never looks upon book; and indeed he was never used to it. He preaches but once a year, though twice on Sunday; for the stuff is still the same, only the dressing a little altered: he has more tricks with a sermon, than a tailor with an old cloak, to turn it, and piece it, and at last quite disguise it with a new preface. If he have waded farther in his profession, and would show reading of his own, his authors are postils, and his school-divinity a catechism. His fashion and demure habit gets him in with some town-precisian, and makes him a guest on Friday nights. You shall know him by his narrow velvet cape, and serge facing; and his ruff, next his hair the shortest thing about him. The companion of his walk is some zealous tradesman, whom he astonishes with strange points, which they both understand alike. His friends and much painfulness may prefer him to thirty pounds a year, and this means to a chambermaid; with whom we leave him now in the bonds of wedlock:—next Sunday you shall have him again.

A GRAVE DIVINE

Is one that knows the burthen of his calling, and hath studied to make his shoulders sufficient; for which he hath not been hasty to launch forth of his port, the university, but expected the ballast of learning, and the wind of opportunity. Divinity is not the beginning but the end of his studies; to which he takes the ordinary stair, and makes the arts his way. He counts it not profaneness to be polished with human reading, or to smooth his way by Aristotle to school-divinity. He has sounded both religions, and anchored in the best, and is a protestant out of judgment, not faction; not because his country, but his reason is on this side. The ministry is his choice, not refuge, and yet the pulpit not his itch, but fear. His discourse is substance, not all rhetoric, and he utters more things than words. His speech is not helped with inforced action, but the matter acts itself. He shoots all his meditations at one butt; and beats upon his text not the cushion; making his hearers, not the pulpit, groan. In citing of popish errors he cuts them with arguments, not cudgels them with barren invectives; and labours more to show the truth of his cants than the spleen. His sermon is

41

limited by the method, not the hour-glass; and his devotion goes along with him out of the pulpit. He comes not up thrice a week, because he would not be idle; nor talks three hours together, because he would not talk nothing: but his tongue preaches at fit times, and his conversation is the every day's exercise. In matters of ceremony, he is not ceremonious, but thinks he owes that reverence to the Church to bow his judgment to it, and make more conscience of schism, than a surplice. He esteems the Church hierarchy as the Church's glory, and however we jar with Rome, would not have our confusion distinguish us. In simoniacal purchases he thinks his soul goes in the bargain, and is loath to come by promotion so dear: yet his worth at length advances him, and the price of his own merit buys him a living. He is no base grater of his tithes, and will not wrangle for the odd egg. The lawyer is the only man he hinders, by whom he is spited for taking up quarrels. He is a main pillar of our church, though not yet dean or canon, and his life our religion's best apology. His death is the last sermon, where, in the pulpit of his bed, he instructs men to die by his example.

From MICROCOSMOGRAPHY, *or* A
PIECE OF THE WORLD CHARACTER-
ISED, by John Earle (1601?–1665).

II

DIVINITY SHOULD NOT BE WANTON

A Suffolk man, Owen Feltham may be presumed to have had a liberal education from the fact that he wrote part of his Resolves Divine, Moral and Political *at the age of eighteen. Little is known about him, however. His character has been judged from his writings to have been that of a sensible man of the world "who without affecting to be a saint, patiently endeavoured to be not too much of a sinner."*

THE defect of preaching has made the pulpit slighted; I mean the much bad oratory we find come from it. It is a wonder to me how men can preach so little, and so long: so long a time, and so little matter; as if they thought to please by the inculcation of their vain tautologies. I see no reason why so high a princess as divinity is should be presented to the people in the sordid rags of the tongue; nor that he who speaks from the Father of Languages should deliver his embassage in an ill one. A man can never speak too well while he speaks not obscurely. Long and diffusive sentences are both tedious to the ear and difficult to retain. A sentence well couched takes both the senses and the understanding. I love not those cart-rope speeches, which are longer than the memory of man can fathom. I see not but that divinity, put into apt *significants*, might ravish as well as poetry. They are sermons but of baser metal, which lead the eyes to slumber. He answered well that, after often asking, said still, that action was the chief part of an orator. Surely that oration is most powerful where the tongue is eloquent, and speaks in a native decency, even in every limb. A good orator should pierce the ear, allure the eye, and invade the mind of his hearer. And this is Seneca's opinion: fit words are better than fine ones: I like not those which are injudiciously employed; but such as are expressively pertinent, which lead the mind to something beside the naked term. And he that speaks thus must not look to speak thus every day. A *kembed* oration will cost both labour and the rubbing of the brain. And *kembed* I wish it, not *frizzled* nor *curled*. Divinity should not be wanton. Harmless jests I like well; but they are fitter for the tavern than the majesty of the temple. Christ taught the people with authority. Gravity becomes the pulpit. I admire the valour of some men who, before their studies, dare ascend the pulpit; and do there take more pains than they have done in their library. But having done this, I wonder not that they there spend sometimes three hours, only to weary the people into sleep. And this makes some such fugitive divines that, like cowards, they run away from their text. Words are not all, nor is matter all, nor gesture; yet together they are. It is very moving in an orator when the soul seems to speak as well as the tongue. St. Augustin says, Tully was admired more for his tongue than his mind; Aristotle more for his mind than his tongue: but Plato for both. And surely nothing is more necessary in an oration, than a judgment able well to conceive and utter. I know God hath

43

chosen by weak things to confound the wise: yet I see not but, in all times, attention has been paid to language. And even the Scriptures (though not the Hebrew) I believe are penned in a tongue of deep expression, wherein almost every word has a metaphorical sense, which illustrates by some allusion. How political is Moses in his Pentateuch! How philosophical Job! How massy and sententious is Solomon in his proverbs! how grave and solemn in his Ecclesiastes; that in the world, there is not such another dissection of the world as it! How were the Jews astonished at Christ's doctrine! How eloquent a pleader is Paul at the bar; in disputation how subtle! And he who reads the Fathers shall find them as if written with a fine pen. . . . I wish no man to be too dark and full of shadow. There is a way to be pleasingly plain; and some have found it. Mercury himself may move his tongue in vain if he has none to hear him but a non-intelligent. They that speak to children assume a pretty lisping. Birds are caught by the counterfeit of their own shrill notes. There is a magic in the tongue which can charm even the rude and untaught. Eloquence is a bridle, wherewith a wise man rides the monster of the world, the people. The affections of the hearer depend upon the tongue of the speaker.

> "Flet, si flere jubes; gaudet, gaudere coactus:
> Et te dante, capit Judex quum non habet iram."—LUCAN.

> "Thou may'st give smiles, or tears which joys do blot;
> Or wrath to Judges, which themselves have not."

I grieve that any thing so excellent as divinity should fall into a sluttish handling. Surely, though other obstructions do eclipse her, yet this is a principal one. I never yet knew a good tongue that wanted ears to hear it. I will honour her in her plain trim; but I would desire her in her graceful jewels; not that they give addition to her goodness, but that she is thereby rendered more persuasive in working on the soul she meets with. When I meet with worth which I cannot overlove, I can well endure that art which is a means to heighten liking.

From RESOLVES DIVINE, MORAL AND POLITICAL, by Owen Feltham (1602?–68).

THE SURROGATE

A WEALTHY man, addicted to his pleasure and profits, finds Religion to be a traffic so entangled, and of so many peddling accounts, that of all mysteries he cannot skill to keep a stock going on that trade. What should he do? Fain would he have the name to be religious; fain would he bear up with his neighbours in that. What does he therefore but resolves to give over toiling and to find himself out some factor to whose care and credit he may commit the whole managing of his religious affairs. . . . To him he adheres; resigns the whole warehouse of his religion, with all the locks and keys, into his study, and indeed makes the very person of that man his religion, esteeming his associating with him a sufficient evidence and commendation of his own piety. So that a man may say his Religion is now no more within himself but . . . goes and comes near him according as that good man frequents the house. He entertains him . . . lodges him . . . and after the Malmsey or some well-spiced beverage, and better breakfasted than He whose appetite would have gladly fed on green figs between Bethany and Jerusalem, his Religion walks abroad at eight, and leaves his kind entertainer in the shop, trading all day without his religion.

From THE AREOPAGITICA, by
John Milton (1608–1674).

13

ON THE NEW FORCES OF CONSCIENCE UNDER THE LONG PARLIAMENT

BECAUSE you have thrown off your Prelate Lord,
And with stiff vows renounced his Liturgy,
To seize the widowed whore Plurality,
From them whose sin ye envied, not abhorred,
Dare ye for this adjure the civil sword

45

To force our consciences that Christ set free,
And ride us with a classic hierarchy,
Taught ye by mere A. S. and Rutherford?
Men whose life, learning, faith, and pure intent,
    Would have been held in high esteem with Paul,
    Must now be named and printed heretics
By shallow Edwards and Scotch What-d'ye-call!
    But we do hope to find out all your tricks,
    Your plots and packing, worse than those of Trent,
            That so the Parliament
May, with their wholesome and preventive shears,
Clip your phylacteries, though baulk your ears,
            And succour our just fears,
When they shall read this clearly in your charge:
New *Presbyter* is but old *Priest* writ large.

By John Milton (1608–1674).

14

THE PRESBYTERS

*The presbyter could be as domineering as any pope. So declared Samuel
Butler in* Hudibras, *the rhyming burlesque on the Parliamentary
Party written at the time of the Restoration.*

Great piety consists in pride;
To rule is to be sanctified:
To domineer, and to control
Both o'er the body and the soul,
Is the most perfect discipline
Of church-rule, and by right divine.
Bel and the Dragon's chaplains were
More moderate than these by far:
For they, poor knaves, were glad to cheat,
To get their wives and children meat;

But these will not be fobbled off so,
They must have wealth and power too,
Or else with blood and desolation,
They'll tear it out o' th' heart o' th' nation,
Sure these themselves from primitive
And heathen priesthood do derive,
When butchers were the only clerks,
Elders and presbyters of kirks;
Whose directory was to kill;
And some believe it is so still.
The only difference is, that then
They slaughtered only beasts, now men.
For then to sacrifice a bullock,
Or, now and then, a child to Moloch,
They count a vile abomination,
But not to slaughter a whole nation.
Presbytery does but translate
The papacy to a free state,
A commonwealth of popery,
Where every village is a see
As well as Rome, and must maintain
A tithe-pig metropolitan;
Where every presbyter and deacon
Commands the keys for cheese and bacon;
And every hamlet's governed
By's holiness, the church's head,
More haughty and severe in 's place,
Than Gregory and Boniface.

From HUDIBRAS, by Samuel Butler (1612–1680).

THE CHURCH'S JESTER

A plea for reconciliation with the Nonconformists issued by Bishop Croft of Hereford in 1675 prompted Andrew Marvell, a republican who was a great favourite with Charles the Second, to write the best known of his prose works, Mr. Smirke or the Divine in Mode. Mr. Smirke confesses that he never sees anyone elevated to a bishopric "but I presently conceived a greater opinion of his wit than ever I held formerly." Other people, as Marvell suggests, are not of Smirke's opinion.

SOME do not stick to affirm that even they, the bishops, come by their wit not by inspiration, not by teaching, but even as the poor laity do light upon it sometimes, by a good mother; which has occasioned the homely Scotch proverb that "an ounce of mother-wit is worth a pound of clergy." And as they come by it as do other men, so they possess it on the same condition: that they cannot transmit it by breathing, touching, or any other natural effluvium, to other persons; not so much as to their most domestic chaplain, or to the closest residentiary. That the king himself, who is no less the spring of that than he is the fountain of honour, yet has never used the dubbing or creating of wits as a flower of his prerogative; much less can the ecclesiastical power confer it with the same ease as they do the holy orders. That whatsoever they can do of that kind is at uttermost, to empower men by their authority and commission, no otherwise than in the licensing of midwives or physicians. But that as to their collating of any internal talent or ability, they could never pretend to it; their grants and their prohibitions are alike invalid, and they can neither capacitate one man to be witty, nor hinder another from being so, further than as the press is at their devotion. Which if it be the case, they cannot be too circumspect in their management, and should be very exquisite,—seeing this way of writing is found so necessary,—in making choice of fit instruments. The Church's credit is more interested in an ecclesiastical droll, than in a lay chancellor. It is no small trust that is reposed in him to whom the bishop shall commit, *omne et omnimodum suum ingenium, tam temporale quam spirituale :* and however it goes with excommunication, they should take good heed to what manner of persons they delegate the keys of laughter. It is not every man that is qualified to sustain the dignity of the church's jester; and should they take as exact a scrutiny of them as of the Nonconformists through their dioceses, the number would appear inconsiderable upon this Easter visitation. Before men be admitted to so important an employment, it were fit they underwent a severe examination; and that it might appear first, whether they have any sense; for without that how can any man pretend—and yet they do—to be ingenious? Then, whether they have any modesty; for without that they can only be scurrilous and impudent. Next, whether they have any truth: for true jests are those that do the greatest execution. And lastly, it were not amiss that they gave some account too of their Christianity; for the world has always been so uncivil as to expect something of that from the clergy, in the design and style even of their most uncanonical writings.

> *From* MR. SMIRKE OR THE DIVINE IN MODE, by Andrew Marvell (1621–78).

16

THE POOR PARSON

In striking contrast with the other clerics among the Canterbury Pilgrims is the poor parson. Dryden, who toward the end of his life made several adaptations from Chaucer and Boccaccio, was recommended by Samuel Pepys to modernise the account of the only ecclesiastic for whom Chaucer had affection and respect.

A PARISH priest was of the pilgrim train;
An awful, reverend, and religious man.
His eyes diffused a venerable grace,
And charity itself was in his face.

49

Rich was his soul, though his attire was poor;
(As God had clothed His own ambassador;)
For such, on earth, his blessed Redeemer bore.
Of sixty years he seemed; and well might last
To sixty more, but that he lived too fast;
Refined himself to soul, to curb the sense;
And made almost a sin of abstinence.
Yet, had his aspect nothing of severe,
But such a face as promised him sincere.
Nothing reserved or sullen was to see:
But sweet regards; and pleasing sanctity:
Mild was his accent, and his action free.
With eloquence innate his tongue was armed:
Though harsh the precept, yet the preacher charmed.
For letting down the golden chain from high,
He drew his audience upward to the sky;
And oft, with holy hymns, he charmed their ears:
(A music more melodious than the spheres.)
For David left him, when he went to rest,
His lyre; and after him he sung the best.
He bore his great commission in his look:
But sweetly tempered awe; and softened all he spoke.
He preached the joys of heaven, and pains of hell;
And warned the sinner with becoming zeal;
But on eternal mercy loved to dwell.
He taught the gospel rather than the law;
And forced himself to drive; but loved to draw.
For fear but freezes minds; but love, like heat,
Exhales the soul sublime, to seek her native seat.
To threats the stubborn sinner oft is hard,
Wrapped in his crimes, against the storm prepared;
But, when the milder beams of mercy play,
He melts, and throws his cumbrous cloak away.
Lightning and thunder (heaven's artillery)
As harbingers before the Almighty fly:
Those but proclaim his style, and disappear;
The stiller sound succeeds, and God is there.

The tithes, his parish freely paid, he took;
But never sued, or cursed with bell and book.
With patience bearing wrong; but offering none;
Since every man is free to lose his own.
The country churls, according to their kind,
(Who grudge their dues, and love to be behind.)
The less he sought his offerings, pinched the more,
And praised a priest contented to be poor.
   Yet of his little he had some to spare,
To feed the famished, and to clothe the bare:
For mortified he was to that degree,
A poorer than himself, he would not see.
"True priests," he said, "and preachers of the Word,
Were only stewards of their sovereign Lord;
Nothing was theirs; but all the public store:
Entrusted riches, to relieve the poor.
Who, should they steal, for want of his relief,
He judged himself accomplice with the thief.
   Wide was his parish; not contracted close
In streets, but here and there a straggling house;
Yet still he was at hand, without request,
To serve the sick; to succour the distressed:
Tempting, on foot, alone, without affright,
The dangers of a dark tempestuous night.
   All this the good old man performed alone,
Nor spared his pains; for curate he had none.
Nor durst he trust another with his care;
Nor rode himself to Paul's, the public fair,
To chaffer for preferment with his gold,
Where bishoprics and sinecures are sold.
But duly watched his flock, by night and day;
And from the prowling wolf redeemed the prey;
And hungry sent the wily fox away.
   The proud he tamed, the penitent he cheered:
Nor to rebuke the rich offender feared.
His preaching much, but more his practice wrought;
(A living sermon of the truths he taught;)

For this by rules severe his life he squared:
That all might see the doctrine which they heard.
"For priests," he said, "are patterns for the rest:
(The gold of heaven, who bear the God impressed;)
But when the precious coin is kept unclean,
The Sovereign's image is no longer seen.
If they be foul on whom the people trust,
Well may the baser brass contract a rust."
   The prelate, for his holy life, he prized;
The worldly pomp of prelacy despised,
His Saviour came not with a gaudy show;
Nor was His kingdom of the world below.
Patience in want, and poverty of mind,
These marks of Church and Churchmen he designed,
And living taught, and dying left behind.
The crown He wore was of the pointed thorn:
In purple, He was crucified, not born.
They who contend for place and high degree,
Are not His sons, but those of Zebedee.
   Not but He knew the signs of earthly power
Might well become Saint Peter's successor;
The holy father holds a double reign,
The prince may keep his pomp, the fisher must be plain.
   Such was the saint; who shone with every grace,
Reflecting, Moses like, his Maker's face.
God saw His image lively was expressed;
And His own work, as in creation, blessed.
   The tempter saw him too with envious eye;
And, as on Job, demanded leave to try.
He took the time when Richard was deposed,
And high and low with happy Harry closed.
This prince, though great in arms, the priest withstood:
Near though he was, yet not the next of blood.
Had Richard, unconstrained, resigned the throne,
A king can give no more than is his own:
The title stood entailed had Richard had a son.

Conquest, an odious name, was laid aside,
Where all submitted, none the battle tried.
The senseless plea of right by providence
Was, by a flattering priest, invented since:
And lasts no longer than the present sway;
But justifies the next who comes in play.

The people's right remains; let those who dare
Dispute their power, when they the judges are.

He joined not in their choice, because he knew
Worse might, and often did from change ensue.
Much to himself he thought; but little spoke;
And, undeprived, his benefice forsook.

Now, through the land, his cure of souls he stretched;
And like a primitive apostle preached.
Still cheerful; ever constant to his call;
By many followed; loved by most; admired by all.
With what he begged, his brethren he relieved;
And gave the charities himself received.
Gave while he taught; and edified the more,
Because he showed, by proof, 'twas easy to be poor.

He went not with the crowd to see a shrine;
But fed us, by the way, with food divine.

In deference to his virtues, I forbear
To show you what the rest in orders were:
This brilliant is so spotless and so bright,
He needs no foil, but shines by his own proper light.

THE CHARACTER OF A GOOD PARSON,
by John Dryden (1631–1700).

53

THE PARSON'S CASE

THAT you, friend Marcus, like a stoic,
Can wish to die in strains heroic,
No real fortitude implies:
Yet, all must own, thy wish is wise.
Thy curate's place, thy fruitful wife,
Thy busy, drudging scene of life,
Thy insolent, illiterate vicar,
Thy want of all-consoling liquor,
Thy threadbare gown, thy cassock rent,
Thy credit sunk, thy money spent,
Thy week made up of fasting-days,
Thy grate unconscious of a blaze,
And to complete thy other curses,
The quarterly demands of nurses,
Are ills you wisely wish to leave,
And fly for refuge to the grave;
And, O, what virtue you express,
In wishing such afflictions less!
    But, now, should Fortune shift the scene,
And make thy curateship a dean:
Or some rich benefice provide,
To pamper luxury and pride;
With labour small, and income great;
With chariot less for use than state;
With swelling scarf, and glossy great;
And license to reside in town:
To shine where all the gay resort,
At concerts, coffee-house, or court:
And weekly persecute his grace
With visits, or to beg a place:
With underlings thy flock to teach,
With no desire to pray or preach;

With haughty spouse in vesture fine,
With plenteous meals and generous wine;
Wouldst thou not wish, in so much ease,
Thy years as numerous as thy days?

By Jonathan Swift (1667–1745).

18

A CURATE'S COMPLAINT OF HARD DUTY

I MARCH'D three miles through scorching sand,
With zeal in heart, and notes in hand;
I rode four more to Great St. Mary,
Using four legs, when two were weary:
To three fair virgins I did tie men,
In the close bands of pleasing Hymen;
I dipp'd two babes in holy water,
And purified their mother after.
Within an hour and eke a half,
I preach'd three congregations deaf;
Where, thundering out, with lungs long-winded,
I chopp'd so fast, that few there minded.
My emblem, the laborious sun,
Saw all these mighty labours done
Before one race of his was run.
All this perform'd by Robert Hewit:
What mortal else could e'er go through it!

By Jonathan Swift (1667–1745).

THE VICAR OF BRAY

In good King Charles's golden days,
　　When loyalty no harm meant,
A zealous high-churchman was I,
　　And so I got preferment.
To teach my Flock I never miss'd
　　Kings were by God appointed,
And damned are those that dare resist
　　Or touch the Lord's anointed.
　　　　And this is law that I'll maintain
　　　　　Until my dying day, sir,
　　　　That whatsoever king shall reign,
　　　　　Still I'll be the Vicar of Bray, sir.

When Royal James possess'd the crown,
　　And Popery grew in fashion
The penal laws I hooted down,
　　And read the Declaration :
The Church of Rome I found would fit
　　Full well my constitution;
And I had been a Jesuit,
　　But for the Revolution.
　　　　And this is law that I'll maintain
　　　　　Until my dying day, sir,
　　　　That whatsoever king shall reign,
　　　　　Still I'll be the Vicar of Bray, sir.

When William was our king declared,
　　To ease the nation's grievance;
With this new wind about I steer'd,
　　And swore to him allegiance.
Old principles I did revoke,
　　Set conscience at a distance
Passive obedience was a joke,
　　A jest was non-resistance.

And this is law that I'll maintain
Until my dying day, sir,
That whatsoever king shall reign,
Still I'll be the Vicar of Bray, sir.

When Royal Anne became our queen,
The Church of England's glory,
Another face of things was seen,
And I became a Tory:
Occasional Conformists base,
I blamed their moderation;
And thought the Church in danger was
By such prevarication.
And this is law that I'll maintain
Until my dying day, sir,
That whatsoever king shall reign,
Still I'll be the Vicar of Bray, sir.

When George in pudding-time came o'er,
And moderate men looked big, sir,
My principles I changed once more,
And so became a Whig, sir;
And thus preferment I procured
From our new faith's defender;
And almost every day abjured
The Pope and the Pretender.
And this is law that I'll maintain
Until my dying day, sir,
That whatsoever king shall reign,
Still I'll be the Vicar of Bray, sir.

Th' illustrious House of Hanover,
And Protestant succession,
To these I do allegiance swear—
While they can keep possession:

For in my faith and loyalty,
    I never more will falter,
And George my lawful king shall be—
    Until the times do alter.
        And this is law that I'll maintain
        Until my dying day, sir,
    That whatsoever king shall reign,
        Still I'll be the Vicar of Bray, sir.

Anonymous.

THE HAPPY LIFE OF A COUNTRY PARSON

PARSON, these things in thy possessing
Are better than the bishop's blessing:—
A wife that makes conserves; a steed
That carries double when there's need;
October store, and best Virginia,
Tithe pig, and mortuary guinea;
Gazettes sent gratis down and frank'd,
For which thy patron's weekly thank'd;
A large Concordance, bound long since;
Sermons to Charles the First when prince;
A Chronicle of ancient standing;
A Chrysostom to smooth thy band in:
The Polyglot—three parts—my text,
Howbeit—likewise—now to my next:
Lo, here the Septuagint—and Paul,
To sum the whole—the close of all.

He that has these may pass his life,
Drink with the 'squire, and kiss his wife;
On Sundays preach, and eat his fill,
And fast on Fridays—if he will;

Toast Church and Queen, explain the news,
Talk with churchwardens about pews,
Pray heartily for some new gift,
And shake his head at Doctor S——t.

IN IMITATION OF DR. SWIFT,
by Alexander Pope (1668-1744).

21

COUNTRY FEUDS

THE fair understanding between Sir Roger and his chaplain, and their mutual concurrence in doing good, is the more remarkable, because the very next village is famous for the differences and contentions that rise between the parson and the 'squire, who live in a perpetual state of war. The parson is always at the 'squire, and the 'squire, to be revenged on the parson, never comes to church. The 'squire has made all his tenants atheists and tithe-stealers; while the parson instructs them every Sunday in the dignity of his order, and insinuates to them, almost in every sermon, that he is a better man than his patron. In short, matters are come to such an extremity, that the 'squire has not said his prayers either in public or private this half year; and that the parson threatens him, if he does not mend his manners, to pray for him in the face of the whole congregation.

Feuds of this nature, though too frequent in the country, are very fatal to the ordinary people; who are so used to be dazzled with riches, that they pay as much deference to the understanding of a man of an estate, as of a man of learning; and are very hardly brought to regard any truth, how important soever it may be, that is preached to them, when they know there are several men of five hundred a year who do not believe it.

From THE SPECTATOR (No. 115),
by Joseph Addison (1672-1719).

THE TREATMENT OF CHAPLAINS

Addison's reflections begin from a letter, supposedly written by a chaplain who served "an honourable family very regularly at devotions." The holy man had been dismissed his post for remaining at table for a second course, one course at dinner being deemed sufficient for menials.

THE case of this gentleman deserves pity, especially if he loves sweetmeats, to which, if I may guess by his letter, he is no enemy. In the mean time, I have often wondered at the indecency of discarding the holiest man from the table, as soon as the most delicious parts of the entertainment are served up, and could never conceive a reason for so absurd a custom. Is it because a liquorish palate, or a sweet tooth (as they call it,), is not consistent with the sanctity of his character? This is but a trifling pretence. No man of the most rigid virtue gives offence by any excesses in plum-pudding or plum-porridge, and that because they are the first parts of the dinner. Is there anything that tends to incitation in sweetmeats more than in ordinary dishes? Certainly not. Sugar-plums are a very innocent diet, and conserves of a much colder nature than our common pickles. I have sometimes thought, that the ceremony of the chaplain's flying away from the dessert was typical and figurative, to mark out to the company how they ought to retire from all the luscious baits of temptation, and deny their appetites the gratifications that are most pleasing to them; or at least to signify, that we ought to stint ourselves in our most lawful satisfactions, and not make our pleasure, but our support, the end of eating. But most certainly, if such a lesson of temperance had been necessary at a table, our clergy would have recommended it to all the lay masters of families, and not have disturbed other men's tables with such unseasonable examples of abstinence. The original, therefore, of this barbarous custom, I take to have been merely accidental. The chaplain retired out of pure complaisance, to make room for the removal of the dishes, or possibly for the ranging of the dessert. This by degrees grew into duty, till at length, as the fashion improved, the good man found himself cut off from the third part of the entertainment; and if the arrogance of the patron goes on, it is not impossible, but, in the next generation, he may see himself reduced to the tithe, or tenth dish of the table; a sufficient caution not to part with any privilege we are once possessed of. It was usual for the priest, in old times, to feast upon the sacrifice, nay, the honey-cake, while the hungry laity looked upon him with great devotion, or, as the late Lord Rochester describes it in a lively manner,

"And while the priest did eat, the people stared."

At present the custom is inverted; the laity feast, while the priest stands by as an humble spectator. This necessarily puts the good man upon making great ravages on all the dishes that stand near him, and distinguishing himself by voraciousness of appetite, as knowing that his time is short. I would fain ask these stiff-necked patrons, whether they would not take it ill of a chaplain that, in his grace after meat, should return thanks for the whole entertainment, with an exception to the dessert? And yet I cannot but think, that in such a proceeding he would but deal with them as they deserved. What would a Roman Catholic priest think, who is always helped first, and placed next the ladies, should he see a clergyman giving his company the slip at the first appearance of the tarts or sweetmeats? Would not he believe that he had the same antipathy to a candied orange, or a piece of puff paste, as some have to a Cheshire cheese, or a breast of mutton? Yet to so ridiculous a height is this foolish custom grown, that even the Christmas pie, which in its very nature is a kind of consecrated cate, and a badge of distinction, is often forbidden to the Druid of the family. Strange! that a sirloin of beef, whether boiled or roasted, when entire, is exposed to his utmost depredations and incisions; but if minced into small pieces, and tossed up with plums and sugar, changes its property, and, forsooth, is meat for his master.

In this case I know not which to censure, the patron or the chaplain; the insolence of power, or the abjectness of dependence.

For my own part, I have often blushed to see a gentleman, whom I know to have much more wit and learning than myself, and who was bred up with me at the University upon the same foot of a liberal education, treated in such an ignominious manner, and sunk beneath those of his own rank, by reason of that character which ought to bring him honour. This deters men of generous minds from placing themselves in such a station of life, and by that means frequently excludes persons of quality from the improving and agreeable conversation of a learned and obsequious friend.

Mr. Oldham lets us know, that he was affrighted from the thought of such an employment, by the scandalous sort of treatment which often accompanies it.

> "Some think themselves exalted to the sky,
> If they light in some noble family:
> Diet, an horse, and thirty pounds a year,
> Besides the advantage of his Lordship's ear,
> The credit of the business, and the state,
> Are things that in a youngster's sense sound great.
> Little the unexperienced wretch does know,
> What slavery he oft must undergo;
> Who though in silken scarf and cassock drest,
> Wears but a gayer livery at best.
> When dinner calls, the implement must wait
> With holy words to consecrate the meat;
> But hold it for a favour seldom known,
> If he be deign'd the honour to sit down.
> Soon as the tarts appear, Sir Crape, withdraw,
> Those dainties are not for a spiritual maw.
> Observe your distance, and be sure to stand
> Hard by the cistern with your cap in hand:
> There for diversion you may pick your teeth,
> Till the kind voider comes for your relief.
> Let others who such meannesses can brook,
> Strike countenance to every great man's look;
> I rate my freedom higher."

This author's raillery is the raillery of a friend, and does not turn the sacred order into ridicule, but is a just censure on such persons as take advantage from the necessities of a man of merit, to impose on him hardships that are by no means suitable to the dignity of his profession.

From THE TATLER (No. 255), by
Joseph Addison (1672–1719).

23

SUCCOUR FOR THE INNOCENT

"Or Virtue Rewarded" was Samuel Richardson's unconsciously ironical sub-title for Pamela, *the story of a maidservant who resisted the brutal advances of her master. Her reward was to marry the bounder. Imprisoned in a country house, she smuggles a letter to Mr. Williams, the curate, asking if none of the local gentry will give her asylum. In his reply, the curate sends discouraging news.*

I AM sorry to tell you that I have had a repulse from Lady Jones. She is concerned at your case, she says, but don't care to make herself enemies. I applied to Lady Darnford, and told her, in the most pathetic manner, your sad story, and shewed her your more pathetic letter. I found her well-disposed; but she would advise with Sir Simon, who is not a man of an extraordinary character for virtue; but he said to his lady, in my presence, "Why, what is all this, my dear, but that our neighbour has a mind to his mother's waiting-maid! And if he takes care she wants for nothing, I don't see any great injury will be done her. He hurts no *family* by this. And I think, Mr. Williams, you, of all men, should not engage in this affair, against your friend and patron." He spoke this in so determined a manner, that the lady said no more, and I had only to beg that no notice should be taken of the matter, as from *me*.

I have hinted your case to Mr. Peters, the minister of this parish; but I am concerned to say, that he imputed selfish views to me, as if I would make an interest in your affections by my zeal. And when I represented the duties of our function, and the like, and protested my disinterestedness, he coldly said, I was very good; but was a young man, and knew little of the world. And though it was a thing to be lamented, yet when he and I should set about to reform mankind in this respect, we should have enough upon our hands; for he said, it was too common and fashionable a case to be withstood by a private clergyman or two: and then uttered some reflections upon the conduct of the present fathers of the church, in regard to the first personages of the realm, as a justification of his coldness on this score.

I represented the different circumstances of your affair; that other women lived evilly by their own consent; but to serve you, was to save an innocence that had but few examples; I then shewed him your letter.

He said it was prettily written: he was sorry for you; and that your good intentions ought to be encouraged: "But what," said he, "would you have *me* do, Mr. Williams?" "Why, suppose, Sir," said I, "you give her shelter in your house with your spouse and niece, till she can get to her friends?" "What, and embroil myself with a man of Mr. B.'s power and fortune! No, not I, I'll assure you! and I would have you consider what you are about. Besides, she owns," continued he, "that he promises to do honourably by her; and her shyness will procure her good terms enough; for he is no covetous nor wicked gentleman, except in this case; and 'tis what all young gentlemen will do."

I am greatly concerned for him, I assure you; but am not discouraged by this ill success, let what will come of it, if I can serve you.

I don't hear as yet that Mr. B. is coming. I am glad of your hint as to that unhappy fellow, John Arnold. Something, perhaps, will strike out from that, which may be useful. As to your packets, if you seal them up, and lay them in the usual place, if you find it not suspected, I will watch an opportunity to convey them; but if they are large, you had best be very cautious. This evil woman, I find, mistrusts me much.

I just hear, that the gentleman is dying whose living Mr. B. has promised me. I have almost a scruple to take it, as I am acting so contrary to his desires; but I hope he'll one day thank me for it. As to money, don't think of it at present. Be assured you may command all in my power without reserve. . . .

From PAMELA, by Samuel
Richardson (1689–1761).

24

THE WISE FOOL

Amused by the priggishness of Richardson's first heroine, Henry Fielding began a burlesque in which the hero, Joseph Andrews, supposed brother to Pamela, was tempted by his mistress much as his sister had been by her master. But Joseph Andrews grew beyond its author's designs, chiefly by the antics of Parson Adams, who takes over the story. Beginning as a mere figure of fun, he is transformed by his humourless but chivalrous humanity into an angel of light.

OF MR. ABRAHAM ADAMS THE CURATE

MR. ABRAHAM ADAMS was an excellent scholar. He was a perfect master of the Greek and Latin languages; to which he added a great share of knowledge in the Oriental tongues; and could read and translate French, Italian, and Spanish. He had applied many years to the most severe study, and had treasured up a fund of learning rarely to be met with in a university. He was, besides, a man of good sense, good parts, and good nature; but was at the same time as entirely ignorant of the ways of this world as an infant just entered into it could possibly be. As he had never any intention to deceive, so he never suspected such a design in others. He was generous, friendly, and brave to an excess; but simplicity was his characteristick: he did, no more than Mr. Colley Cibber, apprehend any such passions as malice and envy to exist in mankind; which was indeed less remarkable in a country parson than in a gentleman who hath passed his life behind the scenes,—a place which hath been seldom thought the school of innocence, and

65

where a very little observation would have convinced the great apologist that those passions have a real existence in the human mind.

His virtue, and his other qualifications, as they rendered him equal to his office, so they made him an agreeable and valuable companion, and had so much endeared and well recommended him to a bishop, that at the age of fifty he was provided with a handsome income of twenty-three pounds a year; which, however, he could not make any great figure with, because he lived in a dear country, and was a little encumbered with a wife and six children. . . .

PARSON ADAMS HAS AMPLE SECURITY

Joseph had rose pretty early this morning; but, though his wounds were far from threatening any danger, he was so sore with the bruises, that it was impossible for him to think of undertaking a journey yet; Mr. Adams, therefore, whose stock was visibly decreased with the expenses of supper and breakfast, and which could not survive that day's scoring, began to consider how it was possible to recruit it. At last he cried, "He had luckily hit on a sure method, and, though it would oblige him to return himself home together with Joseph, it mattered not much." He then sent for Tow-wouse, and, taking him into another room, told him "he wanted to borrow three guineas, for which he would put ample security into his hands." Tow-wouse, who expected a watch, or ring, or something of double the value, answered, "He believed he could furnish him." Upon which Adams, pointing to his saddle-bag, told him, with a face and voice full of solemnity, "that there were in that bag no less than nine volumes of manuscript sermons, as well worth a hundred pounds as a shilling was worth twelve pence, and that he would deposit one of the volumes in his hands by way of pledge; not doubting but that he would have the honesty to return it on his repayment of the money; for otherwise he must be a very great loser, seeing that every volume would at least bring him ten pounds, as he had been informed by a neighbouring clergyman in the country; for," said he, "as to my own part, having never yet dealt in printing, I do not pretend to ascertain the exact value of such things."

Tow-wouse, who was a little surprised at the pawn, said (and not without some truth), "That he was no judge of the price of such kind of goods; and as for money, he really was very short." Adams answered, "Certainly he would not scruple to lend him three guineas on what was undoubtedly worth at least ten." The landlord replied, "He did not believe he had so much money in the house, and besides, he was to make up a sum. He was very confident the books were of much higher value, and heartily sorry it did not suit him." He then cried out, "Coming sir!" though nobody called; and ran downstairs without any fear of breaking his neck.

Poor Adams was extremely dejected at this disappointment, nor knew he what further stratagem to try. He immediately applied to his pipe, his constant friend and comfort in his afflictions; and, leaning over the rails, he devoted himself to meditation, assisted by the inspiring fumes of tobacco.

He had on a nightcap drawn over his wig, and a short greatcoat, which half covered his cassock—a dress which, added to something comical enough in his countenance, composed a figure likely to attract the eyes of those who were not over given to observation. . . .

PARSON ADAMS AROUSES SUSPICION

They now sat cheerfully round the fire, till the master of the house, having surveyed his guests, and conceiving that the cassock, which, having fallen down, appeared under Adams's greatcoat, and the shabby livery on Joseph Andrews, did not well suit with the familiarity between them, began to entertain some suspicions not much to their advantage: addressing himself therefore to Adams, he said, "He perceived he was a clergyman by his dress, and supposed that honest man was his footman." "Sir," answered Adams, "I am a clergyman at your service; but as to that young man, whom you have rightly termed honest, he is at present in nobody's service; he never lived in any other family than that of Lady Booby, from whence he was discharged, I assure you, for no crime." Joseph said, "He did not wonder the gentleman was surprised to see one of Mr. Adams's character condescend to so

67

much goodness with a poor man."—"Child," said Adams, "I should be ashamed of my cloth if I thought a poor man, who is honest, below my notice or my familiarity. I know not how those who think otherwise can profess themselves followers and servants of Him who made no distinction, unless, peradventure, by preferring the poor to the rich.—Sir," said he, addressing himself to the gentleman, "these two poor young people are my parishioners, and I look on them and love them as my children. There is something singular enough in their history, but I have not now time to recount it." The master of the house, notwithstanding the simplicity which discovered itself in Adams, knew too much of the world to give a hasty belief to professions. He was not yet quite certain that Adams had any more of the clergyman in him than his cassock. To try him therefore further, he asked him, "If Mr. Pope had lately published anything new?" Adams answered, "He had heard great commendations of that poet, but that he had never read nor knew any of his works."—"Ho! ho!" says the gentleman to himself, "have I caught you? What!" said he, "have you never seen his Homer?" Adams answered, "he had never read any translation of the classicks." "Why, truly," reply'd the gentleman, "there is a dignity in the Greek language which I think no modern tongue can reach."—"Do you understand Greek, sir?" said Adams hastily. "A little, sir," answered the gentleman. "Do you know, sir, cry'd Adams, "where I can buy an Æschylus? an unlucky misfortune lately happened to mine." . . .

PARSON ADAMS AND LADY BOOBY

"But, sir, our poor is numerous enough already; I will have no more vagabonds settled here."—"Madam," says Adams, "your ladyship is offended with me, I protest, without any reason. This couple were desirous to consummate long ago, and I dissuaded them from it; nay, I may venture to say, I believe I was the sole cause of their delaying it."—"Well," says she, "and you did very wisely and honestly too, notwithstanding she is the greatest beauty in the parish."—"And now, madam," continued he, "I only perform my office to Mr. Joseph."—"Pray, don't mister such

fellows to me," cries the lady. "He," said the parson, "with the consent of Fanny, before my face, put in the banns." "Yes," answered the lady, "I suppose the slut is forward enough; Slipslop tells me how her head runs upon fellows; that is one of her beauties, I suppose. But if they have put in the banns, I desire you will publish them no more without my orders."—"Madam," cries Adams, "if any one puts in a sufficient caution, and assigns a proper reason against them, I am willing to surcease."—"I tell you a reason," says she: "he is a vagabond, and he shall not settle here, and bring a nest of beggars into the parish; it will make us but little amends that they will be beauties."—"Madam," answered Adams, "with the utmost submission to your ladyship, I have been informed by lawyer Scout that any person who serves a year gains a settlement in the parish where he serves."—"Lawyer Scout," replied the lady, "is an impudent coxcomb; I will have no lawyer Scout interfere with me. I repeat to you again, I will have no more incumbrances brought on us: so I desire you will proceed no farther."—"Madam," returned Adams, "I would obey your ladyship in everything that is lawful; but surely the parties being poor is no reason against their marrying. God forbid there should be any such law! The poor have little share enough of this world already; it would be barbarous indeed to deny them the common privileges and innocent enjoyments which nature indulges to the animal creation."—"Since you understand yourself no better," cries the lady, "nor the respect due from such as you to a woman of my distinction, than to affront my ears by such loose discourse, I shall mention but one short word; it is my orders to you that you publish these banns no more; and if you dare, I will recommend it to your master, the doctor, to discard you from his service. I will, sir, notwithstanding your poor family; and then you and the greatest beauty in the parish may go and beg together."
—"Madam," answered Adams, "I know not what your ladyship means by the terms master and service. I am in the service of a Master who will never discard me for doing my duty; and if the doctor (for indeed I have never been able to pay for a licence) thinks proper to turn me from my cure, God will provide me, I hope, another. At least, my family, as well as myself, have hands;

and He will prosper, I doubt not, our endeavours to get our bread honestly with them. Whilst my conscience is pure, I shall never fear what man can do unto me."—"I condemn my humility," said the lady, "for demeaning myself to converse with you so long. I shall take other measures; for I see you are a confederate with them. But the sooner you leave me the better; and I shall give orders that my doors may no longer be open to you. I will suffer no parsons who run about the country with beauties to be entertained here."—"Madam," said Adams, "I shall enter into no persons' doors against their will; but I am assured, when you have enquired farther into this matter, you will applaud, not blame, my proceeding; and so I humbly take my leave:" which he did with many bows, or at least many attempts at a bow.

From JOSEPH ANDREWS, by
Henry Fielding (1707–1754).

25

HINDRANCE TO PREFERMENT

OF Mr. John Pomfret nothing is known but from a slight and confused account prefixed to his poems by a nameless friend, who relates that he was the son of the Rev. Mr. Pomfret, vicar of Luton in Bedfordshire, that he was bred at Cambridge, entered into orders, and was rector of Malden in Bedfordshire, and might have risen in the Church; but that when he applied to Dr. Compton, Bishop of London, for institution to a living of considerable value, to which he had been presented, he found a troublesome obstruction raised by a malicious interpretation of some passage in his *Choice*, from which it was inferred that he considered happiness as more likely to be found in the company of a mistress than of a wife.

This reproach was easily obliterated: for it had happened to Pomfret as to all other men who plan schemes of life, he had departed from his purpose, and was then married.

The malice of his enemies had, however, a very fatal consequence; the delay constrained his attendance in London, where he caught the small-pox, and died in 1703, in the thirty-sixth year of his age.

From LIVES OF THE ENGLISH POETS,
by Samuel Johnson (1709–1784).

26

THE MERITS OF DR. WATTS

HE was one of the first authors that taught the Dissenters to court attention by the graces of language. Whatever they had among them before, whether of learning or acuteness, was commonly obscured and blunted by coarseness and inelegance of style. He showed them that zeal and purity might be expressed and enforced by polished diction.

He continued to the end of his life the teacher of a congregation, and no reader of his works can doubt his fidelity or diligence. In the pulpit, though his low stature, which very little exceeded five feet, graced him with no advantages of appearance, yet the gravity and propriety of his utterance made his discourses very efficacious. I once mentioned the reputation which Mr. Foster had gained by his proper delivery to my friend Dr. Hawkesworth, who told me that in the art of pronunciation he was far inferior to Dr. Watts.

Such was his flow of thoughts, and such his promptitude of language, that in the latter part of his life he did not precompose his cursory sermons, but having adjusted the heads, and sketched out some particulars, trusted for success to his extemporary powers.

He did not endeavour to assist his eloquence by any gesticulations; for, as no corporeal actions have any correspondence with theological truth, he did not see how they could enforce it.

At the conclusion of weighty sentences he gave time, by a short pause, for the proper impression.

To stated and public instruction he added familiar visits and personal application, and was careful to improve the opportunities which conversation offered of diffusing and increasing the influence of religion.

By his natural temper he was quick of resentment; but by his established and habitual practice he was gentle, modest and inoffensive. His tenderness appeared in his attention to children and to the poor. To the poor, while he lived in the family of his friend, he allowed the third part of his annual revenue, though the whole was not a hundred a year; and for children he condescended to lay aside the scholar, the philosopher, and the wit, to write little poems of devotion, and systems of instruction, adapted to their wants and capacities, from the dawn of reason through its gradations of advance in the morning of life. Every man acquainted with the common principles of human action will look with veneration on the writer who is at one time combating Locke, and at another making a catechism for children in their fourth year. A voluntary descent from the dignity of science is perhaps the hardest lesson that humility can teach.

From LIVES OF THE ENGLISH POETS,
by Samuel Johnson (1709–1784).

27

PARSON YORICK

HE was as mercurial and sublimated a composition—as heteroclite a creature in all his declensions——with as much life and whim, and *gaite de cœur* about him, as the kindliest climate could have engendered and put together. With all this sail, poor Yorick carried not one ounce of ballast; he was utterly unpractised in the world; and, at the age of twenty-six, knew just about as well how to steer his course in it as a romping, unsuspicious girl of thirteen: so that upon his first setting out, the brisk gale of his spirits, as you will imagine, ran him foul ten times in a day of somebody's tackling; and as the grave and more slow-paced were oftenest in his way,— you may likewise imagine it was with such he had generally the ill-luck to get the most entangled. For aught I know, there might be some mixture of unlucky wit at the bottom of such *fracas:*——for, to speak the truth, Yorick had an invincible dislike and opposition in his nature to gravity;—not to gravity as such:—for, where gravity was wanted, he would be the most grave or serious of mortal men for days and weeks together;—but he was an enemy to the affectation of it, and declared open war against it only as it appeared a cloak for ignorance or for folly: and then, whenever it fell in his way, however sheltered and protected, he seldom gave it much quarter.

Sometimes, in his wild way of talking, he would say that Gravity was an arrant scoundrel, and he would add—of the most dangerous kind too,—because a sly one—and that, he verily believed, more honest, well-meaning people were bubbled out of their goods and money by it in one twelve-month than by pocket-picking and shop-lifting in seven. In the naked temper which a merry heart discovered, he would say there was no danger—but to itself:—whereas the very essence of gravity was design, and consequently deceit:—it was a taught trick to gain credit of the world for more sense and knowledge than a man was worth; and that, with all its pretensions,—it was no better, but often worse, than what a French wit had long ago defined it,—*viz., A mysterious carriage of the body to cover the defects of the mind;*—which definition of gravity, Yorick, with great imprudence, would say deserved to be written in letters of gold.

But, in plain truth, he was a man unhackneyed and unpractised in the world, and was altogether as indiscreet and foolish on every other subject of discourse where policy is wont to impress restraint. Yorick had no impression but one, and that was what arose from the nature of the deed spoken of; which impression he would usually translate into plain English, without any periphrasis;—and too oft without much distinction of either person, time, or place;—so that when mention was made of a pitiful or an ungenerous proceeding——he never gave himself a moment's time to reflect who was the hero of the piece,——what his station,——or how far he had power to hurt him hereafter;——but if it was a dirty action,— without more ado,—The man was a dirty fellow,—and so on. And as his comments had usually the ill fate to be terminated either in a *bon mot*, or to be enlivened throughout with some drollery or humour of expression, it gave wings to Yorick's indiscretion. In a word, though he never sought, yet, at the same time, as he seldom shunned, occasions of saying what came uppermost, and without much ceremony——he had but too many temptations in life of scattering his wit and his humour, his gibes and his jests, about him.——They were not lost for want of gathering.

.   .   .   .   .

It was Yorick's custom, which I suppose a general one with those of his profession, on the first leaf of every sermon which he composed, to chronicle down the time, the place, and the occasion of its being preached: to this, he was ever wont to add some short comment or stricture upon the sermon itself,—seldom, indeed, much to its credit.—For instance, "This sermon upon the Jewish dispensation,—I don't like it at all;—though I own there is a world of water-landish knowledge in it;—but 'tis all tritical, and most tritically put together.—This is but a flimsy kind of composition. What was in my head when I made it?

—*N.B.* "The excellency of this text is that it will suit any sermon;—and of this sermon, that it will suit any text.

——"For this sermon I shall be hanged,—for I have stolen the greatest part of it. Doctor Paidagunes found me out. ☞ Set a thief to catch a thief."

On the back of half a dozen I find written, *So, so*—and no more; —and upon a couple, *moderato;* by which, as far as one may gather from Alteiri's Italian Dictionary,—but mostly from the authority of a piece of green whipcord, which seemed to have been the unravelling of Yorick's whip-lash, with which he has left us the two sermons marked *Moderato*, and the half dozen of *So so*, tied fast together in one bundle by themselves, one may safely suppose he meant pretty nearly the same thing.

There is but one difficulty in the way of this conjecture, which is this, that the *moderatos* are five times better than the *so sos;*—show ten times more knowledge of the human heart;—have seventy times more wit and spirit in them;—(and, to rise properly in my climax)—discover a thousand times more genius;—and, to crown all, are infinitely more entertaining than those tied up with them:—for which reason, whenever Yorick's *dramatic* sermons are offered to the world, though I shall admit but one out of the whole number of the *so sos*, I shall, nevertheless, adventure to point the two *moderatos* without any sort of scruple.

What Yorick could mean by the words *lentamente,—tenuté,—grave*, and sometimes *adagio,*—as applied to theological compositions, and with which he has characterised some of these sermons, I dare not venture to guess. I am more puzzled still upon finding *a l' octavo alta!* upon one;—*Con strepito* upon the back of another;—*Scicilliana* upon a third;—*Alla capella* upon a fourth;—*Con l' arco* upon this;—*Senza l' arco* upon that.—All I know is that they are musical terms, and have a meaning;—and, as he was a musical man, I will make no doubt but that, by some quaint application of such metaphors to the compositions in hand, they impressed very distinct ideas of their several characters upon his fancy,—whatever they may do upon that of others.

Amongst these, there is that particular sermon which has unaccountably led me into this digression,—The funeral sermon upon poor Le Fevre, wrote out very fairly, as if from a hasty copy.—I take notice of it the more because it seems to have been his favourite composition.—It is upon mortality; and is tied length-ways and cross-ways with a yarn thrumb, and then rolled up and twisted round with a half-sheet of dirty blue paper, which seems to have been once the cast cover of a general review, which to this day smells horribly of horse-drugs.—Whether these marks of humiliation were designed,—I something doubt;—because at the end of the sermon (and not at the beginning of it)—very different from his way of treating the rest, he had wrote —— *Bravo!*

—Though not very offensively,—for it was at two inches, at least, and a half's distance from and below the concluding line of the sermon, at the very extremity of the page, and in that right-hand corner of it which, you know, is generally covered with your thumb;

75

and, to do it justice, it is wrote besides with a crow's quill, so faintly, in a small Italian hand, as scarcely to solicit the eye towards the place, whether your thumb is there or not;—so that, from the *manner of it*, it stands half excused; and being wrote, moreover, with very pale ink, diluted almost to nothing,—'tis more like a *ritratto* of the shadow of Vanity than of Vanity herself—of the two; resembling rather a faint thought of transient applause, secretly stirring up in the heart of the composer, than a gross mark of it, coarsely obtruded upon the world.

With all these extenuations, I am aware that, in publishing this, I do no service to Yorick's character as a modest man—but all men have their failings! and what lessens this still farther, and almost wipes it away, is this,—that the word was struck through some time afterwards (as appears from a different tint of the ink) with a line quite across it, in this manner, ~~BRAVO~~, as if he had retracted, or was ashamed of the opinion he had once entertained of it.

From TRISTRAM SHANDY, by
Laurence Sterne (1713–68).

28

THE CLERICAL NATURALIST

THERE is a wonderful spirit of sociality in the brute creation, independent of sexual attachment: the congregation of gregarious birds in the winter is a remarkable instance.

Many horses, though quiet with company, will not stay one minute in a field by themselves: the strongest fences cannot restrain them. My neighbour's horse will not only not stay by himself abroad, but he will not bear to be left alone in a strange stable without discovering the utmost impatience, and endeavouring to break the rack and manger with his fore feet. He has been known to leap out at a stable window, through which dung was thrown, after company: and yet in other respects is remarkably quiet. Oxen and cows will not fatten by themselves; but will neglect the finest pasture that is not recommended by society. It would be needless to instance sheep, which constantly flock together.

But this propensity seems not to be confined to animals of the same species; for we know a doe, still alive, that was brought up from a little fawn with a dairy of cows; with them it goes a-field, and with them it returns to the yard. The dogs of the house take no notice of this deer, being used to her; but, if strange dogs come by, a chase ensues; while the master smiles to see his favourite securely leading her pursuers over hedge, or gate, or stile, till she returns to the cows, who with fierce lowings and menacing horns, drive the assailants quite out of the pasture.

Even great disparity of kind and size does not always prevent social advances and mutual fellowship. For a very intelligent and observant person has assured me, that in the former part of his life, keeping but one horse, he happened also on a time to have but one solitary hen. These two incongruous animals spent much of their time together in a lonely orchard, where they saw no creature but each other. By degrees an apparent regard began to take place between these two sequestered individuals. The fowl would approach the quadruped with notes of complacency, rubbing herself gently against his legs; while the horse would look down with satisfaction, and move with the greatest caution and circumspection, lest he should trample on his diminutive companion. Thus, by mutual good offices, each seemed to console the vacant hours of the other: so that Milton, when he puts the following sentiment in the mouth of Adam, seems to be somewhat mistaken:—

"Much less can bird with beast, or fish with fowl,
So well converse, nor with the ox the ape."

From NATURAL HISTORY OF SELBORNE,
by Gilbert White (1720–93).

29

TUTORS TO A GENIUS

Entering Magdalen College Oxford at the age of fifteen "with a stock of erudition that might have puzzled a doctor, and a degree of ignorance of which a schoolboy would have been ashamed," Edward Gibbon was astonished by the easy indulgence of his Anglican tutors.

THE fellows or monks of my time were decent easy men, who supinely enjoyed the gifts of the founder; their days were filled by a series of uniform employments; the chapel and the hall, the coffee-house and the common room, till they retired, weary and well satisfied, to a long slumber. From the toil of reading, or thinking, or writing, they had absolved their conscience; and the first shoots of learning and ingenuity withered on the ground, without yielding any fruits to the owners or the public. As a gentleman-commoner, I was admitted to the society of the fellows, and fondly expected that some questions of literature would be the amusing and instructive topics of their discourse. Their conversation stagnated in a round of college business, Tory politics, personal anecdotes, and private scandal: their dull and deep potations excused the brisk intemperance of youth: and their constitutional toasts were not expressive of the most lively loyalty for the house of Hanover.

. . . . .

The first tutor into whose hands I was resigned appears to have been one of the best of the tribe: Dr. Waldegrave was a learned and pious man, of a mild disposition, strict morals, and abstemious life, who seldom mingled in the politics or the jollity of the college. But his knowledge of the world was confined to the University; his learning was of the last, rather than of the present age; his temper was indolent; his faculties, which were not of the first rate, had been relaxed by the climate, and he was satisfied, like his fellows, with the slight and superficial discharge of an important trust. As soon as my tutor had sounded the insufficiency of his disciple in school-learning, he proposed that we should read every morning from ten to eleven the comedies of Terence. The sum of my improvement in the University of Oxford is confined to three or four Latin plays; and even the study of an elegant classic, which might have been illustrated by a comparison of ancient and modern theatres, was reduced to a dry and literal interpretation of the author's text. During the first weeks I constantly attended these lessons in my tutor's room; but as they appeared equally devoid of profit and pleasure, I was once tempted to try the experiment of a formal apology. The apology was accepted with a smile. I repeated the offence with less ceremony; the excuse was admitted with the same indulgence: the slightest motive of laziness or indisposition, the most trifling avocation at home or abroad, was allowed as a worthy impediment; nor did my tutor appear conscious of my absence or neglect. Had the hour of lecture been constantly filled, a single hour was a small portion of my academic leisure. No plan of study was recommended for my use; no exercises were prescribed for his inspection; and, at the most precious season of youth, whole days and weeks were suffered to elapse without labour or amusement, without advice or account.

·　　·　　·　　·　　·

After the departure of Dr. Waldegrave, I was transferred, with his other pupils, to his academical heir, whose literary character did not command the respect of the college. Dr. —— well remembered that he had a salary to receive, and only forgot that he had a duty to perform. Instead of guiding the studies, and watching over the behaviour of his disciple, I was never summoned to attend even the ceremony of a lecture; and, excepting one voluntary visit to his rooms, during the eight months of his titular office, the tutor and pupil lived in the same college as strangers to each other. The want of experience, of advice, and of occupation, soon betrayed me into some improprieties of conduct, ill-chosen company, late hours, and inconsiderate expense. My growing debts might be secret; but my frequent absence was visible and scandalous: and a tour to Bath, a visit into Buckinghamshire, and four excursions to London in the same winter, were costly and dangerous frolics.

They were, indeed, without a meaning, as without an excuse. The irksomeness of a cloistered life repeatedly tempted me to wander; but my chief pleasure was that of travelling; and I was too young and bashful to enjoy, like a manly Oxonian in town, the pleasures of London. In all these excursions I eloped from Oxford; I returned to college; in a few days I eloped again, as if I had been an independent stranger in a hired lodging, without once hearing the voice of admonition, without once feeling the hand of control. Yet my time was lost, my expenses were multiplied, my behaviour abroad was unknown; folly as well as vice should have awakened the attention of my superiors, and my tender years would have justified a more than ordinary degree of restraint and discipline.

It might at least be expected that an ecclesiastical school should inculcate the orthodox principles of religion. But our venerable mother had contrived to unite the opposite extremes of bigotry and indifference: an heretic, or unbeliever was a monster in her eyes; but she was always, or often, or sometimes, remiss in the spiritual education of her own children. According to the statutes of the University, every student, before he is matriculated, must subscribe his assent to the thirty-nine articles of the Church of England, which are signed by more than read, and read by more than believe them. My insufficient age excused me, however, from the immediate performance of this legal ceremony; and the Vice-Chancellor directed me to return, as soon as I should have accomplished my fifteenth year; recommending me, in the meanwhile, to the instruction of my college. My college forgot to instruct: I forgot to return, and was myself forgotten by the first magistrate of the University. Without a single lecture, either public or private, either Christian or Protestant, without any academical subscription, without any episcopal confirmation, I was left by the dim light of my catechism to grope my way to the chapel and communion-table, where I was admitted, without a question, how far, or by what means, I might be qualified to receive the Sacrament.

From AUTOBIOGRAPHY, by
Edward Gibbon (1737–94).

30

SPIRITUAL CONSOLATION

Pressed into the Navy, Roderick Random is stricken with a bilious fever while sailing in the Thunder *in the West Indies.*

WHEN my distemper was at the height, Morgan thought my case desperate; and, after having applied a blister to the nape of my neck, squeezed my hand, bidding me, with a woeful countenance, recommend myself to Got and my Reteemer; then taking his leave, desired the chaplain to come and administer some spiritual consolation to me; but before he arrived, I made shift to rid myself of the troublesome application the Welshman had bestowed on my back. The parson having felt my pulse, inquired into the nature of my complaints, hemmed a little, and began thus: "Mr. Random, God out of his infinite mercy hath been pleased to visit you with a dreadful distemper, the issue of which no man knows. You may be permitted to recover, and live many days on the face of the earth; and, which is more probable, you maybe taken away and cut off in the flower of your youth. It is incumbent on you, therefore, to prepare for the great change, by repenting sincerely of your sins; of this there cannot be a greater sign, than an ingenuous confession, which I conjure you to make, without hesitation or mental reservation; and when I am convinced of your sincerity, I will then give you such comfort as the situation of your soul will admit of. Without doubt, you have been guilty of numberless transgressions to which youth is subject, as swearing, drunkenness, whoredom, and adultery; tell me, therefore, without reserve, the particulars of each, especially the last, that I may be acquainted with the true state of your conscience: for no physicians will prescribe for his patient until he knows the circumstances of his disease." As I was not under any apprehensions of death, I could not help smiling at the chaplain's inquisitive remonstrance, which I told him savoured more of the Roman than of the Protestant church, in recommending auricular confession; a thing, in my opinion, not at all necessary to salvation, and which, for that reason,

I declined. This reply disconcerted him a little; however he explained away his meaning, in making learned distinctions between what was absolutely necessary, and what was only convenient; then proceeded to ask what religion I professed. I answered, that I had not as yet considered the difference of religions, consequently, had not fixed on any one in particular, but that I was bred a presbyterian. At this word the chaplain expressed great astonishment, and said he could not apprehend how a presbyterian was entitled to any post under the English government. Then he asked if I had ever received the sacrament, or taken the oaths; to which questions I replying in the negative, he held up his hands, assured me he could do me no service, wished I might not be in a state of reprobation, and returned to his messmates, who were making merry in the ward-room, round a table well stored with bumbo and wine.

From RODERICK RANDOM, by Tobias
George Smollett (1721–71).

31

ON THE ENGLISH CLERGY AND POPULAR PREACHERS

IT is allowed on all hands, that our English divines receive a more liberal education, and improve that education by frequent study, more than any others of this reverend profession in Europe. In general, also, it may be observed, that a greater degree of gentility is affixed to the character of a student in England than elsewhere; by which means our clergy have an opportunity of seeing better company while young, and of sooner wearing off those prejudices which they are apt to imbibe in the best-regulated universities, and which may be justly termed the vulgar errors of the wise.

Yet, with all these advantages, it is very obvious, that the clergy are nowhere so little thought of, by the populace, as here; and though our divines are foremost with respect to abilities, yet they are found last in the effects of their ministry; the vulgar, in general, appearing no way impressed with a sense of religious duty. I am not for whining at the depravity of the times, or for endeavouring to paint a prospect more gloomy than in nature; but certain it is, no person who has travelled will contradict me, when I aver, that the lower orders of mankind, in other countries, testify, on every occasion, the profoundest awe of religion; while in England they are scarcely awakened into a sense of its duties, even in circumstances of the greatest distress.

This dissolute and fearless conduct foreigners are apt to attribute to climate and constitution; may not the vulgar being pretty much neglected in our exhortations from the pulpit, be a conspiring cause? Our divines seldom stoop to their mean capacities; and they who want instruction most, find least in our religious assemblies.

Whatever may become of the higher orders of mankind, who are generally possessed of collateral motives to virtue, the vulgar should be particularly regarded, whose behaviour in civil life is totally hinged upon their hopes and fears. Those who constitute the basis of the great fabric of society, should be particularly regarded; for, in policy as architecture, ruin is most fatal when it begins from the bottom.

Men of real sense and understanding prefer a prudent mediocrity to a precarious popularity; and fearing to outdo their duty, leave it half done. Their discourses from the pulpit are generally dry, methodical, and unaffecting: delivered with the most insipid calmness; insomuch that should the peaceful preacher lift his head over the cushion, which alone he seems to address, he might discover his audience, instead of being awakened to remorse, actually sleeping over this methodical and laboured composition.

This method of preaching is, however, by some called an address to reason, and not to the passions; this is styled the making of converts from conviction; but such are indifferently acquainted with human nature, who are not sensible that men seldom reason about their debaucheries till they are committed. Reason is but a weak antagonist when headlong passion dictates: in all such cases we should arm one passion against another: it is with the human mind as in nature; from the mixture of two opposites, the result is most frequently neutral tranquillity. Those who attempt to reason us out of our follies, begin at the wrong end, since the attempt naturally presupposes us capable of reason; but to be made capable of this, is one great point of the cure.

There are but few talents requisite to become a popular preacher; for the people are easily pleased, if they perceive any endeavours in the orator to please them; the meanest qualifications will work this effect, if the preacher sincerely sets about it. Perhaps little, indeed very little more is required than sincerity and assurance; and a becoming sincerity is always certain of producing a becoming assurance. "Si vis me flere, dolendum est primum tibi ipsi," is so trite a quotation, that it almost demands an apology to repeat it; yet though all allow the justice of the remark, how few do we find put it in practice! Our orators, with the most faulty bashfulness, seem impressed rather with an awe of their audience, than with a just respect for the truths they are about to deliver: they, of all professions, seem the most bashful, who have the greatest right to glory in their commission.

From ESSAYS, by Oliver
Goldsmith (1728–74).

32

NOT WITHOUT PRIDE

THE temporal concerns of our family were chiefly committed to my wife's management; as to the spiritual, I took them entirely under my own direction. The profits of my living, which amounted to about thirty-five pounds a-year, I made over to the orphans and widows of the clergy of our diocese; for, having a sufficient fortune of my own, I was careless of temporalities, and felt a secret pleasure in doing my duty without reward. I also set a resolution of keeping no curate, and of being acquainted with every man in the parish, exhorting the married men to temperance and the bachelors to matrimony; so that in a few years it was a common saying, that there were three strange wants in Wakefield—a parson wanting pride, young men wanting wives, and alehouses wanting customers.

Matrimony was always one of my favourite topics, and I wrote several sermons to prove its happiness; but there was a peculiar tenet which I made a point of supporting: for I maintained, with Whiston, that it was unlawful for a priest of the church of England, after the death of his first wife, to take a second; or, to express it in one word, I valued myself upon being a strict monogamist.

I was early initiated into this important dispute, on which so many laborious volumes have been written. I published some tracts upon the subject myself, which, as they never sold, I have the consolation of thinking were read only by the happy *few*. Some of my friends called this my weak side; but, alas! they had not, like me, made it the subject of long contemplation. The more I reflected upon it, the more important it appeared. I even went a step beyond Whiston in displaying my principles: as he had engraven upon his wife's tomb that she was the *only* wife of William Whiston; so I wrote a similar epitaph for my wife, though still living, in which I extolled her prudence, economy, and obedience till death; and, having got it copied fair, with an elegant frame, it was placed over the chimney-piece, where it answered several very useful purposes. It admonished my wife of her duty to me, and my fidelity to her; it inspired her with a passion for fame, and constantly put her in mind of her end.

It was thus, perhaps, from hearing marriage so often recommended, that my eldest son, just upon leaving college, fixed his affections upon the daughter of a neighbouring clergyman, who was a dignitary in the Church, and in circumstances to give her a large fortune; but fortune was her smallest accomplishment. Miss Arabella Wilmot was allowed by all (except my two daughters) to be completely pretty. Her youth, health, and innocence were still heightened by complexion so transparent, and such a happy sensibility of look, as even age could not gaze on with indifference. As Mr. Wilmot knew that I could make a very handsome settlement on my son, he was not averse to the match; so both families lived together in all that harmony which generally precedes an expected alliance. Being convinced, by experience, that the days of courtship are the most happy of our lives, I was willing enough to lengthen the period; and the various amusements which the young couple every day shared in each other's company seemed to increase their passion. We were generally awaked in the morning by music, and on fine days rode a-hunting. The hours between breakfast and dinner the ladies devoted to dress and study: they usually read a page, and then gazed at themselves in the glass, which even philosophers might own often presented the page of greatest beauty. At dinner my wife took the lead; for, as she always insisted upon carving everything herself, it being her mother's way, she gave us, upon these occasions, the history of every dish. When we had dined, to prevent the ladies leaving us, I generally ordered the table to be removed; and sometimes, with the music-master's assistance, the girls would give us a very agreeable concert. Walking out, drinking tea, country dances, and forfeits shortened the rest of the day, without the assistance of cards, as I hated all manner of gaming, except backgammon, at which my old friend and I sometimes took a twopenny hit. Nor can I here pass over an ominous circumstance that happened the last time we played together; I only wanted to fling a quatre, and yet I threw deuce-ace five times running.

Some months were elapsed in this manner, till at last it was thought convenient to fix a day for the nuptials of the young couple, who seemed earnestly to desire it. During the preparations for the wedding I need not describe the busy importance of my wife, nor the sly looks of my daughters; in fact my attention was fixed on another object—the completing a tract which I intended shortly to publish in defence of my favourite principle. As I looked upon this as a masterpiece, both for argument and style, I could not, in the pride of my heart, avoid showing it to my old friend Mr. Wilmot, as I made no doubt of receiving his approbation: but not till too late I discovered that he was most violently attached to the contrary opinion, and with good reason; for he was at that time actually courting a fourth wife. This, as may be expected, produced a dispute attended with some acrimony, which threatened to interrupt our intended alliance; but, on the day before that appointed for the ceremony, we agreed to discuss the subject at large.

It was managed with proper spirit on both sides; he asserted that I was heterodox; I retorted the charge, he replied, and I rejoined. In the meantime, while the controversy was hottest, I was called out by one of my relations, who, with a face of concern, advised me to give up the dispute, at least till my son's wedding was over. "How!" cried I; "relinquish the cause of truth, and let him be a husband, already driven to the very verge of absurdity? You might as well advise me to give up my fortune as my argument." "Your fortune," returned my friend, "I am now sorry to inform you, is almost nothing. The merchant in town, in whose hands your money was lodged, has gone off to avoid a statute of bankruptcy, and is thought not to have left a shilling in the pound. I was unwilling to shock you or your family with the account till after the wedding; but now it may serve to moderate your warmth in the argument; for I suppose your own prudence will enforce the necessity of dissembling, at least till your son has the young lady's fortune secure." "Well," returned I, "if what you tell me be true, and I am to be a beggar, it shall never make me a rascal, or induce me to disavow my principles. I'll go this moment and inform the company of my circumstances; and as for the argument, I even here retract my former concessions in the old gentleman's favour, nor will I allow him now to be a husband in any sense of the expression."

It would be endless to describe the different sensations of both families when I divulged the news of our misfortune; but what others felt was slight to what the lovers appeared to endure. Mr. Wilmot, who seemed before sufficiently inclined to break off the match, was by this blow soon determined; one virtue he had in perfection, which was prudence—too often the only one that is left us at seventy-two.

From THE VICAR OF WAKEFIELD,
by Oliver Goldsmith (1728–74).

33

THE VILLAGE PREACHER

NEAR yonder copse, where once the garden smil'd,
And still where many a garden flower grows wild;
There, where a few torn shrubs the place disclose,
The village preacher's modest mansion rose.
A man he was to all the country dear,
And passing rich with forty pounds a year;
Remote from towns he ran his godly race,
Nor e'er had chang'd, nor wish'd to change his place;
Unskilful he to fawn, or seek for power,
By doctrines fashioned to the varying hour;
Far other aims his heart had learned to prize
More bent to raise the wretched than to rise.
His house was known to all the vagrant train,
He chid their wanderings, but reliev'd their pain;
The long remembered beggar was his guest,
Whose beard descending swept his aged breast;
The ruined spendthrift, now no longer proud,
Claimed kindred there, and had his claims allowed;
The broken soldier, kindly bade to stay,
Sat by his fire, and talked the night away;
Wept o'er his wounds, or tales of sorrow done,
Shouldered his crutch, and show'd how fields were won;
Pleased with his guests, the good man learned to glow,
And quite forgot their vices in their woe;
Careless their merits, or their faults to scan,
His pity gave ere charity began.

Thus to relieve the wretched was his pride,
And e'en his failings leaned to Virtue's side;
But in his duty prompt at every call,
He watched and wept, he prayed and felt, for all.

And, as a bird each fond endearment tries
To tempt its new-fledg'd offspring to the skies,
He tried each art, reproved each dull delay,
Allured to brighter worlds, and led the way.

Beside the bed where parting life was layed,
And sorrow, guilt, and pain, by turns dismay'd,
The reverend champion stood. At his control
Despair and anguish fled the struggling soul;
Comfort came down the trembling wretch to raise,
And his last faultering accents whisper'd praise.
At church, with meek and unaffected grace,
His looks adorned the venerable place;
Truth from his lips prevailed with double sway,
And fools, who came to scoff, remained to pray.
The service past, around the pious man,
With ready zeal, each honest rustic ran;
Even children followed with endearing wile,
And plucked his gown, to share the good man's smile.
His ready smile a parent's warmth exprest,
Their welfare pleased him, and their cares distrest;
To them his heart, his love, his griefs were given,
But all his serious thoughts had rest in Heaven.
As some tall cliff, that lifts its awful form,
Swells from the vale, and midway leaves the storm,
Tho' round its breast the rolling clouds are spread,
Eternal sunshine settles on its head.

From THE DESERTED VILLAGE, by
Oliver Goldsmith (1728–74).

34

PARSON WOODFORDE'S TITHE AUDIT

Parson Woodforde, Rector of Longeville in Norfolk during the latter years of the eighteenth century, began a diary at the age of eighteen, and kept it up for forty-five years. It is a fascinating record of the everyday occurrences in the life of a bucolic parson, whose chief pleasures were those of the table, but who was kindly, unpretentious, respectable (though sometimes a bit larky) and faithful in the discharge of his duties.

1799. DECBR. 1, Sunday. We breakfasted, dined, &c. again at home. Mr. Dade (my Curate) called on me this Morning before Divine Service, and I paid him, half a Years serving Weston Church for me, due about this time 15.6.0. Nancy & her Brother went to Church this Morn'. Mr. Custance was at Church and he brought them home in his Coach but he did not come in. Dinner to day, Cod-Fish & a Co. Ducks rosted. Bread given to the Poor at Church to day. Wheat being very dear 50. Shillings per Coomb.

Decbr. 3. Tuesday. We breakfasted, dined, &c. again at home. The Poor complain of the small Quantity of Bread given to them on Sunday at Church almost as much as if they had none given. Dinner to day, Leg of Mutton rosted &c. Nancy's Brother took a ride this Morning to Dr. Thorne's at Mattishall, where he dined & spent the Afternoon—returned to Supper &c. I was but poorly all the whole Day.

Decbr. 4. Wednesday. . . . Sent Briton this Morn' to Norwich after many thing against my Tithe-Audit on Tuesday next—he returned by Tea-time. Dinner to day, a Hare rosted &c. Very indifferent & dull all the day, Weather very dull, very dark & very enervating.

Decbr. 5, Thursday. . . . Mrs. Custance with both her Daughters made us a long Morning Visit. The two young Ladies looked very poorly and very pale. Dinner to day, Skaite & a Neck of Mutton rosted &c. I was something better thank God! this Day. Sent Ben round the Parish this Morning to give notice of my Tithe-Audit on Tuesday next.

Decbr. 9. Monday. We breakfasted, dined, &c. again at home. Mr. Maynard called on us this Morning. Busy to day in preparing for my Tithe Audit to Morrow. Dinner to day, boiled Veal &c.

Decbr. 10, Tuesday. We breakfasted, dined, &c. again at home. This being my Tithe Audit-Day, the following People paid me their respective Compositions for Tithe &c. for the last Year to Michaelmas last. Stephen Andrews Senr., John Pegg for his Father, Michael Andrews, Willm. Bidewell, John Baker, Thos. Reynolds Junr., Js. Jermyn, J_o^n Norton, John Girling Junr., Willm. Howlett, Barnard Dunnell, John Mann, J_o^n Culley, Thos. Baker, Mary Pratt, Charles Cary, Henry Case, John Buck Junr., An. Spraggs, Charles Hardy, John Hubbard, & J_o^n Heavers. I recd. of them upon the whole about —. They dined & stayed at my House, till abt. 11. at Night & went away then highly pleased. I did not see any of them the lest disguised. Dinner, two Legs of Mutton boiled & Capers, Salt-Fish, a Sur-Loin of Beef rosted, with plenty of plumb & plain Puddings &c. Only two Bowls of Punch, four Bottles of Wine four Bottles of Rum—eight Lemons, about three Pounds of Sugar, and at lest six Gallons of strong Beer besides small. My Nephew gave them a Song. It was the pleasantest & most agreeable Tithe-Audit, I ever experienced. Every thing harmonious & agreeable.

Decbr. 12, Thursday. We breakfasted, dined, &c. again at home. Farmer Hugh Bush of this Parish who has been missing from his House ever since Sunday Afternoon December 1st. was this Morning found drowned in a Pond near his House. It is supposed that he destroyed himself. He and Family lived most unhappily. Dinner to day, boiled Beef &c.

Decbr. 13, Friday. We breakfasted, dined &c. again at home. A Coroner's Inquest was this Morn' taken on the Body of the late Farmer Hugh Bush of this Parish by Colls—Coroner—their Verdict was Lunacy. My Servant Ben. Leggatt, attended as one of the Jurors. By all Accounts, his Life was made so unhappy by his Wife & Family and also by his own bad Actions that his Life was miserable. Nancy and her Brother dined and spent the Afternoon at Weston-House. Mr. Press Custance there—none besides but their own Family. They went & returned in Mr. Custance's Coach. They came home about 8. o'clock. I had for my Dinner fryed Beef & Cabbage and a Rabbit rosted &c.

Dec. 14, Saturday. We breakfasted, dined, &c. again at home. Sent Ben this Morning to Norwich with eight Coomb of Wheat to Mr. Bloome for which he owes me (as he sent no Cash) the Sum of 16.12.0 as per his own Note sent back for the same. A great Price, tho' not so great as it was lately. It was a very little time ago up to 50/od. pr. Coomb. Ben returned about 5. o'clock this Evening. Dinner to day, Calfs' Fry &c.

Dec. 15, Sunday. We breakfasted, dined, &c again at home. Mr. Dade read Prayers & Preached this Morn' at Weston-Church. Sent Ben this Morn' to Mr. Stoughton of Sparham to desire him to administer the H. Sacrament at Weston Church on Christmas Day or the Sunday following for Mr. Dade, as he is not in Priests Orders, which he very kindly sent me word that he would do on the Sunday after Christmas-Day. Dinner to day, a Turkey rosted &c. My Nephew had a Letter from his Wife by some of Weston House Family.

From THE DIARY OF A COUNTRY PARSON.

35

A MESSENGER OF GRACE

I VENERATE the man whose heart is warm,
Whose hands are pure, whose doctrine and whose life
Coincident, exhibit lucid proof
That he is honest in the sacred cause.
To such I render more than mere respect,
Whose actions say that they respect themselves.
But loose in morals, and in manners vain,
In conversation frivolous, in dress
Extreme, at once rapacious and profuse,

Frequent in park, with lady at his side,
Ambling and prattling scandal as he goes,
But rare at home, and never at his books,
Or with his pen, save when he scrawls a card
Constant at routs, familiar with a round
Of ladyships, a stranger to the poor;
Ambitious of preferment for its gold,
And well prepared by ignorance and sloth,
By infidelity and love of world,
To make God's work a sinecure; a slave
To his own pleasures and his patron's pride:—
From such apostles, O ye mitred heads,
Preserve the Church! and lay not careless hands
On skulls that cannot teach, and will not learn.
    Would I describe a preacher, such as Paul,
Were he on earth, would hear, approve, and own,
Paul should himself direct me. I would trace
His master-strokes, and draw from his design.
I would express him simple, grave, sincere;
In doctrine uncorrupt; in language plain,
And plain in manner; decent, solemn, chaste,
And natural in gesture; much impress'd
Himself, as conscious of his awful charge,
And anxious mainly that the flock he feeds
May feel it too; affectionate in look,
And tender in address, as well becomes
A messenger of grace to guilty men.
Behold the picture! Is it like?—Like whom?
The things that mount the rostrum with a skip,
And then skip down again; pronounce a text,
Cry hem! and reading what they never wrote,
Just fifteen minutes, huddle up their work,
And with a well-bred whisper close the scene.
    In man or woman, but far most in man,
And most of all in man that ministers
And serves the altar, in my soul I loathe
All affectation. 'Tis my perfect scorn;

Object of my implacable disgust.
What!—will a man play tricks, will he indulge
A silly fond conceit of his fair form
And just proportion, fashionable mien,
And pretty face, in presence of his God?
Or will he seek to dazzle me with tropes,
As with the diamond on his lily hand,
And play his brilliant parts before my eyes
When I am hungry for the bread of life?
He mocks his Maker, prostitutes and shames
His noble office, and, instead of truth,
Displaying his own beauty, starves his flock.
Therefore, avaunt! all attitude and stare,
And start theatric, practised at the glass.
I seek divine simplicity in him
Who handles things divine; and all beside,
Though learn'd with labour, and though much admired
By curious eyes and judgments ill inform'd,
To me is odious as the nasal twang
Heard at conventicle, where worthy men,
Misled by custom, strain celestial themes
Through the press'd nostril, spectacle-bestrid.

From THE TASK, by William
Cowper   (1731–1800).

36

COUNTRY PARSONS

THE ruinous condition of some of the churches gave me great offence; and I could not help wishing that the honest vicar, instead of indulging his genius for improvements, by enclosing his gooseberry bushes within a Chinese rail, and converting half an acre of his glebe-land into a bowling-green, would have applied part of his income to the more laudable purpose of sheltering his parishioners from the weather, during their attendance on divine service. It is no uncommon thing to see the parsonage house well thatched, and in exceeding good repair, while the church perhaps has scarce any other roof than the ivy that grows over it. The noise of owls, bats, and magpies makes the principal part of the church music in many of these ancient edifices; and the walls, like a large map, seem to be portioned out into capes, seas, and promontories, by the various colours by which the damps have stained them. Sometimes, the foundation being too weak to support the steeple any longer, it has been expedient to pull down that part of the building, and to hang the bells under a wooden shed on the ground beside it. This is the case in a parish in Norfolk, through which I lately passed, and where the clerk and the sexton, like the two figures at St. Dunstan's, serve the bells in capacity of clappers, by striking them alternately with a hammer.

In other churches I have observed, that nothing unseemly or ruinous is to be found, except in the clergyman, and the appendages of his person. The squire of the parish, or his ancestors, perhaps to testify their devotion, and leave a lasting monument of their magnificence, have adorned the altar-piece with the richest crimson velvet, embroidered with vine leaves and ears of wheat; and have dressed up the pulpit with the same splendour and expense; while the gentleman, who fills it, is exalted in the midst of all this finery, with a surplice as dirty as a farmer's frock, and a periwig that seems to have transferred its faculty of curling to the band which appears in full buckle beneath it.

But if I was concerned to see several distressed pastors, as well as many of our country churches, in a tottering condition, I was more offended with the indecency of worship in others. I could wish that the clergy would inform their congregations, that there is no occasion to scream themselves hoarse in making the responses; that the town-crier is not the only person qualified to pray with due devotion; and that he who bawls the loudest may nevertheless be the wickedest fellow in the parish. The old women too in the aisle might be told, that their time would be better employed in attending to the sermon, than in fumbling over their tattered testaments till they have found the text; by which time the discourse is near drawing to a conclusion: while a word or two of instruction might not be thrown away upon the younger part of the congregation, to teach them that making posies in summer time, and cracking nuts in autumn, is no part of the religious ceremony.

. . . . .

It is a difficult matter to decide, which is looked upon as the greatest man in a country church, the parson or his clerk. The latter is most certainly held in higher veneration, where the former happens to be only a poor curate, who rides post every Sabbath from village to village, and mounts and dismounts at the church door. The clerk's office is not only to tag the prayers with an Amen, or usher in the sermon with a stave; but he is also the universal father to give away the brides, and the standing godfather to all the new-born bantlings. But in many places there is still a greater man belonging to the church, than either the parson or the clerk himself. The person I mean is the Squire; who, like the King, may be styled Head of the Church in his own parish. If the benefice be in his own gift, the vicar is his creature, and of consequence entirely at his devotion; or, if the care of the church be left to a curate, the Sunday fees of roast beef and plum pudding, and a liberty to shoot in the manor, will bring him as much under the Squire's command as his dogs and horses. For this reason the bell is often kept tolling and the people waiting in the churchyard an hour longer than the usual time; nor must the service begin until the Squire has strutted up the aisle, and seated himself in the great pew in the chancel. The length of the sermon is also measured by the will of the Squire, as formerly by the hour-glass: and I know one parish where the preacher has always the complaisance to conclude his discourse, however abruptly, the minute that the Squire gives the signal, by rising up after his nap. . . .

From LETTERS, by William Cowper (1731–1800).

37

A SHEPHERD OF A DIFFERENT STOCK

HE ceases now the feeble help to crave
Of man; and silent sinks into the grave.
   But ere his death some pious doubts arise,
Some simple fears, which "bold bad" men despise;
Fain would he ask the parish-priest to prove
His title certain to the joys above:
For this he sends the murmuring nurse, who calls
The holy stranger to these dismal walls:
And doth not he, the pious man, appear,
He, "passing rich with forty pounds a year?"
Ah! no; a shepherd of a different stock,
And far unlike him, feeds this little flock:
A jovial youth, who thinks his Sunday's task
As much as God or man can fairly ask;
The rest he gives to loves and labours light,
To fields the morning, and to feasts the night;
None better skill'd the noisy pack to guide,
To urge their chase, to cheer them or to chide;
A sportsman keen, he shoots through half the day,
And, skill'd at whist, devotes the night to play:
Then, while such honours bloom around his head,
Shall he sit sadly by the sick man's bed,
To raise the hope he feels not, or with zeal
To combat fears that e'en the pious feel?
   Now once again the gloomy scene explore,
Less gloomy now; the bitter hour is o'er,
The man of many sorrows sighs no more.—
Up yonder hill, behold how sadly slow
The bier moves winding from the vale below;
There lie the happy dead, from trouble free,
And the glad parish pays the frugal fee:
No more, O Death! thy victim starts to hear
Churchwarden stern, or kingly overseer;

No more the farmer claims his humble bow,
Thou art his lord, the best of tyrants thou!
  Now to the church behold the mourners come,
Sedately torpid and devoutly dumb;
The village children now their games suspend,
To see the bier that bears their ancient friend;
For he was one in all their idle sport,
And like a monarch ruled their little court.
The pliant bow he form'd, the flying ball,
The bat, the wicket, were his labours all;
Him now they follow to his grave, and stand
Silent and sad, and gazing, hand in hand;
While bending low, their eager eyes explore
The mingled relics of the parish poor:
The bell tolls late, the moping owl flies round,
Fear marks the flight and magnifies the sound;
The busy priest, detain'd by weightier care,
Defers his duty till the day of prayer;
And, waiting long, the crowd retire distress'd,
To think a poor man's bones should lie unbless'd.

From THE VILLAGE, by
George Crabbe (1754–1832).

38

HIS RULING PASSION

To what famed college we our Vicar owe,
To what fair country, let historians show:
Few now remember when the mild young man,
Ruddy and fair, his Sunday-task began;
Few live to speak of that soft soothing look
He cast around, as he prepared his book;
It was a kind of supplicating smile,
But nothing hopeless of applause the while;

And when he finished, his corrected pride
Felt the desert, and yet the praise denied.
Thus he his race began, and to the end
His constant care was, no man to offend;
No haughty virtues stirr'd his peaceful mind;
Nor urged the Priest to leave the Flock behind;
He was his Master's Soldier, but not one
To lead an army of his Martyrs on:
Fear was his ruling passion; yet was Love,
Of timid kind, once known his heart to move;
It led his patient spirit where it paid
Its languid offerings to a listening Maid:
She, with her widow'd Mother, heard him speak,
And sought awhile to find what he would seek:
Smiling he came, he smiled when he withdrew,
And paid the same attention to the two;
Meeting or parting without joy or pain,
He seem'd to come that he might go again.
    The wondering girl, no prude, but something nice,
At length was chill'd by his unmelting ice;
She found her tortoise held such sluggish pace,
That she must turn and meet him in the chase:
This not approving, she withdrew, till one
Came who appear'd with livelier hope to run;
Who sought a readier way the heart to move,
Than by faint dalliance of unfixing love.

    Fiddling and fishing were his arts: at times
He alter'd sermons, and he aim'd at rhymes;
And his fair friends, not yet intent on cards,
Oft he amused with riddles and charades.
    Mild were his doctrines, and not one discourse
But gain'd in softness what it lost in force.

In him his flock found nothing to condemn;
Him sectaries liked,—he never troubled them.

99

No trifles fail'd his yielding mind to please,
And all his passions sunk in early ease;
Nor one so old has left this world of sin,
More like the being that he enter'd in.

By George Crabbe (1754–1832).

39

PASTOR OF A JOVIAL FOLD

THE vicar at the table's front presides,
Whose presence a monastic life derides;
The reverend wig, in sideway order placed,
The reverend band, by rubric stains disgraced,
The leering eye, in wayward circles roll'd,
Mark him the pastor of a jovial fold,
Whose various texts excite a loud applause,
Favouring the bottle, and the good old cause.
See! the dull smile which fearfully appears,
When gross indecency her front uprears;
The joy conceal'd, the fiercer burns within,
As masks afford the keenest gust to sin;
Imagination helps the reverend sire,
And spreads the sails of sub-divine desire;
But when the gay immoral joke goes round,
When shame and all her blushing train are drown'd,
Rather than hear his God blasphemed, he takes
The last loved glass, and then the board forsakes.
Not that religion prompts the sober thought,
But slavish custom has the practice taught;
Besides, this zealous son of warm devotion
Has a true Levite bias for promotion.
Vicars must with discretion go astray,
Whilst bishops may be damn'd the nearest way.

By George Crabbe (1754–1832).

THE DISSENTING MINISTER

A DISSENTING minister is a character not so easily to be dispensed with, and whose place cannot be well supplied. It is a pity that this character has worn itself out; that that pulse of thought and feeling has ceased almost to beat in the heart of the nation, who, if not remarkable for sincerity and plain downright well-meaning, are remarkable for nothing. But we have known some such, in happier days, who had been brought up and lived from youth to age in the one constant belief in God and of His Christ, and who thought "all other things but dross compared with the glory to be hereafter revealed." Their youthful hopes and vanity had been mortified in them even in their boyish days, by the neglect and supercilious regards of the world; and they turned to look into their own minds for something else to build their hopes and confidence upon. They were true priests. They set up an image in their own minds—it was truth; they worshipped an idol there—it was justice. They looked on man as their brother, and only bowed the knee to the Highest. Separate from the world, they walked humbly with their God, and lived in thought with those who had borne testimony of a good conscience, with the spirits of just men in all ages. . . . Their sympathy was not with the oppressors, but the oppressed. They cherished in their thoughts—and wished to transmit to their posterity—those rights and privileges for asserting which their ancestors had bled on scaffolds, or had pined in dungeons, or in foreign climes. Their creed, too, was "Glory to God, peace on earth, goodwill to man." This creed, since profaned and rendered vile, they kept fast through good report and evil report. This belief they had, that looks at something out of itself, fixed as the stars, deep as the firmament; that makes of its own heart an altar to truth, a place of worship for what is right, at which it does reverence with praise and prayer like a holy thing, apart and content; that feels that the greatest Being in the universe is always near it; and that all things work together for the good of His creatures, under His guiding hand. This covenant they kept, as the stars keep their courses; this principle they stuck by, for want of knowing better, as it sticks by them to the last. It grows with their growth, it does not wither in their decay. It lives when the almond tree flourishes, and is not bowed down with the tottering knees. It glimmers with the last feeble eyesight, smiles in the faded cheek like infancy, and lights a path before them to the grave!

From THE ESSAYS of
William Hazlitt (1778–1828).

41
MEMORABLE SERMON

MY father lived ten miles from Shrewsbury, and was in the habit of exchanging visits with Mr. Rowe, and with Mr. Jenkins of Whitchurch (nine miles farther on) according to the custom of Dissenting Ministers in each other's neighbourhood. A line of communication is thus established, by which the flame of civil and religious liberty is kept alive, and nourishes its smouldering fire unquenchable, like the fires in the Agamemnon of Æschylus, placed at different stations, that waited for ten long years to announce with their blazing pyramids the destruction of Troy. Coleridge had agreed to come over to see my father, according to the courtesy of the country, as Mr. Rowe's probable successor; but in the meantime I had gone to hear him preach the Sunday after his arrival. A poet and a philosopher getting up into a Unitarian pulpit to preach the Gospel, was a romance in these degenerate days, a sort of revival of the primitive spirit of Christianity, which was not to be resisted.

It was in January, 1798, that I rose one morning before daylight, to walk ten miles in the mud, and went to hear this celebrated person preach. Never, the longest day I have to live, shall I have such another walk as this cold, raw, comfortless one, in the winter of the year 1798. *Il y a des impressions que ni le tems ni les circonstances peuvent effacer. Dusse-je vivre des siècles entiers, le doux tems de ma jeunesse ne peut renaître pour moi, ni s'effacer jamais dans ma mémoire.* When I got there, the organ was playing the 100th psalm, and, when it was done, Mr. Coleridge rose and gave out his text, "And he went up into the mountain to pray, HIMSELF, ALONE." As he gave out this text, his voice "rose like a steam of rich distilled perfumes," and when he came to the last two words, which he pronounced loud, deep, and distinct, it seemed to me, who was then young, as if the sounds had echoed from the bottom of the human heart, and as if that prayer might have floated in solemn silence through the universe. The idea of St. John came into mind, "of one crying in the wilderness, who had his loins girt about, and whose food was locusts and wild honey." The preacher then launched into his subject, like an eagle dallying with the wind. The sermon was upon peace and war; upon church and state—not their alliance, but their separation—on the spirit of the world and the spirit of Christianity, not as the same, but as opposed to one another. He talked of those who had "inscribed the cross of Christ on banners dripping with human gore." He made a poetical and pastoral excursion,—and to shew the fatal effects of war, drew a striking contrast between the simple shepherd boy, driving his team afield, or sitting under the hawthorn, piping to his flock, "as though he should never be old," and the same poor country-lad, crimped, kidnapped, brought into town, made drunk at an alehouse, turned into a wretched drummer-boy, with his hair sticking on end with powder and pomatum, a long cue at his back, and tricked out in the loathsome finery of the profession of blood.

Such were the notes our once-lov'd poet sung. And for myself, I could not have been more delighted if I had heard the music of the spheres.

From THE ESSAYS of
William Hazlitt (1778–1828).

42
BLIND LEADERS

THE first of Quakers and by trade a shoemaker . . . was a Man; and the Temple of Immensity, wherein as man he had been sent to minister was full of holy mystery to him.

The Clergy of the neighbourhood, the ordained Watchers and Interpreters of that same holy mystery, listened with unaffected tedium to his consultations and advised him, as the solution of such doubts, "to drink beer and dance with the girls." Blind leaders of the blind! For what end were their tithes levied and eaten; for what were their shovel-hats scooped out, and their surplices and cassock-aprons girt on; and such a church-repairing, and chaffering, and organing, and other racketing, held over that spot of God's earth,—if man were but a Patent Digester, and the belly with its adjuncts the grand Reality? Fox turned from them, with tears and sacred scorn, back to his Leather-parings and his Bible.

From SARTOR RESARTUS, by
Thomas Carlyle (1795–1881).

43

SCHEIN PRIESTER

MEANWHILE, in our era of the World, those same Church-Clothes have gone sorrowfully out-at-elbows: nay, far worse, many of them have become mere hollow Shapes, or Masks, under which no living Figure or Spirit any longer dwells; but only spiders and unclean beetles, in horrid accumulation, drive their trade; and the mask still glares on you with its glass-eyes, in ghastly affectation of Life,—some generation-and-half after Religion has quite withdrawn from it, and in unnoticed nooks is weaving for herself new Vestures, wherewith to reappear, and bless us, or our sons or grandsons. As a Priest, or Interpreter of the Holy, is the noblest and highest of all men, so is a Sham-priest (*Schein-priester*) the falsest and basest; neither is it doubtful that his Canonicals, were they Popes' Tiaras, will one day be torn from him, to make bandages for the wounds of mankind; or even to burn into tinder, for general scientific or culinary purposes. . . .

From SARTOR RESARTUS, by
Thomas Carlyle (1795–1881).

BROTHER SAMSON

From the distress and confusion of the Victorian era, its Luddite and Chartist riots, growing pauperism and increasing class antagonism, Carlyle looks back to the twelfth century, when, as an old record tells, a certain Abbot Samson ruled and reformed the monastery of St. Edmundsbury. From the example set by the priestly disciplinarian, Carlyle then returns to the reforms needed in nineteenth-century society.

THEY call him "Norfolk *Barrator*," or litigious person; for indeed, being of grave taciturn ways, he is not universally a favourite; he has been in trouble more than once. The reader is desired to mark this Monk. A personable man of seven-and-forty; stout-made, stands erect as a pillar; with bushy eyebrows, the eyes of him beaming into you in a really strange way; the face massive, grave, with "a very eminent nose;" his head almost bald, its auburn remnants of hair, and the copious ruddy beard, getting slightly streaked with gray.

.   .   .   .   .

A learned man, of devout grave nature; has studied at Paris, has taught in the Town Schools here, and done much else; can preach in three languages, and, like Dr. Caius, "has had losses" in his time. A thoughtful, firm-standing man; much loved by some, not loved by all; his clear eyes flashing into you, in an almost inconvenient way!

Abbot Hugo, as we said, had his own difficulties with him; Abbot Hugo had him in prison once, to teach him what authority was, and how to dread the fire in future. For Brother Samson, in the time of the Antipopes, had been sent to Rome on business; and, returning successful, was too late,—the business had all misgone in the interim! . . . But let us hear Brother Samson, as to his mode of travelling:

"You know what trouble I had for that Church of Woolpit; how I was despatched to Rome in the time of the Schism between Pope Alexander and Octavian; and passed through Italy at that season, when all clergy carrying letters for our Lord Pope Alexander were laid hold of, and some were clapt in prison, some hanged; and some, with nose and lips cut off, were sent forward to our Lord the Pope, for the disgrace and confusion of him (*in dedecus et confusionem ejus*). I, however, pretended to be Scotch, and putting on the garb of a Scotchman, and taking the gesture of one, walked along; and when anybody mocked at me, I would brandish my staff in the manner of that weapon they call *gaveloc*,[1] uttering comminatory words after the way of the Scotch. To those that met and questioned me who I was, I made no answer but: '*Ride, ride Rome; turne Cantwereberei.*'[2] Thus did I, to conceal myself and my errand, and get safer to Rome under the guise of a Scotchman.

"Having at last obtained a Letter from our Lord the Pope according to my wishes, I turned homewards again. I had to pass through a certain strong town on my road; and lo, the soldiers thereof surrounded me, seizing me, and saying: 'This vagabond (*iste solivagus*), who pretends to be Scotch, is either a spy, or has Letters from the false Pope Alexander.' And whilst they examined every stitch and rag of me, my leggings (*caligas*), breeches, and even the old shoes that I carried over my shoulder in the way of the Scotch,—I put my hand into the leather scrip I wore, wherein our Lord the Pope's Letter lay, close by a little jug (*ciffus*) I had for drinking out of; and the Lord God so pleasing, and St. Edmund, I got out both the Letter and the jug together; in such a way that, extending my arm aloft, I held the Letter hidden between jug and hand: they saw the jug, but the Letter they saw not. And thus I escaped out of their hands in the name of the Lord. Whatever money I had they took from me; wherefore I had to beg from door to door, without any payment (*sine omni expensa*) till I came to England again. But hearing that the Woolpit Church was already given to Geoffry Ridell, my soul was struck with sorrow because I had laboured in vain. Coming home, therefore, I sat me down secretly under the Shrine of St. Edmund, fearing lest our Lord Abbot should seize and imprison me, though I had done no mischief;

[1] Javelin, missile pike. "Gaveloc" is still the Scotch name for "crowbar."
[2] Does this mean, "Rome forever; Canterbury *not*" (which claims an unjust Supremacy over us)! Mr. Rokewood is silent. Dryasdust would perhaps explain it, in the course of a week or two of talking; did one dare to question him!

nor was there a monk who durst speak to me, nor a laic who durst bring me food except by stealth."[1]

Such resting and welcoming found Brother Samson, with his worn soles, and strong heart! He sits silent, revolving many thoughts, at the foot of St. Edmund's Shrine. In the wide Earth, if it be not Saint Edmund, what friend or refuge has he? Our Lord Abbot, hearing of him, sent the proper officer to lead him down to prison, and clap "foot-gyves on him" there. Another poor official furtively brought him a cup of wine; bade him "be comforted in the Lord." Samson utters no complaint; obeys in silence. "Our Lord Abbot, taking counsel of it, banished me to Acre, and there I had to stay long."

Our Lord Abbot next tried Samson with promotions; made him Subsacristan, made him Librarian, which he liked best of all, being passionately fond of Books: Samson, with many thoughts in him, again obeyed in silence; discharged his offices to perfection, but never thanked our Lord Abbot,—seemed rather as if looking into him, with those clear eyes of his. Whereupon Abbot Hugo said, *Se nunquam vidisse*, He had never seen such a man; whom no severity would break to complain, and no kindness soften into smiles or thanks:—a questionable kind of man!

In this way, not without troubles, but still in an erect clear-standing manner, has Brother Samson reached his forty-seventh year; and his ruddy beard is getting slightly grizzled. He is endeavouring, in these days, to have various broken things thatched in; nay perhaps to have the Choir itself completed, for he can bear nothing ruinous.

From PAST AND PRESENT, by
Thomas Carlyle (1795–1881).

45

DISTASTEFUL NOTORIETY

IT is curious to reflect what might have been the issue, had Roman Popery happened to pass this Luther by; to go on in its great wasteful orbit, and not come athwart his little path, and force him

[1] *Jocelini Chronica*, p. 36.

to assault it! Conceivable enough that, in this case, he might have held his peace about the abuses of Rome; left Providence, and God on high to deal with them! A modest quiet man; not prompt he to attack irreverently persons in authority. His clear task, as I say, was to do his own duty; to walk wisely in this world of confused wickedness, and save his own soul alive. But the Roman High-priesthood did come athwart him: afar off at Wittenberg he, Luther, could not get lived in honesty for it; he remonstrated, resisted, came to extremity; was struck at, struck again, and so it came to wager of battle between them! This is worth attending to in Luther's history. Perhaps no man of so humble, peaceable a disposition ever filled the world with contention. We cannot but see that he would have loved privacy, quiet diligence in the shade; that it was against his will he ever became a notoriety. Notoriety: what would that do for him? The goal of his march through this world was the Infinite Heaven; an indubitable goal for him: in a few years, he should either have attained that, or lost it forever! We will say nothing at all, I think, of that sorrowfulest of theories, of its being some mean shopkeeper grudge, of the Augustine Monk against the Dominican, that first kindled the wrath of Luther, and produced the Protestant Reformation. We will say to the people who maintain it, if indeed any such exist now: Get first into the sphere of thought by which it is so much as possible to judge of Luther, or of any man like Luther, otherwise than distractedly; we may then begin arguing with you.

The Monk Tetzel, sent out carelessly in the way of trade, by Leo Tenth,—who merely wanted to raise a little money, and for the rest seems to have been a Pagan rather than a Christian, so far as he was anything,—arrived at Wittenberg, and drove his scandalous trade there. Luther's flock bought Indulgences; in the confessional of his Church, people pleaded to him that they had already got their sins pardoned. Luther, if he would not be found wanting at his own post, a false sluggard and coward at the very centre of the little space of ground that was his own and no other man's, had to step forth against Indulgences, and declare aloud that *they* were a futility and sorrowful mockery, that no man's sins could be pardoned by *them*. It was the beginning of the whole

Reformation. We know how it went; forward from this first public challenge of Tetzel, on the last day of October, 1517, through remonstrance and argument;—spreading ever wider, rising ever higher; till it became unquenchable, and enveloped all the world. Luther's heart's-desire was to have this grief and other griefs amended; his thought was still far from introducing separation in the Church, or revolting against the Pope, Father of Christendom. The elegant Pagan Pope cared little about this Monk and his doctrines; wished, however, to have done with the noise of him: in a space of some three years, having tried various softer methods, he thought good to end it by *fire*. He dooms the Monk's writings to be burnt by the hangman, and his body to be sent bound to Rome—probably for a similar purpose.

From HEROES AND HERO-WORSHIP,
by Thomas Carlyle (1795–1881).

46

EPISTLE TO THE REV. JOHN M'MATH

Enclosing a copy of "Holy Willie's Prayer" which he had requested.

I OWN 'twas rash, an' rather hardy,
That I a simple, country bardie,
Shou'd meddle wi' a pack sae sturdy,
        Wha, if they ken me,
Can easy, wi' a single wordie,
        Louse h—ll upon me.

But I gae mad at their grimaces,
Their sighin' cantin', grace proud faces,
Their three-mile prayers, an' half-mile graces,
        Their raxin conscience,
Whase greed, revenge, and pride disgraces
        Waur not their nonsense.

There's Gaw'n, misca'd waur than a beast,
Wha has mair honor in his breast
Than mony scores as guid's the priest
　　　　Wha sae abused him:
And may a bard no crack his jest
　　　　What way they've us'd him?

　　　・　　　・　　　・　　　・　　　・

God knows, I'm no the thing I shou'd be,
Nor am I even the thing I cou'd be,
But twenty times I rather would be
　　　　An atheist clean,
Than under gospel colours hid be
　　　　Just for a screen.

An honest man may like a glass,
An honest man may like a lass,
But mean revenge, an' malice fause
　　　　He'll still disdain,
An' then cry zeal for gospel laws,
　　　　Like some we ken.

They take religion in their mouth;
They talk o' mercy, grace, an' truth,
For what? to gie their malice skouth
　　　　On some puir wight,
An' hunt him down, owre right and ruth,
　　　　To ruin streicht.

　　　・　　　・　　　・　　　・　　　・

O Ayr! my dear, my native ground,
Within thy presbyterial bound
A candid liberal band is found
　　　　Of public teachers,
As men, as christians too, renown'd,
　　　　An' manly preachers.

Sir, in that circle you are nam'd,
Sir, in that circle you are fam'd;
An' some, by whom your doctrine's blam'd
    (Which gies ye honour)
Even, sir, by them your heart's esteem'd,
    An' winning manner.

Pardon this freedom I have ta'en,
An' if impertinent I've been,
Impute it not, good sir, in ane
    Whase heart ne'er wrang'd ye,
But to his utmost would befriend
    Ought that belang'd ye.

                By Robert Burns (1759–96).

ON HEARING IT ASSERTED FALSEHOOD IS EXPRESSED IN THE REV. DR. BABINGTON'S VERY LOOKS

That there is a falsehood in his looks,
    I must and will deny:
They tell their master is a knave,
    And sure they do not lie.

                By Robert Burns

47
THE VISION OF HABAKKUK MUCKLEWRATH

The fanaticism of the Covenanters who in 1679 murdered James Sharp, Archbishop of St. Andrews, and carried on a hopeless struggle against Government troops until routed at Bothwell Brig provided Scott with the theme of one of his early romances.

"I OPINE," said Poundtext,—for, like the other divines of the period, he had no hesitation in offering his advice upon military matters of which he was profoundly ignorant,—"I opine, that we should take in and raze that stronghold of the woman Lady Margaret Bellenden, even though we should build a fort and raise a mount against it; for the race is a rebellious and a bloody race, and their hand has been heavy on the children of the Covenant, both in the former and the latter times. Their hook hath been in our noses, and their bridle betwixt our jaws."

"What are their means and men of defence?" said Burley. "The place is strong; but I cannot conceive that two women can make it good against a host."

"There is also," said Poundtext, "Harrison the steward, and John Gudyill, even the lady's chief butler, who boasteth himself a man of war from his youth upward, and who spread the banner against the good cause with that man of Belial, James Grahame of Montrose."

"Pshaw!" returned Burley scornfully, "a butler!"

"Also, there is that ancient malignant," replied Poundtext, "Miles Bellenden of Charnwood, whose hands have been dipped in the blood of the saints."

"If that," said Burley, "be Miles Bellenden, the brother of Sir Arthur, he is one whose sword will not turn back from battle; but he must now be stricken in years."

"There was word in the country as I rode along," said another of the council, "that so soon as they heard of the victory which has been given to us, they caused shut the gates of the Tower, and called in men, and collected ammunition. They were ever a fierce and a malignant house."

"We will not, with my consent," said Burley, "engage in a siege which may consume time. We must rush forward, and follow our advantage by occupying Glasgow; for I do not fear that the troops we have this day beaten, even with the assistance of my Lord Ross's regiment, will judge it safe to await our coming."

"Howbeit," said Poundtext, "we may display a banner before the Tower, and blow a trumpet, and summon them to come forth. It may be that they will give over the place into our mercy, though they be a rebellious people. And we will summon the women to come forth from their stronghold, that is, Lady Margaret Bellenden and her granddaughter, and Jenny Dennison, which is a girl of an ensnaring eye, and the other maids, and we will give them a safe conduct, and send them in peace to the city, even to the town of Edinburgh. But John Gudyill, and Hugh Harrison, and Miles Bellenden, we will restrain with fetters of iron, even as they, in times bypast, have done to the martyred saints."

"Who talks of safe conduct and of peace?" said a shrill, broken, and overstrained voice, from the crowd.

"Peace, brother Habakkuk," said Macbriar, in a soothing tone, to the speaker.

"I will not hold my peace," reiterated the strange and unnatural voice; "is this a time to speak of peace, when the earth quakes, and the mountains are rent, and the rivers are changed into blood, and the two-edged sword is drawn from the sheath to drink gore as if it were water, and devour flesh as the fire devours dry stubble?"

While he spoke thus, the orator struggled forward to the inner part of the circle, and presented to Morton's wondering eyes a figure worthy of such a voice and such language. The rags of a dress which had once been black, added to the tattered fragments of a shepherd's plaid, composed a covering scarce fit for the purposes of decency, much less for those of warmth or comfort. A long beard, as white as snow, hung down on his breast, and mingled with bushy, uncombed, grizzled hair, which hung in elf-locks around his wild and staring visage. The features seemed to be extenuated by penury and famine, until they hardly retained the likeness of a human aspect. The eyes, gray, wild, and wandering, evidently betokened a bewildered imagination. He held in his hand a rusty sword, clotted with blood, as were his long lean hands, which were garnished at the extremity with nails like eagle's claws.

"In the name of Heaven! who is he?" said Morton, in a whisper to Poundtext, surprised, shocked, and even startled, at this ghastly apparition, which looked more like the resurrection of some cannibal priest, or Druid red from his human sacrifice, than like an earthly mortal.

"It is Habakkuk Mucklewrath," answered Poundtext, in the same tone, "whom the enemy have long detained in captivity in forts and castles, until his understanding hath departed from him, and, as I fear, an evil demon hath possessed him. Nevertheless, our violent brethren will have it, that he speaketh of the spirit, and that they fructify by his pouring forth."

Here he was interrupted by Mucklewrath, who cried in a voice that made the very beams of the roof quiver, "Who talks of peace and safe conduct? who speaks of mercy to the bloody house of the malignants? I say take the infants and dash them against the stones; take the daughters and the mothers of the house and hurl them from the battlements of their trust, that the dogs may fatten on their blood, as they did on that of Jezebel, the spouse of Ahab, and that their carcasses may be dung to the face of the field even in the portion of their fathers!"

"He speaks right," said more than one sullen voice from behind; "we will be honoured with little service in the great cause, if we already make fair weather with Heaven's enemies."

"This is utter abomination and daring impiety," said Morton, unable to contain his indignation. "What blessing can you expect in a cause in which you listen to the mingled ravings of madness and atrocity?"

"Hush, young man!" said Kettledrummle, "and reserve thy censure for that for which thou canst render a reason. It is not for thee to judge into what vessels the spirit may be poured."

"We judge of the tree by the fruit," said Poundtext, "and allow not that to be of divine inspiration that contradicts the divine laws."

"You forget, brother Poundtext," said Macbriar, "that these are the latter days, when signs and wonders shall be multiplied."

Poundtext stood forward to reply; but, ere he could articulate a word, the insane preacher broke in with a scream that drowned all competition.

"Who talks of signs and wonders? Am not I Habakkuk Mucklewrath, whose name is changed to Magor-Missabib, because I am made a terror unto myself and unto all that are around me?—I heard it—When did I hear it?—Was it not in the Tower of the Bass, that overhangeth the wide wild sea?—And it howled in the winds, and it roared in the billows, and it screamed, and it whistled, and it clanged, with the screams and the clang and the whistle of the sea-birds, as they floated, and flew, and dropped, and dived, on the bosom of the waters. I saw it—Where did I see it?—Was it not from the high peaks of Dumbarton, when I looked westward upon the fertile land, and northward on the wild Highland hills; when the clouds gathered and the tempest came, and the lightnings of heaven flashed in sheets as wide as the banners of an host?— What did I see?—Dead corpses and wounded horses, the rushing together of battle, and garments rolled in blood.—What heard I?— The voice that cried, 'Slay, slay—smite—slay utterly—let not your eye have pity! slay utterly, old and young, the maiden, the child, and the woman whose head is gray.—Defile the house and fill the courts with the slain!' "

"We receive the command," exclaimed more than one of the company. "Six days he hath not spoken nor broken bread, and now his tongue is unloosed:—We receive the command; as he hath said, so will we do."

From OLD MORTALITY, by
Sir Walter Scott (1771–1832).

48

THE STICKIT MINISTER

DOMINIE SAMPSON was of low birth, but having evinced, even from his cradle, an uncommon seriousness of disposition, the poor parents were encouraged to hope that their *bairn*, as they expressed it, "might wag his pow[1] in a pulpit yet." With an ambitious view to such consummation, they pinched and pared, rose early and lay down late, ate dry bread and drank cold water, to secure to Abel the means of learning. Meantime, his tall, ungainly figure, his taciturn and grave manners, and some grotesque habits of

[1] Head.

swinging his limbs, and screwing his visage, while reciting his task, made poor Sampson the ridicule of all his school-companions. The same qualities secured him at Glasgow college a plentiful share of the same sort of notice. Half the youthful mob "of the yards" used to assemble regularly to see Dominie Sampson (for he had already attained that honourable title) descend the stairs from the Greek class, with his Lexicon under his arm, his long misshapen legs sprawling abroad, and keeping awkward time to the play of his immense shoulder-blades, as they raised and depressed the loose and threadbare black coat which was his constant and only wear. When he spoke, the efforts of the professor (professor of divinity though he was) were totally inadequate to restrain the inextinguishable laughter of the students, and sometimes even to repress his own. The long, sallow visage, the goggle eyes, the huge under-jaw, which appeared not to open and shut by an act of volition, but to be dropped and hoisted up again by some complicated machinery within the inner man,—the harsh and dissonant voice, and the screech-owl notes to which it was exalted when he was exhorted to pronounce more distinctly,—all added fresh subject for mirth to the torn cloak and shattered shoe, which have afforded legitimate subjects of raillery against the poor scholar, from Juvenal's time downward. It was never known that Sampson either exhibited irritability at this ill usage, or made the least attempt to retort upon his tormentors. He slunk from college by the most secret paths he could discover, and plunged himself into his miserable lodgings, where, for eighteenpence a week, he was allowed the benefit of a straw mattress, and, if his landlady was in good humour, permission to study his task by her fire. Under all these disadvantages, he obtained a competent knowledge of Greek and Latin, and some acquaintance with the sciences.

In progress of time, Abel Sampson, probationer of divinity, was admitted to the privileges of a preacher. But, alas! partly from his own bashfulness, partly owing to a strong and obvious disposition to risibility which pervaded the congregation upon his first attempt, he became totally incapable of proceeding in his intended discourse, gasped, grinned, hideously rolled his eyes till the congregation thought them flying out of his head, shut the Bible, stumbled down the pulpit-stairs, trampling upon the old women who generally take their station there, and was ever after designated as a "stickit minister." And thus he wandered back to his own country, with blighted hopes and prospects, to share the poverty of his parents. As he had neither friend nor confidant, hardly even an acquaintance, no one had the means of observing closely how Dominie Sampson bore a disappointment which supplied the whole town with a week's sport. It would be endless even to mention the numerous jokes to which it gave birth, from a ballad, called "Sampson's Riddle," written upon the subject by a smart young student of humanity, to the sly hope of the Principal, that the fugitive had not, in imitation of his mighty namesake, taken the college gates along with him in his retreat.

To all appearance, the equanimity of Sampson was unshaken. He sought to assist his parents by teaching a school, and soon had plenty of scholars, but very few fees. In fact, he taught the sons of farmers for what they chose to give him, and the poor for nothing; and, to the shame of the former be it spoken, the pedagogue's gains never equalled those of a skilful ploughman. He wrote, however, a good hand, and added something to his pittance by copying accounts and writing letters for Ellangowan. By degrees, the Laird, who was much estranged from general society, became partial to that of Dominie Sampson. Conversation, it is true, was out of the question, but the Dominie was a good listener, and stirred the fire with some address. He attempted even to snuff the candles, but was unsuccessful, and relinquished that ambitious post of courtesy after having twice reduced the parlour to total darkness. So his civilities, thereafter, were confined to taking off his glass of ale in exactly the same time and measure with the Laird, and in uttering certain indistinct murmurs of acquiescence at the conclusion of the long and winding stories of Ellangowan.

From GUY MANNERING, by
Sir Walter Scott (1771–1832).

49

FIT ONLY FOR THE KIRK

HE was decidedly the best scholar at the little parish school; and so gentle was his temper and disposition, that he was rather admired than envied by the little mob who occupied the noisy mansion, although he was the declared favourite of the master. Several girls, in particular (for in Scotland they are taught with the boys), longed to be kind to and comfort the sickly lad, who was so much cleverer than his companions. The character of Reuben Butler was so calculated as to offer scope both for their sympathy and their admiration, the feelings, perhaps, through which the female sex (the more deserving part of them at least) is more easily attached.

But Reuben, naturally reserved and distant, improved none of these advantages; and only became more attached to Jeanie Deans, as the enthusiastic approbation of his master assured him of fair prospects in future life, and awakened his ambition. In the meantime, every advance that Reuben made in learning (and, considering his opportunities, they were uncommonly great), rendered him less capable of attending to the domestic duties of his grandmother's farm. While studying the *pons asinorum* in Euclid, he suffered every *cuddie* upon the common to trespass upon a large field of peas belonging to the Laird, and nothing but the active exertions of Jeanie Deans, with her little dog Dustiefoot, could have saved great loss and consequent punishment. Similar miscarriages marked his progress in his classical studies. He read Virgil's *Georgics* till he did not know bere from barley; and had nearly destroyed the crofts of Beersheba while attempting to cultivate them according to the practice of Columella and Cato the Censor.

These blunders occasioned grief to his grand-dame, and disconcerted the good opinion which her neighbour, Davie Deans, had for some time entertained of Reuben.

"I can see naething ye can mak of that silly callant, neighbour Butler," said he to the old lady, "unless ye train him to the wark o' the ministry. And ne'er was there mair need of poorfu' preachers that e'en now in these cauld Gallio days, when men's hearts are hardened like the nether millstone, till they come to regard none of these things. It's evident this puir callant of yours will never be able to do a usefu' day's wark, unless it be as an ambassador from our Master; and I will make it my business to procure a license when he is fit for the same, trusting he will be a shaft cleanly polished, and meet to be used in the body of the kirk; and that he shall not turn again, like the sow, to wallow in the mire of heretical extremes and defections, but shall have the wings of a dove, though he hath lain among the pots."

The poor widow gulped down the affront to her husband's principles, implied in this caution, and hastened to take Butler from the High School, and encourage him in the pursuit of mathematics and divinity, the only physics and ethics that chanced to be in fashion at the time.

From THE HEART OF MIDLOTHIAN,
by Sir Walter Scott (1771–1832).

50

THE PASTOR OF CAIRNVRECKAN

MAJOR MELVILLE had been versed in camps and cities; he was vigilant by profession, and cautious from experience; had met with much evil in the world, and therefore, though himself an upright magistrate and an honourable man, his opinions of others were always strict, and sometimes unjustly severe. Mr. Morton, on the contrary, had passed from the literary pursuits of a college, where he was beloved by his companions, and respected by his teachers, to the ease and simplicity of his present charge, where his opportunities of witnessing evil were few, and never dwelt upon but in order to encourage repentance and amendment; and where the love and respect of his parishioners repaid his affectionate zeal in their behalf, by endeavouring to disguise from him what they knew would give him the most acute pain, namely, their own occasional transgressions of the duties which it was the business of his life to recommend. Thus it was a common saying in the neighbourhood (though both were popular characters), that the laird knew only the ill in the parish, and the minister only the good.

A love of letters, though kept in subordination to his clerical studies and duties, also distinguished the pastor of Cairnvreckan, and had tinged his mind in earlier days with a slight feeling of romance, which no after incidents of real life had entirely dissipated. The early loss of an amiable young woman, whom he had married for love, and who was quickly followed to the grave by an only child, had also served, even after the lapse of many years, to soften a disposition naturally mild and contemplative. His feelings on the present occasion were therefore likely to differ from those of the severe disciplinarian, strict magistrate, and distrustful man of the world.

When the servants had withdrawn, the silence of both parties continued, until Major Melville, filling his glass, and pushing the bottle to Mr. Morton, commenced.

"A distressing affair this, Mr. Morton. I fear this youngster has brought himself within the compass of a halter."

"God forbid!" answered the clergyman.

"Marry, and amen," said the temporal magistrate; "but I think even your merciful logic will hardly deny the conclusion."

"Surely, Major," answered the clergyman, "I should hope it might be averted, for aught we have heard to-night?"

"Indeed!" replied Melville. "But, my good parson, you are one of those who would communicate to every criminal the benefit of clergy."

"Unquestionably I would: Mercy and long-suffering are the grounds of the doctrine I am called to teach."

"True, religiously speaking; but mercy to a criminal may be gross injustice to the community. I don't speak of this young fellow in particular, who I heartily wish may be able to clear himself, for I like both his modesty and his spirit. But I fear he has rushed upon his fate."

"And why? Hundreds of misguided gentlemen are now in arms against the Government, many, doubtless, upon principles which education and early prejudice have gilded with the names of patriotism and heroism;—Justice, when she selects her victims from such a multitude (for surely all will not be destroyed), must regard the moral motive. He whom ambition, or hope of personal advantage, has led to disturb the peace of a well-ordered government, let him fall a victim to the laws; but surely youth, misled by the wild visions of chivalry and imaginary loyalty, may plead for pardon."

"If visionary chivalry and imaginary loyalty come within the predicament of high treason," replied the magistrate, "I know no court in Christendom, my dear Mr. Morton, where they can sue out their Habeas Corpus."

"But I cannot see that this youth's guilt is at all established to my satisfaction," said the clergyman.

From WAVERLEY, by Sir
Walter Scott (1771–1832).

51

CLERICAL PEDAGOGUES

THE Upper and the Lower Grammar Schools were held in the same room; and an imaginary line only divided their bounds. Their character was as different as that of the inhabitants on the two sides of the Pyrenees. The Rev. James Boyer was the Upper Master; but the Rev. Matthew Feilde presided over that portion of the apartment, of which I had the good fortune to be a member. We lived a life as careless as birds. We talked and did just what we pleased, and nobody molested us. We carried an accidence, or a grammar, for form; but, for any trouble it gave us, we might take two years in getting through the verbs deponent, and another two in forgetting all that we had learned about them. There was now and then the formality of saying a lesson, but if you had not learned it, a brush across the shoulders (just enough to disturb a fly) was the sole remonstrance. Feilde never used the rod; and in truth he wielded the cane with no great good will—holding it "like a dancer." It looked in his hands rather like an emblem than an instrument of authority; and an emblem, too, he was ashamed of. He was a good easy man, that did not care to ruffle his own peace, nor perhaps set any great consideration upon the value of juvenile time. He came among us, now and then, but often staid away whole days from us; and when he came, it made no difference to us—he had his private room to retire to, the short time he staid, to be out of the sound of our noise. Our mirth and uproar went on. We had classics of our own, without being beholden to "insolent Greece or haughty Rome," that passed current among us—Peter Wilkins—the Adventures of the Hon. Captain Robert Boyle—the Fortunate Blue-coat Boy—and the like. Or we cultivated a turn for mechanic and scientific operations; making little sun-dials of paper; or weaving those ingenious parentheses, called *cat-cradles*; or making dry peas to dance upon the end of a tin pipe; or studying the art military over that laudable game "French and English," and a hundred other such devices to pass away the time—mixing the useful with the agreeable—as would have made the souls of Rousseau and John Locke chuckle to have seen us.

Matthew Feilde belonged to that class of modest divines who affect to mix in equal proportion the *gentleman*, the *scholar*, and the *Christian*; but, I know not how, the first ingredients generally found to be the predominating dose in the composition. He was engaged in gay parties, or with his courtly bow at some episcopal levée, when he should have been attending upon us. He had for many years the classical charge of a hundred children, during the four or five first years of their education; and his very highest form seldom proceeded further than two or three of the introductory fables of Phædrus. How things were suffered to go on thus, I cannot guess. Boyer, who was the proper person to have remedied these abuses, always affected, perhaps felt, a delicacy in interfering in a province not strictly his own. I have not been without my suspicions, that he was not altogether displeased at the contrast we presented to his end of the school. We were a sort of Helots to his young Spartans. He would sometimes, with ironic deference, send to borrow a rod of the Under Master, and then, with Sardonic grin, observe to one of his upper boys, "how neat and fresh the twigs looked." While his pale students were battering their brains over Xenophon and Plato, with a silence as deep as that enjoined by the Samite, we were enjoying ourselves at our ease in our little Goshen. We saw a little into the secrets of his discipline, and the prospect did but the more reconcile us to our lot. His thunders rolled innocuous for us; his storms came near, but never touched us; contrary to Gideon's miracle, while all around were drenched, our fleece was dry. His boys turned out the better scholars; we, I suspect, have the advantage in temper. His pupils cannot speak of him without something of terror allaying their gratitude; the remembrance of Feilde comes back with all the soothing images of indolence, and summer slumbers, and work like play, and innocent idleness, and Elysian exemptions, and life itself a "playing holiday."

Though sufficiently removed from the jurisdiction of Boyer, we were near enough (as I have said) to understand a little of his system. We occasionally heard sounds of the *Ululantes*, and caught glances of Tartarus. B. was a rabid pedant. His English style was crampt to barbarism. His Easter anthems (for his duty obliged him to those periodical flights) were grating as scrannel pipes.— He would laugh—ay, and heartily—but then it must be at Flaccus's quibble about *Rex*—or at the *tristis severitas in vultu*, or *inspicere in patinas*, of Terence—thin jests, which at their first broaching could hardly have had *vis* enough to move a Roman muscle.—He had two wigs, both pedantic, but of different omen. The one serene, smiling, fresh powdered, betokening a mild day. The other, an old discoloured, unkempt, angry caxon, denoting frequent and bloody execution. Woe to the school, when he made his morning appearance in his *passy*, or *passionate wig*. No comet expounded surer.—J.B. had a heavy hand. I have known him double his knotty fist at a poor trembling child (the maternal milk hardly dry upon its lips) with a "Sirrah, do you presume to set your wits at me?"—Nothing was more common than to see him make a headlong entry into the school-room, from his inner recess, or library, and, with turbulent eye, singling out a lad, roar out, "Od's my life, sirrah" (his favourite aduration,) "I have a great mind to whip you," then, with as sudden a retracting impulse, fling back into his lair—and, after a cooling lapse of some minutes

123

(during which all but the culprit had totally forgotten the context) drive headlong out again, piecing out his imperfect sense, as if it had been some Devil's Litany, with the expletory yell—"*and I* WILL *too.*"

From THE ESSAYS OF ELIA, by
Charles Lamb (1775–1834)

52

AN EQUIVOCAL GRACE

I ONCE drank tea in company with two Methodist divines of different persuasions, whom it was my fortune to introduce to each other for the first time that evening. Before the first cup was handed round, one of these reverend gentlemen put it to the other, with all due solemnity, whether he chose to *say anything*. It seems it is the custom with some sectaries to put up a short prayer before this meal also. His reverend brother did not at first quite apprehend him, but upon an explanation, with little less importance he made answer that it was not a custom known in his church: in which courteous evasion the other acquiescing for good manners' sake, or in compliance with a weak brother, the supplementary or tea grace was waived altogether. With what spirit might not Lucian have painted two priests, of *his* religion, playing into each other's hands the compliment of performing or omitting a sacrifice,—the hungry God meantime, doubtful of his incense, with expectant nostrils hovering over the two flamens, and (as between two stools) going away in the end without his supper.

A short form upon these occasions is felt to want reverence; a long one, I am afraid, cannot escape the charge of impertinence. I do not quite approve of the epigrammatic conciseness with which that equivocal wag (but my pleasant school-fellow) C. V. L., when importuned for a grace, used to inquire, first slyly leering down the table, "Is there no clergyman here?"—significantly adding, "Thank G——."

From THE ESSAYS OF ELIA, by
Charles Lamb (1775–1834).

53

THE AMIABLE MR. ELTON

*The Rev. Mr. Elton was all gush and graciousness until he discovered
that Emma was not herself in love with him, but had mistakenly
supposed him to be in love with her humble friend, Harriet Smith.
Mr. Elton thereupon takes a wife, and begins to take on a new character.*

THE ball proceeded pleasantly. The anxious cares, the incessant
attentions of Mrs. Weston, were not thrown away. Every body
seemed happy; and the praise of being a delightful ball, which is
seldom bestowed till after a ball has ceased to be, was repeatedly
given in the very beginning of the existence of this. Of very
important, very recordable events, it was not more productive
than such meetings usually are. There was one, however, which
Emma thought something of.—The two last dances before supper
were begun, and Harriet had no partner;—the only young lady
sitting down;—and so equal had been hitherto the number of
dancers, that how there could be any one disengaged was the
wonder!—But Emma's wonder lessened soon afterwards, on seeing
Mr. Elton sauntering about. He would not ask Harriet to dance
if it were possible to be avoided; she was sure he would not—and
she was expecting him every moment to escape into the card-room.

Escape, however, was not his plan. He came to the part of the
room where the sitters-by were collected, spoke to some, and
walked about in front of them, as if to show his liberty, and his
resolution of maintaining it. He did not omit being sometimes
directly before Miss Smith, or speaking to those who were close
to her.—Emma saw it. She was not yet dancing, she was working
her way up from the bottom, and had therefore leisure to look
around, and by only turning her head a little she saw it all. When
she was half way up the set, the whole group were exactly behind
her, and she would no longer allow her eyes to watch; but Mr.
Elton was so near, that she heard every syllable of a dialogue which
just then took place between him and Mrs. Weston; and she
perceived that his wife, who was standing immediately above her,

was not only listening also, but even encouraging him by significant glances.—The kind-hearted, gentle Mrs. Weston had left her seat to join him and say, "Do not you dance, Mr. Elton?" to which his prompt reply was, "Most readily, Mrs. Weston, if you will dance with me."

"Me!—oh! no—I would get you a better partner than myself. I am no dancer."

"If Mrs. Gilbert wishes to dance," said he, "I shall have great pleasure, I am sure—for, though beginning to feel myself rather an old married man, and that my dancing days are over, it would give me very great pleasure at any time to stand up with an old friend like Mrs. Gilbert."

"Mrs. Gilbert does not mean to dance, but there is a young lady disengaged whom I should be very glad to see dancing—Miss Smith." "Miss Smith—oh!—I had not observed.—You are extremely obliging—and if I were not an old married man.—But my dancing days are over, Mrs. Weston. You will excuse me. Any thing else I should be most happy to do, at your command—but my dancing days are over."

Mrs. Weston said no more; and Emma could imagine with what surprise and mortification she must be returning to her seat. This was Mr. Elton! the amiable, obliging, gentle Mr. Elton.—She looked round for a moment; he had joined Mr. Knightley at a little distance, and was arranging himself for settled conversation, while smiles of high glee passed between him and his wife.

From EMMA, by Jane
Austen (1775–1817).

54
MR. COLLINS SEEKS A WIFE

Learning that upon the death of Mr. Bennett he will inherit the family estate, Mr. Collins resolves by way of amends to marry one of Mr. Bennett's two daughters "if he found they were as handsome and amiable as they were represented by common report."

MRS. BENNETT and Kitty walked off, and as soon as they were gone Mr. Collins began,—

"Believe me, my dear Miss Elizabeth, that your modesty, so far from doing you any disservice, rather adds to your other perfections. You would have been less amiable in my eyes had there *not* been this little unwillingness; but allow me to assure you that I have your respected mother's permission for this address. You can hardly doubt the purport of my discourse, however your natural delicacy may lead you to dissemble; my attentions have been too marked to be mistaken. Almost as soon as I entered the house I singled you out as the companion of my future life. But before I am run away with by my feelings on this subject, perhaps it will be advisable for me to state my reasons for marrying, and, moreover, for coming into Hertfordshire with the design of selecting a wife, as I certainly did."

The idea of Mr. Collins, with all his solemn composure, being run away with by his feelings, made Elizabeth so near laughing that she could not use the short pause he allowed in any attempt to stop him further, and he continued,—

"My reasons for marrying are, first, that I think it a right thing for every clergyman in easy circumstances (like myself) to set the example of matrimony in his parish; secondly, that I am convinced it will add very greatly to my happiness; and thirdly, which perhaps I ought to have mentioned earlier, that it is the particular advice and recommendation of the very noble lady whom I have the honour of calling patroness. Twice has she condescended to give me her opinion (unasked too!) on this subject; and it was but the very Saturday night before I left Hunsford—between our pools at quadrille, while Mrs. Jenkinson was arranging Miss De Bourgh's footstool—that she said, 'Mr. Collins, you must marry. A clergyman like you must marry. Choose properly, choose a gentlewoman, for *my* sake and for your *own*; let her be an active, useful sort of person, not brought up high, but able to make a small income go a good way. This is my advice. Find such a woman as soon as you can, bring her to Hunsford, and I will visit her.' Allow me, by the way, to observe, my fair cousin, that I do not reckon the notice and kindness of Lady Catherine de Bourgh as among the least of the advantages in my power to offer. You will find her manners beyond anything I can describe; and your wit and vivacity, I think, must be acceptable to her, especially when tempered with the silence and respect which her rank will inevitably excite. Thus much for my general intention in favour of matrimony; it remains to be told why my views were directed to Longbourn instead of my own neighbourhood, where, I assure you, there are many amiable young women. But the fact is, that being, as I am, to inherit this estate after the death of your honoured father (who, however, may live many years longer), I could not satisfy myself without resolving to choose a wife from among his daughters, that the loss to them might be as little as possible when the melancholy event takes place which, however, as I have already said, may not be for several years. This has been my motive, my fair cousin, and I flatter myself it will not sink me in your esteem. And now nothing remains for me but to assure you in the most animated language of the violence of my affection. To fortune I am perfectly indifferent, and shall make no demand of that nature on your father, since I am well aware that it could not be complied with, and that one thousand pounds in the four per cents., which will not be yours till after your mother's decease, is all that you may ever be entitled to. On that head, therefore, I shall be uniformly silent, and you may assure yourself that no ungenerous reproach shall ever pass my lips when we are married."

It was absolutely necessary to interrupt him now.

"You are too hasty, sir," she cried. "You forget that I have made no answer. Let me do it without further loss of time. Accept my thanks for the compliment you are paying me. I am very sensible of the honour of your proposals, but it is impossible for me to do otherwise than decline them."

"I am not now to learn," replied Mr. Collins, with a formal wave of the hand, "that it is usual with young ladies to reject the addresses of the man whom they secretly mean to accept, when he first applies for their favour; and that sometimes the refusal is repeated a second or even a third time. I am, therefore, by no means discouraged by what you have just said, and shall hope to lead you to the altar ere long."

"Upon my word, sir," cried Elizabeth, "your hope is rather an extraordinary one after my declaration. I do assure you that I am not one of those young ladies (if such young ladies there are) who are so daring as to risk their happiness on the chance of being asked a second time. I am perfectly serious in my refusal. You could not make *me* happy, and I am convinced that I am the last woman in the world who would make *you* so. Nay, were your friend Lady Catherine to know me, I am persuaded she would find me in every respect ill qualified for the situation."

"Were it certain that Lady Catherine would think so," said Mr. Collins, very gravely; "but I cannot imagine that her ladyship would at all disapprove of you. And you may be certain that when I have the honour of seeing her again I shall speak in the highest terms of your modesty, economy, and other amiable qualifications."

"Indeed, Mr. Collins, all praise of me will be unnecessary. You must give me leave to judge for myself, and pay me the compliment of believing what I say. I wish you very happy and very rich, and by refusing your hand do all in my power to prevent your being otherwise. In making me the offer, you must have satisfied the delicacy of your feelings with regard to my family, and may take possession of Longbourn estate whenever it falls, without any self-reproach. This matter may be considered, therefore, as finally settled." And rising as she thus spoke, she would have quitted the room, had not Mr. Collins thus addressed her,—

"When I do myself the honour of speaking to you next on the subject, I shall hope to receive a more favourable answer than you have now given me; though I am far from accusing you of cruelty at present, because I know it to be the established custom of your sex to reject a man on the first application, and perhaps you have even now said as much to encourage my suit as would be consistent with the true delicacy of the female character."

"Really, Mr. Collins," cried Elizabeth, with some warmth, "you puzzle me exceedingly. If what I have hitherto said can appear to you in the form of encouragement, I know not how to express my refusal in such a way as may convince you of its being one."

"You must give me leave to flatter myself, my dear cousin, that your refusal of my addresses are merely words of course. My reasons for believing it are briefly these:—It does not appear to me that my hand is unworthy of your acceptance, or that the establishment I can offer would be any other than highly desirable. My situation in life, my connections with the family of De Bourgh, and my relationship to your own, are circumstances highly in my favour; and you should take it into further consideration that, in spite of your manifold attractions, it is by no means certain that another offer of marriage may ever be made to you. Your portion is, unhappily, so small that it will in all likelihood undo the effects of your loveliness and amiable qualifications. As I must, therefore, conclude that you are not serious in your rejection of me, I shall choose to attribute it to your wish of increasing my love by suspense, according to the usual practice of elegant females."

"I do assure you, sir, that I have no pretensions whatever to that kind of elegance which consists in tormenting a respectable man. I would rather be paid the compliment of being believed sincere. I thank you again and again for the honour you have done me in your proposals, but to accept them is absolutely impossible. My feelings in every respect forbid it. Can I speak plainer? Do not consider me now as an elegant female intending to plague you, but as a rational creature speaking the truth from her heart."

"You are uniformly charming!" cried he, with an air of awkward gallantry; "and I am persuaded that, when sanctioned by the express authority of both your excellent parents, my proposals will not fail of being acceptable."

To such perseverance in wilful self-deception Elizabeth would make no reply, and immediately and in silence withdrew, determined that, if he persisted in considering her repeated refusals as flattering encouragement, to apply to her father, whose negative might be uttered in such a manner as must be decisive, and whose behaviour at least could not be mistaken for the affectation and coquetry of an elegant female.

From PRIDE AND PREJUDICE,
by Jane Austen (1775–1817).

55

MR. BLOOMBURY AND MR. SWAN

The conflict between the Evangelical and Broad Church Parties that is reflected in several Victorian novels, including Trollope's Barchester Towers, *is the theme of one of Landor's* Imaginary Conversations.

SWAN: Whither are you walking so fast, Mr. Bloombury?

BLOOMBURY: My dear brother in Christ, Mr. Swan, I am truly happy to meet you. A fine fresh pleasant day! Any news? I am going to visit Lord Coleraine, who has been attacked by an apoplexy.

SWAN: Such was the report I heard yesterday. Accidents of this kind, when they befall the light and thoughtless, shock us even more than when it pleases God to inflict them on the graver and the better. What is more awful than to confront so unexpectedly the gay in spirit with the king of terrors? Sincerely as I grieve to hear of this appalling visitation, it is consolatory to think that his lordship has brought himself to such a comfortable and cheering frame of mind.

BLOOMBURY: Has he, Mr. Swan? Methinks it is rather early, if he has.

SWAN: He must be sensible of his situation, or he would not have required your spiritual aid.

BLOOMBURY: He require it! no more than a rank heathen or unchristened babe. He shall have it though. I will awaken him; I will prick him; I will carry to him the sword of faith; it shall pierce his heart.

SWAN: Gently with the rowels on a foundered steed.

BLOOMBURY: Mr. Swan, our pulpits should not smell of the horse-cloth. I never heard that text before.

SWAN: You have heard many a worse.

BLOOMBURY: Profane! there are none but from the Bible.

SWAN: The application and intent make them more or less good. *Smite* is in that book; *do not smite* is there also. Now which is best?

BLOOMBURY: Both are excellent if they are there: we can only know which is best by opening the volume of grace, and the text that we open first is for our occasion the best of the two.

SWAN: There is no logic to place against this. Of course you are intimately acquainted with Lord Coleraine. You can remind him of faults which it is still in his power to correct; of wrongs . . .

BLOOMBURY: I can, and will. When I was in the Guards, he won a trifle of money from me: I shall bring him to a proper sense of his sinfulness in having done it.

SWAN: In winning your money?

BLOOMBURY: He may make some reparation to society for his offence.

SWAN: He could not have won your money if you had not played with him.

BLOOMBURY: I was young: he ought to have taught me better.

SWAN: He did, if he won much.

BLOOMBURY: He won fifty guineas.

SWAN: How? and were you, Mr. Bloombury, ever a gamester?

BLOOMBURY: At that time I was not under grace.

SWAN: Well, really now I would converse with a dying man on other topics. Comfort him; prepare him for his long journey.

BLOOMBURY: Ay, sing to him; read to him Shakespeare and Cervantes and Froissart! Make him believe that man is better than a worm, lovelier than a toad, wiser than a deaf adder. Mr. Swan, you are a virtuous man (I mean no offence by calling you so), a good neighbour, a cordial friend, but you are not touched.

SWAN: Bloombury, if you are sincere, you will acknowledge that, among your evangelicals, this touching for the most part begins with the pocket, or its environs.

BLOOMBURY: O for shame! such indecency I never heard! This comes from your worldly and university view of things, your drinkings and cricketings.

SWAN: Too frequently. We want drilling in our armour of faith from the Horse-guards: we want teaching from those who pay fifty guineas the lesson. I am not so unchristian as to deny that you are adepts in the practice of humility, but it is quite of a new kind. You are humble while you speak, but the reverse when you are spoken to; and, if it were not for your sanctification, I should call you the most arrogant and self-sufficient of sectarians.

BLOOMBURY: We are of the church; the true English church.

SWAN: Few sects are not, opposite as they may be. Take the general spirit and practice of it, and tell me what church under heaven is more liberal and forbearing.

BLOOMBURY: Because you forego and forget the most prominent of the thirty-nine articles. There is the sword in them.

SWAN: Let it lie there, in God's name.

BLOOMBURY: There is doctrine.

SWAN: I take what I understand of it, and would not give a pinch of snuff for the rest. Our Saviour has taught me whatever is useful to know in Christianity. If churches, or any members of them, wanted more from his apostles, I hope they enjoyed what they wanted. The coarser Gentiles must needs have cheese and garlic upon their bread of life: my stomach won't digest them. Those who like the same fare may take it; only let them, when their mouths are full of it, sit quiet, and not open them upon me. We are at the house, I think. Good morning . . . A word at parting. May not that musk about you hurt the sick man?

BLOOMBURY: What musk? I protest I never have used any.

SWAN: Then the creature that bears it has run between your legs, and rubbed its fur against your dress but lately. Adieu.

From IMAGINARY CONVERSATIONS, by
Walter Savage Landor (1775–1864).

56

THE BOOKWORM

A LOW snug parsonage seemed coeval with the church. The front of it was perfectly matted with a yew-tree that had been trained against its walls, through the dense foliage of which apertures had been formed to admit light into the small antique lattices. As we passed this sheltered nest, the parson issued forth and preceded us.

I had expected to see a sleek well-conditioned pastor, such as is often found in a snug living in the vicinity of a rich patron's table; but I was disappointed. The parson was a little, meagre, black-looking man, with a grizzled wig that was too wide, and stood off from each ear; so that his head seemed to have shrunk away within it, like a dried filbert in its shell. He wore a rusty coat, with great skirts, and pockets that would have held the church Bible and prayer-book; and his small legs seemed still smaller, from being planted in large shoes decorated with enormous buckles.

I was informed by Frank Bracebridge that the parson had been a chum of his father's at Oxford, and had received this living shortly after the latter had come to his estate. He was a complete black-letter hunter, and would scarcely read a work printed in the Roman character. The editions of Caxton and Wynkin de Worde were his delight; and he was indefatigable in his researches after such old English writers as have fallen into oblivion from their worthlessness. In deference, perhaps, to the notions of Mr. Bracebridge, he had made diligent investigations into the festive rites and holiday customs of former times; and had been as zealous in the inquiry as if he had been a boon companion; but it was merely with that plodding spirit with which men of adust temperament follow up any track of study, merely because it is denominated learning; indifferent to its intrinsic nature, whether it be the illustration of the wisdom, or of the ribaldry and obscenity of antiquity. He had pored over these old volumes so intensely, that they seemed to have been reflected into his countenance indeed; which, if the face be an index of the mind, might be compared to a title-page of black-letter.

On reaching the church-porch, we found the parson rebuking the grey-headed sexton for having used mistletoe among the greens with which the church was decorated. It was, he observed, an unholy plant, profaned by having been used by the Druids in their mystic ceremonies; and though it might be innocently employed in the festive ornamenting of halls and kitchens, yet it had been deemed by the Fathers of the Church as unhallowed, and totally unfit for sacred purposes. So tenacious was he on this point, that the poor sexton was obliged to strip down a great part of the humble trophies of his taste, before the parson would consent to enter upon the service of the day.

.   .   .   .   .

The parson gave us a most erudite sermon on the rites and ceremonies of Christmas, and the propriety of observing it not merely as a day of thanksgiving, but of rejoicing; supporting the correctness of his opinions by the earliest usages of the Church, and enforcing them by the authorities of Theophilus of Cesarea, St. Cyprian, St. Chrysostom, St. Augustine and a cloud more of saints and Fathers from whom he made copious quotations. I was a little at a loss to perceive the necessity of such a mighty array of forces to maintain a point which no one present seemed inclined to dispute; but I soon found that the good man had a legion of ideal adversaries to contend with; having in the course of his researches on the subject of Christmas got completely embroiled in the sectarian controveries of the Revolution when the Puritans made such a fierce assault upon the ceremonies of the Church,

135

and poor old Christmas was driven out of the land by proclamation of parliament. The worthy parson lived but with times past, and knew but a little of the present.

From THE SKETCH BOOK, by
Washington Irving (1783–1859).

57

THE GREY FRIAR

WHY are thy looks so blank, grey friar?
    Why are thy looks so blue?
Thou seem'st more pale and lank, grey friar,
    Than thou wast used to do:—
    Say, what has made thee rue?

Thy form was plump, and a light did shine
    In thy round and ruby face,
Which showed an outward visible sign
    Of an inward spiritual grace:—
    Say, what has changed thy case?

Yet will I tell thee true, grey friar,
    I very well can see,
That, if thy looks are blue, grey friar,
    'Tis all for love of me,—
    'Tis all for love of me.

But breathe not thy vows to me, grey friar,
    Oh, breathe them not, I pray;
For ill beseem in a reverend friar,
    The love of a mortal may;
    And I needs must say thee nay.

But could'st thou think my heart to move
  With that pale and silent scowl?
Know, he who would win a maiden's love,
  Whether clad in cap or cowl,
  Must be more of a lark than an owl.

From NIGHTMARE ABBEY, by
Thomas Love Peacock (1785–1866).

58

DR. GASTER NODS

THE Reverend Doctor Gaster seated himself in the corner of a sofa near Miss Philomela Poppyseed. Miss Philomela detailed to him the plan of a very moral and aristocratical novel she was preparing for the press, and continued holding forth, with her eyes half shut, till a long-drawn nasal tone from the reverend divine compelled her suddenly to open them in all the indignation of surprise. The cessation of the hum of her voice awakened the reverend gentleman, who, lifting up first one eyelid, then the other, articulated, or rather murmured, "Admirably planned, indeed!"

"I have not quite finished, sir," said Miss Philomela, bridling. "Will you have the goodness to inform me where I left off?"

The doctor hummed awhile, and at length answered, "I think you had just laid it down at a position, that a thousand a year is an indispensable ingredient in the passion of love, and that no man who is so far gifted by *nature*, can reasonably presume to feel that passion himself, or be correctly the object of it with a well-educated female."

"That, sir," said Miss Philomela, highly incensed, "is the fundamental principle which I lay down in the first chapter, and which the whole four volumes, of which I detailed to you the outline, are intended to set in a strong practical light."

"Bless me!" said the doctor, "what a nap I must have had!"

From HEADLONG HALL, by Thomas
Love Peacock (1785–1866).

RELIGION AND ETHICS

THE REV. SAMUEL H., was at the time of my father's death a curate at some church in Manchester or in Salford. This gentleman represented a class—large enough at all times by necessity of human nature, but in those days far larger than at present—that class, I mean, who sympathise with no spiritual sense or spiritual capacities in man; who understand by religion simply a respectable code of ethics—leaning for support upon some great mysteries dimly traced in the background, and commemorated in certain great church festivals by the *elder* churches of Christendom; as, *e.g.*, by the English, which does not stand as to age on the Reformation epoch, by the Romish, and by the Greek. He had composed a body of about 330 sermons, which thus, at the rate of two every Sunday, revolved through a cycle of three years; that period being modestly assumed as sufficient for insuring to their eloquence total oblivion. Possibly to a cynic, some shorter cycle might have seemed equal to that effect, since their topics rose but rarely above the level of prudential ethics; and the style, though scholarly, was not impressive. As a preacher, Mr. H. was sincere, but not earnest. He was a good and conscientious man; and he made a high valuation of the pulpit as an organ of civilisation for co-operating with books; but it was impossible for any man, starting from the low ground of themes so unimpassioned and so desultory as the benefits of industry, the danger from bad companions, the importance of setting a good example, or the value of perseverance—to pump up any persistent stream of earnestness either in himself or in his auditors.

From THE OPIUM-EATER, by
Thomas de Quincey (1785–1859).

TO THE DEAN AND CHAPTER

OH, very reverend Dean and Chapter,
　　Exhibitors of giant men,
Hail to each surplice-back'd adapter
　　Of England's dead, in her stone den!
Ye teach us properly to prize
　　Two-shilling Grays, and Gays, and Handels,
And, to throw light upon our eyes,
　　Deal in Wax Queens like old wax candles.

Oh, reverend showmen, rank and file,
　　Call in your shillings, two and two;
March with them up the middle aisle,
　　And cloister them from public view.
Yours surely are the dusty dead,
　　Gladly ye look from bust to bust,
And set a price on each great head,
　　And make it come down with the dust.

Oh, as I see you walk along
　　In ample sleeves and ample back,
A pursy and well-order'd throng,
　　Thoroughly fed, thoroughly black!
In vain I strive me to be dumb,—
　　You keep each bard like fatted kid,
Grind bones for bread like Fee-faw-fum!
　　And drink from skulls as Byron did!

The profitable Abbey is
　　A sacred 'Change for stony stock,
Not that a speculation 'tis—
　　The profit's founded on a rock.
Death and the Doctors in each nave
　　Bony investments have inurn'd,
And hard 'twould be to find a grave
　　From which "no money is returned!"

Here many a pensive pilgrim, brought
  By reverence for those learnëd bones,
Shall often come and walk your short
  Two-shilling fare upon the stones—[1]
Ye have that talisman of Wealth
  Which puddling chemists sought of old
Till ruin'd out of hope and health—
  The Tomb's the stone that turns to gold!

Oh, licensed cannibals, ye eat
  Your dinners from your own dead race,
Think Gray, preserved—a "funeral meat,"
  And Dryden, devil'd—after grace,
A relish;—and you take your meal
  From Rare Ben Jonson underdone,
Or, whet your holy knives on Steele,
  To cut away at Addison!

Rare is your show, ye righteous men!
  Priestly Politos,—rare, I ween;
But should ye not outside the Den
  Paint up what in it may be seen?
A long green Shakspeare, with a deer
  Grasp'd in the many folds it died in,—
A Butler stuff'd from ear to ear,
  Wet White Bears weeping o'er a Dryden!

Put up in Poet's Corner, near
  The little door, a platform small;
Get there a monkey—never fear,
  You'll catch the gapers, one and all!
Stand each of ye a Body Guard,
  A Trumpet under either fin,
And yell away in Palace Yard
  "All dead! All dead! Walk in! Walk in!"

                    By Thomas Hood (1799–1845).

[1] "Since this poem was written, Doctor Ireland and those in authority under
him have reduced the fares. It is gratifying to the English people to know that
while butcher's meat is rising tombs are falling."—*Note in Third Edition.*

61

WHEN THE BISHOPS WERE BLESSED

Bent on restoring the papal authority in Britain, James II in 1681 ordered the clergy on two successive Sundays to read a Declaration of Indulgence, proclaiming liberty of worship to Dissenters and Catholics alike. The Primate and seven bishops petitioned the King against the order. Angered by what he termed "rebellion," the King was further incensed when by some means never satisfactorily explained the petition was circulated throughout London. He caused the bishops to be charged with seditious libel, and committed to the Tower.

IT was known all over London that the Bishops were before the Council. The public anxiety was intense. A great multitude filled the courts of Whitehall and all the neighbouring streets. Many people were in the habit of refreshing themselves at the close of a summer day with the cool air of the Thames. But on this evening the whole river was alive with wherries. When the Seven came forth under a guard, the emotions of the people broke through all restraint. Thousands fell on their knees and prayed aloud for the men who had, with the Christian courage of Ridley and Latimer, confronted a tyrant inflamed by all the bigotry of Mary. Many dashed into the stream, and, up to their waists in ooze and water, cried to the holy fathers to bless them. All down the river, from Whitehall to London Bridge, the royal barge passed between lines of boats, from which arose a shout of "God bless your Lordships." The King, in great alarm, gave orders that the garrison of the Tower should be doubled, that the Guards should be held ready for action, and that two companies should be detached from every regiment in the kingdom, and sent up instantly to London. But the force on which he relied as the means of coercing the people shared all the feelings of the people. The very sentinels who were under arms at the Traitors' Gate reverently asked for a blessing from the martyrs whom they were to guard. Sir Edward Hales was Lieutenant of the Tower. He was little inclined to treat his prisoners with kindness. For he was an apostate from that Church for which they suffered; and he held several lucrative posts by virtue of that dispensing power against which they had protested. He learned with indignation that his soldiers were drinking the health of the Bishops. He ordered his officers to see that it was done no more. But the officers came back with a report that the thing could not be prevented, and that no other health was drunk in the garrison. Nor was it only by carousing that the troops showed their reverence for the fathers of the Church. There was such a show of devotion throughout the Tower that pious divines thanked God for bringing good out of evil, and for making the persecution of His faithful servants the means of saving many souls. All day the coaches and liveries of the first nobles of England were seen round the prison gates. Thousands of humbler spectators constantly covered Tower Hill. But among the marks of public respect and sympathy which the prelates received there was one which more than all the rest enraged and alarmed the King. He learned that a deputation of ten Nonconformist ministers had visited the Tower. He sent for four of these persons, and himself upbraided them. They courageously answered that they thought it their duty to forget past quarrels, and to stand by the men who stood by the Protestant religion.

From THE HISTORY OF ENGLAND, by
Thomas, Lord Macaulay (1800–1859).

62

THE COUNTRY CLERGYMAN'S TRIP TO CAMBRIDGE
An Election Ballad, 1827.

As I sat down to breakfast in state,
    At my living of Tithing-cum-Boring,
With Betty beside me to wait,
    Came a rap that almost beat the door in.

I laid down my basin of tea,
  And Betty ceased spreading the toast,
"As sure as a gun, sir," said she,
  "That must be the knock of the post."

A letter—and free—bring it here—
  I have no correspondent who franks.
No! yes! can it be? Why, my dear,
  'Tis our glorious, our Protestant Bankes.
"Dear sir, as I know you desire
  That the Church should receive due protection,
I humbly presume to require
  Your aid at the Cambridge election.

"It has lately been brought to my knowledge,
  That the Ministers fully design
To suppress each cathedral and college,
  And eject every learned divine.
To assist this detestable scheme
  Three nuncios from Rome are come over;
They left Calais on Monday by steam,
  And landed to dinner at Dover.

"An army of grim Cordeliers,
  Well furnished with relics and vermin,
Will follow, Lord Westmoreland fears,
  To effect what their chiefs may determine.
Lollards' Tower, good authorities say,
  Is again fitting up as a prison;
And a wood-merchant told me to-day
  'Tis a wonder how faggots have risen,

"The finance scheme of Canning contains
  A new Easter-offering tax;
And he means to devote all the gains
  To a bounty on thumb-screws and racks.

143

Your living, so neat and compact—
    Pray, don't let the news give you pain!—
Is promised, I know·for a fact,
    To an olive-faced Padre from Spain."

I read, and I felt my heart bleed,
    Sore wounded with horror and pity;
So I flew with all possible speed,
    To our Protestant champion's committee.
True gentlemen, kind and well-bred!
    No fleering! no distance! no scorn!
They asked after my wife, who is dead,
    And my children who never were born.

They then, like high-principled Tories,
    Called our Sovereign unjust and unsteady,
And assailed him with scandalous stories,
    Till the coach for the voters was ready.
That coach might be well called a casket
    Of learning and brotherly love:
There were parsons in boot and in basket;
    There were parsons below and above.

There were Sneaker and Griper, a pair
    Who stick to Lord Mulesby like leeches;
A smug chaplain of plausible air,
    Who writes my Lord Goslingham's speeches;
Dr. Buzz, who alone is a host,
    Who, with arguments weighty as lead,
Proves six times a week in the *Post*
    That flesh somehow differs from bread;

Dr. Nimrod, whose orthodox toes
    Are seldom withdrawn from the stirrup;
Dr. Humdrum, whose eloquence flows,
    Like droppings of sweet poppy syrup;

Dr. Rosygill puffing and fanning,
    And wiping away perspiration;
Dr. Humbug, who proved Mr. Canning
    The beast in St. John's Revelation.

A layman can scarce form a notion
    Of our wonderful talk on the road;
Of the learning, the wit, and devotion,
    Which almost each syllable showed:
Why divided allegiance agrees
    So ill with our free constitution;
How Catholics swear as they please,
    In hope of the priest's absolution;

How the Bishop of Norwich had bartered
    His faith for a legate's commission;
How Lyndhurst, afraid to be martyred,
    Had stooped to a base coalition;
How Papists are cased from compassion
    By bigotry, stronger than steel;
How burning would soon come in fashion,
    And how very bad it must feel.

We were all so much touched and excited
    By a subject so direly sublime,
That the rules of politeness were slighted,
    And we all of us talked at a time;
And in tones, which each moment grew louder,
    Told how we should dress for the show,
And where we should fasten the powder,
    And if we should bellow or no.

Thus from subject to subject we ran,
    And the journey passed pleasantly o'er,
Till at last Dr. Humdrum began;
    From that time I remember no more.

At Ware he commenced his prelection,
  In the dullest of clerical drones:
And when next I regained recollection
  We were rumbling o'er Trumpington stones.

By Thomas, Lord
Macaulay (1800–1859).

63

POISONING THE WELLS

*It was in 1865 that Charles Kingsley made the attack on John Henry
Newman that provoked the* Apologia Pro Vita Sua. *Newman had
lapsed into obscurity after his conversion to Rome, and his orthodoxy
was under suspicion in Italy at the very time that his sincerity was
being impugned in England. He wrote the* Apologia *that lifted him to
a new pinnacle of fame in seven weeks "constantly in tears, and
constantly crying out with distress."*

I REALLY feel sad for what I am obliged now to say. I am in warfare
with him, but I wish him no ill;—it is very difficult to get up
resentment towards persons whom one has never seen. It is easy
enough to be irritated with friends or foes *vis-à-vis*; but, though
I am writing with all my heart against what he has said of me, I
am not conscious of personal unkindness towards himself. I think
it necessary to write as I am writing, for my own sake, and for
the sake of the Catholic Priesthood; but I wish to impute nothing
worse to him than that he has been furiously carried away by his
feelings. Yet what shall I say of the upshot of all his talk of my
economies and equivocations and the like? What is the precise
work which it is directed to effect? I am at war with him; but there
is such a thing as legitimate warfare: war has its laws; there are
things which may fairly be done, and things which may not be
done. I say it with shame and with stern sorrow;—he has attempted
a great transgression; he has attempted (as I may call it) to *poison*

the wells. I will quote him and explain what I mean. . . . He says,—

"I am henceforth in doubt and fear, as much as any honest man can be, *concerning every word* Dr. Newman may write. *How can I tell that I shall not be the dupe of some cunning equivocation*, of one of the three kinds laid down as permissible by the blessed Alfonso da Liguori and his pupils, even when confirmed by an oath, because 'then we do not deceive our neighbour, but allow him to deceive himself?' . . . It is admissible, therefore, to use words and sentences which have a double signification, and leave the hapless hearer to take which of them he may choose. *What proof have I, then, that by 'mean it? I never said it!' Dr. Newman does not signify*, I did not say it, but I did mean it?"

Now these insinuations and questions shall be answered in their proper places; here I will but say that I scorn and detest lying, and quibbling, and double-tongued practice, and slyness, and cunning, and smoothness, and cant, and pretence, quite as much as any Protestants hate them; and I pray to be kept from the snare of them. But all this is just now by the bye; my present subject is my Accuser; what I insist upon here is this unmanly attempt of his, in his concluding pages, to cut the ground from under my feet;—to poison by anticipation the public mind against me, John Henry Newman, and to infuse into the imaginations of my readers, suspicion and mistrust of everything that I may say in reply to him. This I call *poisoning the wells.*

"I am henceforth in *doubt and fear*," he says, "as much as any *honest* man can be, *concerning every word* Dr. Newman may write. *How can I tell that I shall not be the dupe of some cunning equivocation?*" . . .

Well, I can only say, that, if his taunt is to take effect, I am but wasting my time in saying a word in answer to his calumnies; and this is precisely what he knows and intends to be its fruit. I can hardly get myself to protest against a method of controversy so base and cruel, lest in doing so, I should be violating my self-respect and self-possession; but most base and most cruel it is. We all know how our imagination runs away with us, how suddenly and at what a pace;—the saying, "Cæsar's wife should not be

147

suspected," is an instance of what I mean. The habitual prejudice, the humour of the moment, is the turning-point which leads us to read a defence in a good sense or a bad. We interpret it by our antecedent impressions. The very same sentiments, according as our jealousy is or is not awake, or our aversion stimulated, are tokens of truth or of dissimulation and pretence. There is a story of a sane person being by mistake shut up in the wards of a Lunatic Asylum, and that, when he pleaded his cause to some strangers visiting the establishment, the only remark he elicited in answer was, "How naturally he talks! you would think he was in his senses." Controversies should be decided by the reason; is it legitimate warfare to appeal to the misgivings of the public mind and to its dislikings? Any how, if my accuser is able thus to practise upon my readers, the more I succeed, the less will be my success. If I am natural, he will tell them "Ars est celare artem;" if I am convincing, he will suggest that I am an able logician; if I show warmth, I am acting the indignant innocent; if I am calm, I am thereby detected as a smooth hypocrite; if I clear up difficulties, I am too plausible and perfect to be true. The more triumphant are my statements, the more certain will be my defeat.

So will it be if my Accuser succeeds in his manœuvre; but I do not for an instant believe that he will. Whatever judgment my readers may eventually form of me from these pages, I am confident that they will believe me in what I shall say in the course of them. I have no misgiving at all, that they will be ungenerous or harsh towards a man who has been so long before the eyes of the world; who has so many to speak of him from personal knowledge; whose natural impulse it has ever been to speak out; who has ever spoken too much rather than too little; who would have saved himself many a scrape, if he had been wise enough to hold his tongue; who has ever been fair to the doctrines and arguments of his opponents; who has never slurred over facts and reasonings which told against himself; who has never given his name or authority to proofs which he thought unsound, or to testimony which he did not think at least plausible; who has never shrunk from confessing a fault when he felt that he had committed one; who has ever consulted for others more than for himself; who has given up much that he loved and prized and could have retained, but that he loved honesty better than name, and Truth better than dear friends. . . .

From APOLOGIA PRO VITA SUA, by John Henry, Cardinal Newman (1801–1890).

64

THE VICAR

SOME years ago, ere time and taste
    Had turned our parish topsy-turvy,
When Darnel Park was Darnel Waste,
    And roads as little known as scurvy,
The man who lost his way, between
    St. Mary's Hill and Sandy Thicket,
Was always shown across the green,
    And guided to the Parson's wicket.

Back flew the bolt of lissom lath;
    Fair Margaret, in her tidy kirtle,
Led the lorn traveller up the path,
    Through clean-clipt rows of box and myrtle;
And Don and Sancho, Tramp and Tray,
    Upon the parlour steps collected,
Wagged all their tails, and seemed to say—
    Our master knows you—you're expected!

Uprose the Reverend Dr. Brown,
    Uprose the Doctor's winsome marrow;
The lady laid her knitting down,
    Her husband clasped his ponderous Barrow;
Whate'er the stranger's caste or creed,
    Pundit or Papist, saint or sinner,
He found a stable for his steed,
    And welcome for himself, and dinner.

If, when he reached his journey's end,
    And warmed himself in Court or College,
He had not gained an honest friend
    And twenty curious scraps of knowledge,—
If he departed as he came,
    With no new light on love or liquor,—
Good sooth, the traveller was to blame,
    And not the Vicarage, nor the Vicar.

His talk was like a spring, which runs
    With rapid change from rocks to roses;
It slipped from politics to puns,
    It passed from Mahomet to Moses;
Beginning with the laws which keep
    The planets in their radiant courses,
And ending with some precept deep
    For dressing eels, or shoeing horses.

He was a shrewd and sound Divine,
    Of loud Dissent the mortal terror;
And when, by dint of page and line,
    He 'stablished Truth, or startled Error,
The Baptist found him far too deep;
    The Deist sighed with saving sorrow;
And the lean Levite went to sleep,
    And dreamed of tasting pork to-morrow.

His sermons never said or showed
    That Earth is foul, that Heaven is gracious,
Without refreshment on the road
    From Jerome or from Athanasius:
And sure a righteous zeal inspired
    The hand and head that penned and planned them,
For all who understood admired,
    And some who did not understand them.

He wrote, too, in a quiet way,
  Small treatises, and smaller verses,
And sage remarks on chalk and clay,
  And hints to noble Lords—and nurses;
True histories of last year's ghost,
  Lines to a ringlet, or a turban,
And trifles for the *Morning Post*,
  And nothings for Sylvanus Urban.

He did not think all mischief fair,
  Although he had a knack of joking;
He did not make himself a bear,
  Although he had a taste for smoking;
And when religious sects ran mad,
  He held, in spite of all his learning,
That if a man's belief is bad,
  It will not be improved by burning.

And he was kind, and loved to sit
  In the low hut or garnished cottage,
And praise the farmer's homely wit,
  And share the widow's homelier pottage:
At his approach complaint grew mild;
  And when his hand unbarred the shutter,
The clammy lips of fever smiled
  The welcome which they could not utter.

By Winthrop Mack-
worth Praed (1802–39).

65

MOVED BY THE HOLY GHOST

WHEN wealth accrues to a chaplaincy, a bishopric, or rectorship,
it requires moneyed men for its stewarts, who will give it another
direction than to the mystics of their day. Of course, money will
do after its kind, and will steadily work to unspiritualise and

unchurch the people to whom it was bequeathed. The class certain
to be excluded from all preferment are the religious—and driven
to other churches;—which is nature's *vis medicatrix*.

The curates are ill-paid, and the prelates are overpaid. This
abuse draws into the church the children of the nobility, and
other unfit persons, who have a taste for expense. Thus a Bishop
is only a surpliced merchant. Through his lawn, I can see the
bright buttons of the shopman's coat glitter. A wealth like that of
Durham makes almost a premium on felony. Brougham, in a
speech in the House of Commons on the Irish elective franchise,
said, "How will the reverend Bishops of the other house be able
to express their due abhorrence of the crime of perjury, who
solemnly declare in the presence of God, that when they are called
upon to accept a living, perhaps of £4000 a year, at that very
instant, they are moved by the Holy Ghost to accept the office
and administration thereof, and for no other reason whatever."
The modes of initiation are more damaging than custom-house
oaths. The Bishop is elected by the Dean and Prebends of the
cathedral. The Queen sends these gentlemen a *congé d'élire*, or
leave to elect; but also sends them the name of the person whom
they are to elect. They go into the cathedral, chant and pray,
and beseech the Holy Ghost to assist them in their choice; and,
after these invocations, invariably find that the dictates of the
Holy Ghost agree with the recommendations of the Queen.

The church at this moment is much to be pitied. She has nothing
left but possession. If a Bishop meets an intelligent gentleman,
and reads fatal interrogations in his eyes, he has no resource but
to take wine with him. False position introduces cant, perjury,
simony, and ever a lower class of mind and character into the
clergy: and, when the hierarchy is afraid of science and education,
afraid of piety, afraid of tradition, and afraid of theology, there is
nothing left but to quit a church which is no longer one.

From ENGLISH TRAITS, by Ralph
Waldo Emerson (1803–82).

66

THE EXTEMPORE PREACHER

WHEN two days had passed, Sunday came; I breakfasted by myself in the solitary dingle; and then, having set things a little to rights, I ascended to Mr. Petulengro's encampment. I could hear church-bells ringing around in the distance, appearing to say, "Come to church, come to church," as clearly as it was possible for church-bells to say. I found Mr. Petulengro seated by the door of his tent, smoking his pipe, in rather an ungenteel undress. "Well, Jasper," said I, "are you ready to go to church; for if you are, I am ready to accompany you?" "I am not ready, brother," said Mr. Petulengro, "nor is my wife; the church, too, to which we shall go is three miles off; so it is of no use to think of going there this morning, as the service would be three-quarters over before we got there; if, however, you are disposed to go in the afternoon, we are your people." Thereupon I returned to my dingle, where I passed several hours in conning the Welsh Bible, which the preacher, Peter Williams, had given me.

At last I gave over reading, took a slight refreshment, and was about to emerge from the dingle, when I heard the voice of Mr. Petulengro calling me. I went up again to the encampment, where I found Mr. Petulengro, his wife, and Tawno Chikno, ready to proceed to church. Mr. and Mrs. Petulengro were dressed in Roman fashion, though not in the full-blown manner in which they had paid their visit to Isopel and myself. Tawno had on a clean white slop, with a nearly new black beaver, with very broad rims, and the nap exceedingly long. As for myself, I was dressed in much the same manner as that in which I departed from London, having on, in honour of the day, a shirt perfectly clean, having washed one on purpose for the occasion, with my own hands, the day before, in the pond of tepid water in which the newts and efts were in the habit of taking their pleasure. We proceeded for upwards of a mile, by footpaths through meadows and corn-fields; we crossed various stiles; at last, passing over one, we found ourselves in a road, wending along which for a considerable distance, we at last came in sight of a church, the bells of which had been tolling distinctly in our ears for some time; before, however, we reached the churchyard the bells had ceased their melody. It was surrounded by lofty beech-trees of brilliant green foliage. We entered the gate, Mrs. Petulengro leading the way, and proceeded to a small door near the east end of the church.

.   .   .   .   .

Still following Mrs. Petulengro, we proceeded down the chancel and along the aisle; notwithstanding the singing, I could distinctly hear as we pass many a voice whispering, "Here come the gypsies! here come the gypsies!" I felt rather embarrassed, with a somewhat awkward doubt as to where we were to sit; none of the occupiers of the pews, who appeared to consist almost entirely of farmers, with their wives, sons, and daughters, opened a door to admit us. Mrs. Petulengro, however, appeared to feel not the least embarassment, but tripped along the aisle with the greatest nonchalance. We passed under the pulpit, in which stood the clergyman in his white surplice, and reached the middle of the church, where we were confronted by the sexton dressed in long blue coat, and holding in his hand a wand. This functionary motioned towards the lower end of the church, where were certain benches, partly occupied by poor people and boys. Mrs. Petulengro, however, with a toss of her head, directed her course to a magnificent pew, which was unoccupied, which she opened and entered, followed closely by Tawno Chikno, Mr. Petulengro, and myself. The sexton did not appear by any means to approve of the arrangement, and as I stood next the door laid his finger on my arm, as if to intimate that myself and companions must quit our aristocratical location. I said nothing, but directed my eyes to the clergyman, who uttered a short and expressive cough; the sexton looked at him for a moment, and then, bowing his head, closed the door—in a moment more the music ceased. I took up a prayer-book, on which was engraved an earl's coronet. The clergyman uttered, "I will arise, and go to my father." England's sublime liturgy had commenced.

.   .   .   .   .

The liturgy was over, during the reading of which my companions behaved in a most unexceptional manner, sitting down and rising up when other people sat down and rose, and holding in their hands prayer-books which they found in the pew, into which they stared intently, though I observed that, with the exception of Mrs. Petulengro, who knew how to read a little, they held the books by the top, and not the bottom, as is the usual way. The clergyman now ascended the pulpit, arrayed in his black gown. The congregation composed themselves to attention, as did also my companions, who fixed their eyes upon the clergyman with a certain strange immovable stare, which I believe to be peculiar to their race. The clergyman gave out his text, and began to preach. He was a tall, gentlemanly man, seemingly between fifty and sixty, with greyish hair; his features were very handsome, but with a somewhat melancholy cast: the tones of his voice were rich and noble, but also with somewhat of melancholy in them. The text which he gave out was the following one, "In what would a man be profited, provided he gained the whole world, and lost his own soul?"

And on this text the clergyman preached long and well: he did not read his sermon, but spoke it extempore; his doing so rather surprised and offended me at first; I was not used to such a style of preaching in a church devoted to the religion of my country. I compared it within my mind with the style of preaching used by the high-church rector in the old church of pretty D . . . , and I thought to myself it was very different, and being very different I did not like it, and I thought to myself how scandalised the people of D . . . would have been had they heard it, and I figured to myself how indignant the high-church clerk would have been had any clergyman got up in the church of D . . . and preached in such a manner. Did it not savour strongly of dissent, methodism, and similar low stuff? Surely it did; why, the Methodist I had heard preach on the heath above the old city, preached in the same manner—at least he preached extempore; ay, and something like the present clergyman, for the Methodist spoke very zealously and with great feeling, and so did the present clergyman; so I, of course, felt rather offended with the clergyman for speaking

155

with zeal and feeling. However, long before the sermon was over I forgot the offence which I had taken, and listened to the sermon with much admiration, for the eloquence and powerful reasoning with which it abounded.

Oh, how eloquent he was, when he talked of the inestimable value of a man's soul, which he said endured for ever, whilst his body, as every one knew, lasted at most for a very contemptible period of time; and how forcibly he reasoned on the folly of man, who, for the sake of gaining the whole world—a thing, he said, which provided he gained he could only possess for a part of the time, during which his perishable body existed—should lose his soul, that is, cause that precious deathless portion of him to suffer indescribable misery time without end.

There was one part of his sermon which struck me in a very particular manner: he said, "That there were some people who gained something in return for their souls; if they did not get the whole world, they got a part of it—lands, wealth, honour or renown; mere trifles he allowed, in comparison with the value of a man's soul, which is destined either to enjoy delight, or suffer tribulation time without end; but which in the eyes of the worldly, had a certain value, and which afforded a certain pleasure and satisfaction. But there were also others who lost their souls, and got nothing for them—neither lands, wealth, renown, nor consideration, who were poor outcasts, and despised by everybody. My friends," he added, "if the man is a fool who barters his soul for the whole world, what a fool he must be who barters his soul for nothing."

The eyes of the clergyman, as he uttered these words, wandered around the whole congregation; and when he had concluded them, the eyes of the whole congregation were turned upon my companions and myself.

From THE ROMANY RYE, by
George Borrow (1803–81).

67

LINES FROM A LETTER TO A YOUNG CLERICAL FRIEND

A STRENGTH Thy service cannot tire,
   A faith which doubts can never dim,
A heart of love, a lip of fire,
   O Freedom's God! be Thou to him!

Speak through him words of power and fear,
   As through Thy prophet bards of old,
And let a scornful people hear
   Once more Thy Sinai-thunders rolled.

For lying lips Thy blessing seek,
   And hands of blood are raised to Thee,
And on Thy children, crushed and weak,
   The oppressor plants his kneeling knee.

Let then, O God! Thy servant dare
   Thy truth in all its power to tell,
Unmask the priestly thieves, and tear
   The Bible from the grasp of hell!

From hollow rite and narrow span
   Of law and sect by Thee released,
Oh, teach him that the Christian man
   Is holier than the Jewish priest.

Chase back the shadows, gray and old,
   Of the dead ages, from his way,
And let his hopeful eyes behold
   The dawn of Thy millennial day;

That day when fettered limb and mind
   Shall know the truth which maketh free,
And he alone who loves his kind
   Shall, childlike, claim the love of Thee!

         By John Greenleaf Whittier (1807–92).

68

THE CHURCHWARDEN AND THE CURATE

"This is written," explained Tennyson, "in the dialect which was current in my youth at Spilsby and in the country round about it."

I

Eh? good daäy! good daäy! thaw it bean't not mooch of a daäy,
Nasty, casselty[1] weather! an' mea haäfe down wi' my haäy![2]

II

How be the farm gittin on? noäways. Gittin on i'deeäd!
Why, tonups was haäfe on 'em fingers an' toäs,[3] an' the mare
   brokkenkneeäd,
An' pigs didn't sell at fall,[4] an' wa lost wer Haldeny cow,
An' it beäts ma to knaw wot she died on, but wool's looking oop
   ony how.

III

An' soä they've maäde tha a parson, an' thou'll git along, niver fear,
Fur I beän chuch-warden mysen i' the parish fur fifteen year.
Well—sin ther beä chuch-wardens, ther mun be parsons an' all,
An' if t'ōne stick alongside t'uther[5] the church weänt happen a fall.

   [1] "Casselty," casualty, chance weather.
   [2] "Haäfe down wi' my haäy," while my grass is only half-mown.
   [3] "Fingers and toes," a disease in turnips.
   [4] "Fall," autumn.
   [5] "If t'ōne stick alongside t'uther," if the one hold by the other. One
is pronounced like "own."

IV

Fur I wur a Baptis wonst, an' ageän the toithe an' the raäte,
Till I fun[1] that it warn't not the gaäinist[2] waäy to the narra Gaäte.
An' I can't abeär 'em, I can't, fur a lot on 'em coom'd ta-year[3]—
I wur down wi' the rheumatis then—to *my* pond to wesh thessens
   theere—
Sa I sticks like the ivin[4] as long as I lives to the owd chuch now,
Fur they wesh'd their sins i' *my* pond, an' I doubts they poison'd
   the cow.

V

Ay, an' ya seed the Bishop. They says 'at he coom'd fra nowt—
Burn i' traäde. Sa I warrants 'e niver said haäfe wot 'e thowt,
But 'e creeäpt an' 'e crawl'd along, till 'e feeäld 'e could howd
   'is oän,
Then 'e married a greät Yerl's darter, an' sits o' the Bishop's throän.

VI

Now I'll gie tha a bit o' my mind an' tha weant be taakin' offence,
Fur thou be a big scholard now wi' a hoonderd haäcre o' sense—
But sich an obstropulous[5] lad—naay, naay—fur I minds tha sa
   well,
Tha'd niver not hopple[6] thy tongue, an' the tongue's sit afire o'
   Hell,
As I says to my missis to-daay, when she hurl'd a plaäte at the cat
An' anoother ageän my noäse. Ya was niver so bad as that.

VII

But I minds when i' Howlaby beck won daäy ya was ticklin' o' trout,
An' keeäper 'e seed ya an roon'd, an' 'e beal'd[7] to ya 'Lad coom
   hout'

[1] "Fun," found.   [2] "Gaäinist," nearest.
[3] "Ta-year," this year.   [4] "Ivin," ivy.
[5] "Obstropulous," obstreperous—here the Curate makes a sign of
deprecation.
[6] "Hopple" or "hobble," to tie the legs of a skittish cow when she is
being milked.
[7] "Beal'd," bellowed.

An' ya stood oop naäkt i' the beck, an' ya tell'd 'im to knaw
    his awn plaäce
An' ya call'd 'im a clown, ya did, an' ya thraw'd the fish i' 'is faäce,
An' 'e torn'd[1] as red as a stag-tuckey's[2] wattles, but theer an' then
I coämb'd 'im down, fur I promised ya'd niver not do it ageän.

VIII

An' I cotch'd tha wonst i' my garden, when thou was a height-
    year-howd,[3]
An' I fun thy pockets as full o' my pippins as iver they'd 'owd,[4]
An' thou was as peärky[5] as owt, an' tha maäde me as mad as mad,
But I says to tha 'keeap 'em, an' welcome' fur thou was the Parson's
    lad.

IX

An Parson 'e 'ears on it all, an' then taäkes kindly to me,
An' then I wur chose Chuch-warden an' coom'd to the top o' the
    tree,
Fur Quoloty's hall my friends, an' they maäkes ma a help to the
    poor,
When I gits the plaäte fuller o' Soondays nor ony chuch-warden
    afoor,
Fur if iver thy feyther 'ed riled me I kep' mysen meeäk as a lamb,
An' saw by the Graäce o' the Lord, Mr. Harry, I ham wot I ham.

X

But Parson 'e *will* speäk out, saw, now 'e be sixty-seven,
He'll niver swap Owlby an' Scratby fur owt but the Kingdom o'
    Heaven;
An' thou'll be 'is Curate 'ere, but, if iver tha means to git 'igher,
Tha mun tackle the sins o' the Wo'ld,[6] an' not the faults o' the
    Squire.

[1] In such words as "torned" (turned), "hurled," the *r* is hardly audible.
[2] "Stag-tuckey," turkey-cock.
[3] "Height-year-howd," eight-year-old.
[4] "Owd," hold.   [5] "Peärky," pert.   [6] "Wo'ld," the world. Short *o*.

An' I reckons tha'll light of a livin' somewheers i' the Wowd[1] or
  the Fen,
If tha cottons down to thy betters, an' keeäps thysen to thysen.
But niver not speäk plaain out, if tha wants to git forrards a bit,
But creeäp along the hedge-bottoms, an' thou'll be a Bishop yit.

XI

Naäy, but tha *mun* speäk hout to the Baptises here i' the town,
Fur moäst on 'em talks ageän tithe, an' I'd like tha to preäch 'em
  down,
Fur *they*'ve bin a-preächin' *mea* down, they heve, an' I haätes
  'em now,
Fur they leäved their nasty sins i' *my* pond, an' it poison'd the cow.

By Alfred, Lord Tennyson (1809–92).

69

THE RECTOR OF QUEEN'S CRAWLEY

THE REVEREND BUTE CRAWLEY was a tall, stately, jolly, shovel-
hatted man, far more popular in his county than the baronet, his
brother. At college he pulled stroke-oar in the Christchurch boat,
and had thrashed all the best bruisers of the "town." He carried
his taste for boxing and athletic exercises into private life: there
was not a fight within twenty miles at which he was not present,
nor a race, nor a coursing match, nor a regatta, nor a ball, nor an
election, nor a visitation dinner, nor indeed a good dinner in the
whole county, but he found means to attend it. You might see his
bay mare and gig-lamps a score of miles away from his Rectory
House, whenever there was any dinner-party at Fuddleston, or
at Roxby, or at Wapshot Hall, or at the great lords of the county,
with all of whom he was intimate. He had a fine voice; sang "A

1 "Wowd," wold.

southerly wind and a cloudy sky;" and gave the "whoop" in chorus with general applause. He rode to hounds in a pepper-and-salt frock, and was one of the best fishermen in the county.

Mrs. Crawley, the rector's wife, was a smart little body, who wrote this worthy divine's sermons. Being of a domestic turn, and keeping the house a great deal with her daughters, she ruled absolutely within the Rectory, wisely giving her husband full liberty without. He was welcome to come and go, and dine abroad as many days as his fancy dictated, for Mrs. Crawley was a saving woman and knew the price of port wine. Ever since Mrs. Bute carried off the young rector of Queen's Crawley (she was of a good family, daughter of the late Lieut.-Colonel Hector MacTavish, and she and her mother played for Bute and won him at Harrogate), she had been a prudent and thrifty wife to him. In spite of her care, however, he was always in debt. In took him at least ten years to pay off his college bills contracted during his father's life-time. In the year 179-, when he was just clear of these incumbrances, he gave the odds of 100 to 1 (in twenties) against Kangaroo, who won the Derby.

The rector was obliged to take up the money at a ruinous interest, and had been struggling ever since. His sister helped him with a hundred now and then, but of course his great hope was in her death—when "Hang it" (as he would say), "Matilda *must* leave me half her money."

So that the baronet and his brother had every reason which two brothers possibly can have for being by the ears. Sir Pitt had had the better of Bute in innumerable family transactions. Young Pitt not only did not hunt; but set up a meeting-house under his uncle's very nose. Rawdon, it was known, was to come in for the bulk of Miss Crawley's property. These money transactions— these speculations in life and death—these silent battles for reversionary spoil—make brothers very loving toward each other in Vanity Fair. I, for my part, have known a five-pound note to interpose and knock up half a century's attachment between two brethren; and can't but admire, as I think what a fine and durable thing Love is among worldly people.

"Why did you ask that scoundrel, Rawdon Crawley, to dine?" said the rector to his lady, as they were walking home through the park. "*I* don't want the fellow. He looks down upon us country people as so many blackamoors. He's never content unless he gets my yellow-sealed wine, which costs me ten shillings a bottle, hang him! Besides, he's such an infernal character: he's a gambler—he's a drunkard—he's a profligate in every way. He's killed a man in a duel—he's over head and ears in debt, and he's robbed me and mine of the best part of Miss Crawley's fortune. Waxy says she has him"—here the rector shook his fist at the moon, with something very like an oath, and added in a melancholious tone—"——, down in her will for fifty thousand; and there won't be above thirty to divide."

"I think she's going," said the rector's wife. "She was very red in the face when we left dinner. I was obliged to unlace her."

"She drank seven glasses of champagne," said the reverend gentleman, in a low voice; "and filthy champagne it is, too, that my brother poisons us with—but you women never know what's what."

"We know nothing," said Mrs. Bute Crawley.

"She drank cherry-brandy after dinner," continued his Reverence, "and took curaçoa with her coffee. *I* wouldn't take a glass for a five-pound note: it kills me with heartburn. She can't stand it, Mrs. Crawley—she must go—flesh and blood won't bear it! and I lay five to two, Matilda drops in a year."

Indulging in these solemn speculations, and thinking about his debts, and his son Jim at college, and Frank at Woolwich, and the four girls who were no beauties, poor things, and would not have a penny but what they got from the aunt's expected legacy, the rector and his lady walked on for a while.

"Pitt can't be such an infernal villain as to sell the reversion of the living. And that Methodist milksop of an eldest son looks to Parliament," continued Mr. Crawley, after a pause.

"Sir Pitt Crawley will do anything," said the rector's wife. "We must get Miss Crawley to make him promise it to James."

"Pitt will promise anything," replied the brother. "He promised he'd pay my college bills, when my father died: he promised he'd build the new wing to the Rectory: he promised he'd let me have Jibb's field and the Six-acre Meadow—and much he executed his promises! And it's to this man's son—this scoundrel, gambler, swindler, murderer of a Rawdon Crawley that Matilda leaves the bulk of her money. I say it's unchristian. By Jove, it is. The infamous dog that has got every vice except hypocrisy, and that belongs to his brother."

"Hush, my dearest love! we're in Sir Pitt's grounds," interposed his wife.

"I say he *has* got every vice, Mrs. Crawley. Don't ma'am, bully *me*. Didn't he shoot Captain Firebrace? Didn't he rob young Lord Dovedale at the Cocoa-Tree? Didn't he cross the fight between Bill Soames and the Cheshire Trump, by which I lost forty pound? You know he did; and as for the women, why, you heard that before me, in my own magistrate's room——"

"For Heaven's sake, Mr. Crawley," said the lady, "spare me the details."

"And you ask this villain into your house!" continued the exasperated rector. "You, the mother of a young family, the wife of a clergyman of the Church of England. By Jove!"

"Bute Crawley, you are a fool," said the rector's wife scornfully.

"Well, ma'am, fool or not—and I don't say, Martha, I'm so clever as *you* are, I never did. But I won't meet Rawdon Crawley, that's flat. I'll go over to Huddleston, that I will, and see his black greyhound, Mrs. Crawley; and I'll run Launcelot against him for fifty. By Jove, I will; or against any dog in England. But I won't meet that beast Rawdon Crawley."

"Mr. Crawley, you are intoxicated, as usual," replied his wife. And the next morning, when the rector woke, and called for small beer, she put him in mind of his promise to visit Sir Huddleston Fuddleston, on Saturday, and as he knew he should have a *wet night*, it was agreed that he might gallop back again in time for church on Sunday morning. Thus it will be seen that the parishioners of Crawley were equally happy in their squire and in their rector.

From VANITY FAIR, by William Makepeace Thackeray (1811–63).

70

SMALLPOX VISITS CASTLEWOOD

ONE day in the year 1694 (I have good reason to remember it), Doctor Tusher ran into Castlewood House, with a face of consternation, saying that the malady had made its appearance at the blacksmith's house in the village, and that one of the maids there was down in the smallpox.

. . . . .

Little Lady Beatrix screamed out at Doctor Tusher's news; and my lord cried out, "God bless me!" He was a brave man, and not afraid of death in any shape but this. He was very proud of his pink complexion and fair hair—but the idea of death by smallpox scared him beyond all other ends. "We will take the children and ride away to-morrow to Walcote:" this was my lord's small house, inherited from his mother, near to Winchester.

"That is the best refuge in case the disease spreads," said Doctor Tusher. "'Tis awful to think of it beginning at the ale-house; half the people of the village have visited that to-day, or the blacksmith's which is the same thing. My clerk Nahum lodges with them—I can never go into my reading-desk and have that fellow so near me. I *won't* have that man near me."

"If a parishioner dying in the smallpox sent to you, would you not go?" asked my lady, looking up from her frame of work, with her calm blue eyes.

"By the Lord, *I* wouldn't," said my lord.

"We are not in a Popish country; and a sick man doth not absolutely need absolution and confession," said the Doctor. "'Tis true they are a comfort and a help to him when attainable, and to be administered with hope of good. But in a case where the life of a parish priest in the midst of his flock is highly valuable to them, he is not called upon to risk it (and therewith the lives, future prospects, and temporal, even spiritual welfare of his own family) for the sake of a single person, who is not very likely in a condition even to understand the religious message whereof the

165

priest is the bringer—being uneducated, and likewise stupefied or delirious by disease. If your ladyship or his lordship, my excellent good friend and patron, were to take it——"

"God forbid!" cried my lord.

"Amen," continued Doctor Tusher. "Amen to that prayer, my very good lord! for your sake I would lay my life down"—and, to judge from the alarmed look of the Doctor's purple face, you would have thought that that sacrifice was about to be called for instantly.

> *From* HENRY ESMOND, by William
> Makepeace Thackeray (1811–63).

71

THE MAYFAIR INCUMBENT

HIS hermitage is situated in Walpole Street let us say, on the second floor of a quiet mansion, let out to hermits by a nobleman's butler, whose wife takes care of the lodgings. His cells consist of a refectory, a dormitory, and an adjacent oratory where he keeps his shower-bath and boots—the pretty boots trimly stretched on boot-trees and blacked to a nicety (not varnished) by the boy who waits on him. The barefooted business may suit superstitious ages and gentlemen of Alcantara, but does not become Mayfair and the nineteenth century. If Saint Pedro walked the earth now with his eyes to the ground he would know fashionable divines by the way in which they were shod. Charles Honeyman's is a sweet foot. I have no doubt as delicate and plump and rosy as the white hand with its two rings, which he passes in impassioned moments through his slender flaxen hair.

A sweet odour pervades his sleeping apartment—not that peculiar and delicious fragrance with which the Saints of the Roman Church are said to gratify the neighbourhood where they repose—but oils, redolent of the richest perfumes of Macassar, essences (from Truefitt's or Delcroix's) into which a thousand flowers have expressed their sweetest breath, await his meek head on rising; and infuse the pocket-handkerchief with which he dries and draws so many tears. For he cries a good deal in his sermons, to which the ladies about him contribute showers of sympathy.

By his bedside are slippers lined with blue silk and worked of an ecclesiastical pattern, by some of the faithful who sit at his feet. They come to him in anonymous parcels: they come to him in silver paper: boys in buttons (pages who minister to female grace!) leave them at the door for the Rev. C. Honeyman, and slip away without a word. Purses are sent to him—pen-wipers—a portfolio with the Honeyman arms—yea, braces have been known to reach him by the post (in his days of popularity), and flowers, and grapes, and jelly when he was ill, and throat comforters, and lozenges for his dear bronchitis. In one of his drawers is the rich silk cassock presented to him by his congregation at Leatherhead (when the young curate quitted that parish for London duty), and on his breakfast-table the silver teapot, once filled with sovereigns and presented by the same devotees. The devoteapot he has, but the sovereigns, where are they.

What a different life this is from our honest friend of Alcantara, who eats once in three days! At one time if Honeyman could have drunk tea three times in an evening, he might have had it. The glass on his chimney-piece is crowded with invitations, not merely cards of ceremony (of which there are plenty) but dear little confidential notes from sweet friends of his congregation. "Oh, dear Mr. Honeyman," writes Blanche, "what a sermon that was! I cannot go to bed to-night without thanking you for it." "Do, *do*, dear Mr. Honeyman," writes Beatrice, "lend me that delightful sermon. And can you come and drink tea with me and Selina, and my aunt? Papa and mamma dine out, but you *know* I am always your faithful Chesterfield Street." And so on. He has all the domestic accomplishments; he plays on the violoncello: he sings a delicious second, not only in sacred but in secular music. He has a thousand anecdotes, laughable riddles, droll stories (of the utmost correctness, you understand) with which he entertains females of all ages; suiting his conversation to stately matrons, deaf old dowagers (who can hear his clear voice better than the loudest roar of their stupid sons-in-law), mature spinsters, young beauties dancing through the season, even rosy little slips out of the nursery, who cluster round his beloved feet. Societies fight for him to preach their charity sermon. You read in the papers:—"The Wapping Hospital for Wooden-legged Seamen. On Sunday the 23rd, Sermons will be preached in behalf of this charity, by the Lord BISHOP OF TOBAGO in the morning, in the afternoon by the Rev. C. HONEYMAN, A.M., Incumbent of, etc." "Clergyman's Grandmothers' Fund. Sermons in aid of this admirable institution will be preached on Sunday, 4th May, by the Very Rev. The DEAN OF PIMLICO, and the Rev. C. HONEYMAN, A.M." When the Dean of Pimlico has his illness, many people think Honeyman will have the Deanery; that he ought to have it, a hundred female voices vow and declare; though it is said that a right reverend head at headquarters shakes dubiously when his name is mentioned for preferment. His name is spread wide, and not only women but men come to hear him. Members of Parliament, even Cabinet Ministers, sit under him: Lord Dozeley of course is seen in a front pew: where was a public meeting without Lord Dozeley? The men come away from his sermons and say, "It's very pleasant, but I don't know what the deuce makes all you women crowd so to hear the man." "Oh, Charles! if you would but go oftener!" sighs Lady Anna Maria. "Can't you speak to the Home Secretary? Can't you do something for him?" "We can ask him to dinner next Wednesday if you like," says Charles. "They say he's a pleasant fellow out of the wood. Besides there is no use in doing anything for him," Charles goes on. "He can't make less than a thousand a year out of his chapel, and that is better than anything any one can give him. A thousand a year, beside the rent of the wine-vaults below the chapel."

"Don't, Charles!" says his wife, with a solemn look. "Don't ridicule things in that way."

From THE NEWCOMES, by William
Makepeace Thackeray (1811–63).

72

BISHOP BLOUGRAM'S APOLOGY

The famous dramatic monologue from which this extract is taken gave some offence at the time of publication because Blougram, the worldly prelate who makes a casuistical defence of his position in the Church, was taken as a portrait of Cardinal Wiseman. Browning is said to have admitted the likeness, but denied the insult, since Blouhram (in Browning's estimation) makes a successful defence.

So, you despise me, Mr. Gigadibs.
No deprecation,—nay, I beg you, sir!
Beside 'tis our engagement: don't you know,
I promised, if you'd watch a dinner out,
We'd see truth dawn together?—truth that peeps
Over the glass's edge when dinner's done,
And body gets its sop and hold its noise
And leaves soul free a little. Now's the time—
'Tis break of day! You do despise me then.
And if I say, "despise me,"—never fear—
I know you do not in a certain sense—
Not in my arm-chair for example: here,
I well imagine you respect my place
(Status, *entourage*, worldly circumstance)
Quite to its value—very much indeed
—Are up to the protesting eyes of you
In pride at being seated here for once—
You'll turn it to such capital account!
When somebody, through years and years to come,
Hints of the bishop—names me—that's enough—
"Blougram? I knew him"—(into it you slide)
"Dined with him once, a Corpus Christi Day,
All alone, we two—he's a clever man—
And after dinner,—why, the wine you know,—
Oh, there was wine, and good!—what with the wine. . . .
'Faith, we began upon all sorts of talk!

He's no bad fellow, Blougram—he had seen
Something of mine he relished—some review—
He's quite above their humbug in his heart,
Half-said as much, indeed—the thing's his trade—
I warrant, Blougram's sceptical at times—
How otherwise? I liked him, I confess!"
Che che, my dear sir, as we say at Rome,
Don't you protest now! It's fair give and take;
You have had your turn and spoken your home-truths:
The hand's mine now, and here you follow suit.

Thus much conceded, still the first fact stays—
You do despise me; your ideal of life
Is not the bishop's—you would not be I—
You would like better to be Goethe, now,
Or Buonaparte—or, bless me, lower still,
Count D'Orsay,—so you did what you preferred,
Spoke as you thought, and, as you cannot help,
Believed or disbelieved, no matter what,
So long as on that point, whate'er it was,
You loosed your mind, where whole and sole yourself.
—That, my ideal never can include,
Upon that element of truth and worth
Never be based! for say they make me Pope
(They can't—suppose it for our argument)
Why, there I'm at my tether's end—I've reached
My height, and not a height which pleases you.
An unbelieving Pope won't do, you say.
It's like those eerie stories nurses tell,
Of how some actor played Death on a stage
With pasteboard crown, sham orb and tinselled dart,
And called himself the monarch of the world,
Then, going in the tire-room afterward
Because the play was done, to shift himself,
Got touched upon the sleeve familiarly
The moment he had shut the closet door
By Death himself. Thus God might touch a Pope

At unawares, ask what his baubles mean,
And whose part he presumed to play just now?
Best be yourself, imperial, plain and true!
So, drawing comfortable breath again,
You weigh and find whatever more or less
I boast of my ideal realised
Is nothing in the balance when opposed
To your ideal, your grand simple life,
Of which you will not realise one jot.
I am much, you are nothing; you would be all,
I would be merely much—you beat me there.
No, friend, you do not beat me,—hearken why.
The common problem, yours, mine, every one's,
Is not to fancy what were fair in life
Provided it could be,—but finding first
What may be, then find how to make it fair
Up to our means—a very different thing!
No abstract intellectual plan of life
Quite irrespective of life's plainest laws,
But one, a man, who is man and nothing more,
May lead within a world which (by your leave)
Is Rome or London—not Fool's-paradise.
Embellish Rome, idealise away,
Make Paradise of London if you can,
You're welcome, nay, you're wise.

And now what are we? unbelievers both,
Calm and complete, determinately fixed
To-day, to-morrow, and for ever, pray?
You'll guarantee me that? Not so, I think!
In no-wise! all we've gained is, that belief,
As unbelief before, shakes us by fits,
Confounds us like its predecessor. Where's
The gain? how can we guard our unbelief,
Make it bear fruit to us?—the problem here.
Just when we are safest, there's a sunset-touch,
A fancy from a flower-bell, some one's death,

A chorus-ending from Euripides,—
And that's enough for fifty hopes and fears
As old and new at once as Nature's self,
To rap and knock and enter in our soul,
Take hands and dance there, a fantastic ring,
Round the ancient idol, on his base again,—
The grand Perhaps! we look on helplessly,—
There the old misgivings, crooked questions are—
This good God,—what He could do, if He would,
Would, if He could—then must have done long since:
If so, when, where, and how? some way must be,—
Once feel about, and soon or late you hit
Some sense, in which it might be, after all.
Why not, "The Way, the Truth, the Life?"

By Robert Browning (1812–89).

73

GIUSEPPE CAPONSACCHI

A high-born seventeenth-century Italian with notable family connections in the Church, Giuseppe Caponsacchi was from boyhood destined for the priesthood and high office. Becoming involved in a murder trial, he explains to the court how lightly his qualms at ordination were set aside.

I HAD a right
To the self-same office, bishop in the egg,
So, grew i' the garb and prattled in the school,
Was made expect, from infancy almost,
The proper mood o' the priest; till time ran by
And brought the day when I must read the vows,
Declare the world renounced and undertake
To become priest and leave probation,—leap

Over the ledge into the other life,
Having gone tripplingly hitherto up to the height
O'er the wan water. Just a vow to read!

I stopped short awe-struck. "How shall holiest flesh
Engage to keep such vow inviolate,
How much less mine? I know myself too weak,
Unworthy! Choose a worthier stronger man!"
And the very Bishop smiled and stopped my mouth
In its mid-protestation. "Incapable?
Qualmish of conscience? Thou ingenuous boy!
Clear up the clouds and cast they scruples far!
I satisfy thee there's an easier sense
Wherein to take such vow than suits the first
Rough rigid reading. Mark what makes all smooth,
Nay, has been even a solace to myself!
The Jews who needs must, in their synagogue,
Utter sometimes the holy name of God,
A thing their superstition boggles at,
Pronounce aloud the ineffable sacrosanct,—
How does their shrewdness help them? In this wise;
Another set of sounds they substitute,
Jumble so consonants and vowels—how
Should I know?—that there grows from out the old
Quite a new word that means the very same—
And o'er the hard place slide they with a smile.
Giuseppe Maria Caponsacchi mine,
Nobody wants you in these latter days
To prop the Church by breaking your back bone,—
As the necessary way was once, we know,
When Diocletian flourished and his like.
That building of the buttress-work was done
By martyrs and confessors: let it bide,
Add not a brick, but, where you see a chink,
Stick in a sprig of ivy or root a rose
Shall make amends and beautify the pile!
We profit as you were the painfullest

O' the martyrs, and you prove yourself a match
For the cruelest confessor ever was,
If you march boldly up and take your stand
Where their blood soaks, their bones yet strew the soil,
And cry 'Take notice, I the young and free
And well-to-do i' the world, thus leave the world,
Cast in my lot thus with no gay young world
But the grand old Church: she tempts me of the two!'
Renounce the world? Nay, keep and give it us!
Let us have you, and boast of what you bring.
We want the pick o' the earth to practise with,
Not its offscouring, halt and deaf and blind
In soul and body. . . ."

From THE RING AND THE BOOK,
by Robert Browning (1812–89).

74

PUTTING THE CASE

Surely the goods of this world, it occurred in an accidental way
to Bishop to remark, could scarcely be directed into happier
channels than when they accumulated under the magic touch of
the wise and sagacious, who, while they knew the just value of
riches (Bishop here tried to look as if he were rather poor himself),
were aware of their importance, judiciously governed and rightly
distributed, to the welfare of our brethren at large.

Mr. Merdle with humility expressed his conviction that Bishop
couldn't mean him, and with inconsistency expressed his high
gratification in Bishop's good opinion.

Bishop then—jauntily stepping out a little with his well-shaped
right leg, as though he said to Mr. Merdle "don't mind the apron;
a mere form!"—put this case to his good friend:

Whether it had occurred to his good friend, that Society might
not unreasonably hope that one so blest in his undertakings, and

whose example on his pedestal was so influential with it, would shed a little money in the direction of a mission or so to Africa?

Mr. Merdle signifying that the idea should have his best attention, Bishop put another case:

Whether his good friend had at all interested himself in the proceedings of our Combined Additional Endowed Dignitaries Committee, and whether it had occurred to him that to shed a little money in *that* direction might be a great conception finely executed?

Mr. Merdle made a similar reply, and Bishop explained his reason for inquiring.

Society looked to such men as his good friend to do such things. It was not that *he* looked to them, but that Society looked to them. Just as it was not Our Committee who wanted the Additional Endowed Dignitaries, but it was Society that was in a state of the most agonising uneasiness of mind until it got them. He begged to assure his good friend that he was extremely sensible of his good friend's regard on all occasions for the best interests of Society; and he considered that he was at once consulting those interests, and expressing the feeling of Society, when he wished him continued prosperity, continued increase of riches, and continued things in general.

Bishop then betook himself up-stairs, and the other magnates gradually floated up after him until there was no one left below but Mr. Merdle. That gentleman, after looking at the table-cloth until the soul of the chief butler glowed with a noble resentment, went slowly up after the rest, and became of no account in the stream of people on the grand staircase. Mrs. Merdle was at home, the best of the jewels were hung out to be seen, Society got what it came for, Mr. Merdle drank twopennyworth of tea in a corner and got more than he wanted.

Among the evening magnates was a famous physician, who knew everybody and whom everybody knew. On entering at the door, he came upon Mr. Merdle drinking his tea in a corner, and touched him on the arm.

Mr. Merdle started. "Oh! It's you!"

"Any better to-day?"

"No," said Mr. Merdle, "I am no better."

"A pity I didn't see you this morning. Pray come to me to-morrow, or let me come to you."

"Well!" he replied. "I will come to-morrow as I drive by."

Bar and Bishop had both been bystanders during this short dialogue, and as Mr. Merdle was swept away by the crowd, they made their remarks upon it to the Physician. Bar said there was a certain point of mental strain beyond which no man could go; that the point varied with various textures of brain and peculiarities of constitution, as he had had occasion to notice in several of his learned brothers; but, the point of endurance passed by a line's breadth, depression and dyspepsia ensued. Not to intrude on the sacred mysteries of medicine, he took it, now (with the Jury droop and persuasive eye-glass), that this was Merdle's case? Bishop said that when he was a young man, and had fallen for a brief space into the habit of writing sermons on Saturdays, a habit which all young sons of the church should sedulously avoid, he had frequently been sensible of a depression, arising as he supposed from an over-taxed intellect, upon which the yolk of a new-laid egg, beaten up by the good woman in whose house he at that time lodged, with a glass of sound sherry, nutmeg, and powdered sugar, acted like a charm. Without presuming to offer so simple a remedy to the consideration of so profound a professor of the great healing art, he would venture to inquire whether the strain being by way of intricate calculations, the spirits might not (humanly speaking) be restored to their tone by a gentle and yet generous stimulant?

From LITTLE DORRIT, by
Charles Dickens (1812–70).

75
THE DEPUTY SHEPHERD

HE was a prim-faced, red-nosed man, with a long, thin countenance, and a semi-rattlesnake sort of eye—rather sharp, but decidedly bad. He wore very short trousers, and black-cotton stockings, which, like the rest of his apparel, were particularly rusty. His looks were starched, but his white neckerchief was not, and its long limp ends straggled over his closely-buttoned waistcoat in a very uncouth and unpicturesque fashion. A pair of old, worn beaver gloves, a broad-brimmed hat, and a faded green umbrella, with plenty of whalebone sticking through the bottom, as if to counterbalance the want of a handle at the top, lay on a chair beside him, and, being disposed in a very tidy and careful manner, seemed to imply that the red-nosed man, whoever he was, had no intention of going away in a hurry.

* * * * *

The appearance of the red-nosed man had induced Sam, at first sight, to more than half suspect that he was the deputy shepherd of whom his estimable parent had spoken. The moment he saw him eat, all doubt on the subject was removed, and he perceived at once that if he purposed to take up his temporary quarters where he was, he must make his footing good without delay. He therefore commenced proceedings by putting his arm over the half-door of the bar, coolly unbolting it, and leisurely walking in.

"Mother-in-law," said Sam, "how are you?"

"Why, I do believe he is a Weller!" said Mrs. W., raising her eyes to Sam's face, with no very gratified expression of countenance.

"I rayther think he is," said the imperturbable Sam; "and I hope this here reverend gen'l'm'n 'll excuse me saying that I wish I was *the* Weller as owns you, mother-in-law."

This was a double-barrelled compliment. It implied that Mrs. Weller was a most agreeable female, and also that Mr. Stiggins had a clerical appearance. It made a visible impression at once; and Sam followed up his advantage by kissing his mother-in-law.

"Get along with you!" said Mrs. Weller, pushing him away.

"For shame, young man!" said the gentleman with the red nose.

"No offence, sir, no offence," replied Sam; "you're wery right, though; it ain't the right sort o' thing, wen mothers-in-law is young and good looking, is it, sir?"

"It's all vanity," said Mr. Stiggins.

"Ah, so it is," said Mrs. Weller, setting her cap to rights.

Sam thought it was, too, but he held his peace.

177

The deputy shepherd seemed by no means best pleased with Sam's arrival; and when the first effervescence of the compliment had subsided, even Mrs. Weller looked as if she could have spared him without the smallest inconvenience. However, there he was; and as he couldn't be decently turned out, they all three sat down to tea.

"And how's father?" said Sam.

At this inquiry, Mrs. Weller raised her hands, and turned up her eyes, as if the subject were too painful to be alluded to.

Mr. Stiggins groaned.

"What's the matter with that 'ere gen'l'm'n?" inquired Sam.

"He's shocked at the way your father goes on in," replied Mrs. Weller.

"Oh, he is, is he?" said Sam.

"And with too good reason," added Mrs. Weller, gravely.

Mr. Stiggins took up a fresh piece of toast, and groaned heavily.

"He is a dreadful reprobate," said Mrs. Weller.

"A man of wrath!" exclaimed Mr. Stiggins. He took a large semi-circular bite out of the toast, and groaned again.

Sam felt very strongly disposed to give the reverend Mr. Stiggins something to groan for, but he repressed his inclination, and merely asked, "What's the old 'un up to, now?"

"Up to, indeed!" said Mrs. Weller. "Oh, he has a hard heart. Night after night does this excellent man—don't frown, Mr. Stiggins: I *will* say you *are* an excellent man—come and sit here, for hours together, and it has not the least effect upon him."

"Well, that is odd," said Sam; "it 'ud have a wery considerable effect upon me, if I wos in his place; I know that."

"The fact is, my young friend," said Mr. Stiggins solemnly, "he has an obderrate bosom. Oh, my young friend, who else could have resisted the pleading of sixteen of our fairest sisters, and withstood their exhortations to subscribe to our noble society for providing the infant negroes in the West Indies with flannel waist-coats and moral pocket-handkerchiefs?"

"What's a moral pocket ankercher?" said Sam: "I never see one o' them articles o' furniter."

"Those which combine amusement with instruction, my young

178

friend," replied Mr. Stiggins: "blending select tales with wood-cuts."

"Oh, I know," said Sam; "them as hangs up in the linen-drapers' shops, with beggars' petitions and all there 'ere upon 'em?"

Mr. Stiggins began a third round of toast, and nodded assent.

"And he wouldn't be persuaded by the ladies, wouldn't he?" said Sam.

"Sat and smoked his pipe, and said the infant negroes were—what did he say the infant negroes were?" said Mrs. Weller.

"Little humbugs," replied Mr. Stiggins, deeply affected.

"Said the infant negroes were little humbugs," repeated Mrs. Weller. And they both groaned at the atrocious conduct of the old gentleman.

A great many more iniquities of a similar nature might have been disclosed, only the toast being all eaten, the tea having got very weak, and Sam holding out no indications of meaning to go, Mr. Stiggins suddenly recollected that he had a most pressing appointment with the shepherd, and took himself off accordingly.

From PICKWICK PAPERS, by
Charles Dickens (1812–70)

76

RESPECT FOR THE DEAN

WHOSOEVER has observed that sedate and clerical bird, the rook, may perhaps have noticed that when he wings his way homeward towards nightfall, in a sedate and clerical company, two rooks will suddenly detach themselves from the rest, will retrace their flight for some distance, and will there poise and linger; conveying to mere men the fancy that it is of some occult importance to the body politic, that this artful couple should pretend to have renounced connection with it.

Similarly, service being over in the old cathedral with the square tower, and the choir scuffling out again, and divers venerable persons of rook-like aspect dispersing, two of these latter retrace their steps, and walk together in the echoing Close.

Not only is the day waning, but the year. The low sun is fiery and yet cold behind the monastery ruin, and the Virginia creeper on the cathedral wall has showered half its deep-red leaves down on the pavement. There has been rain this afternoon, and a wintry shudder goes among the little pools on the cracked uneven flagstones, and through the giant elm-trees as they shed a gust of tears. Their fallen leaves lie strewn thickly about. Some of these leaves, in a timid rush, seek sanctuary within the low arched cathedral door; but two men coming out resist them, and cast them forth again with their feet; this done, one of the two locks the door with a goodly key, and the other flits away with a folio music-book.

"Mr. Jasper was that, Tope?"

"Yes, Mr. Dean."

"He has stayed late."

"Yes, Mr. Dean. I have stayed for him, your Reverence. He has been took a little poorly."

"Say 'taken,' Tope—to the Dean," the younger rook interposes in a low tone with this touch of correction, as who should say: "You may offer bad grammar to the laity, or the humbler clergy, not to the Dean."

Mr. Tope, Chief Verger and Showman, and accustomed to be high with excursion parties, declines with a silent loftiness to perceive that any suggestion has been tendered to him.—

"And when and how has Mr. Jasper been taken—for, as Mr. Crisparkle has remarked, it is better to say taken—taken—" repeats the Dean; "when and how has Mr. Jasper been Taken——"

"Taken, sir," Tope deferentially murmurs.

"—Poorly, Tope?"

"Why, sir, Mr. Jasper was that breathed——"

"I wouldn't say 'That breathed,' Tope," Mr. Crisparkle interposes with the same touch as before. "Not English—to the Dean."

"Breathed to that extent," the Dean (not unflattered by this indirect homage) condescendingly remarks, "would be preferable."

"Mr. Jasper's breathing was so remarkably short"—thus dis-

creetly does Mr. Tope work his way round the sunken rock—
"when he came in, that it distressed him mightily to get his notes
out: which was perhaps the cause of his having a kind of fit on
him after a little. His memory grew DAZED." Mr. Tope, with his
eyes on the Reverend Mr. Crisparkle, shoots this word out, as
defying him to improve upon it: "and a dimness and giddiness
crept over him as strange as ever I saw: though he didn't seem
to mind it particularly, himself. However, a little time and a little
water brought him out of his DAZE." Mr. Tope repeats the word
and its emphasis, with the air of saying: "As I *have* made a success,
I'll make it again."

"And Mr. Jasper has gone home quite himself, has he?" asked
the Dean.

"Your Reverence, he has gone home quite himself. And I'm
glad to see he's having his fire kindled up, for it's chilly after the
wet, and the Cathedral had both a damp feel and a damp touch
this afternoon, and he was very shivery."

They all three look towards an old stone gatehouse crossing the
Close, with an arched thoroughfare passing beneath it. Through
its latticed window, a fire shines out upon the fast-darkening scene,
involving in shadow the pendent masses of ivy and creeper covering
the building's front. As the deep Cathedral-bell strikes the hour,
a ripple of wind goes through these at their distance, like a ripple
of the solemn sound that hums through tomb and tower, broken
niche and defaced statue, in the pile close at hand.

"Is Mr. Jasper's nephew with him?" the Dean asks.

"No, sir," replied the Verger, "but expected. There's his own
solitary shadow betwixt his two windows—the one looking this
way, and the one looking down into the High Street—drawing his
own curtains now."

"Well, well," says the Dean, with a sprightly air of breaking up
the little conference, "I hope Mr. Jasper's heart may not be too
much set upon his nephew. Our affections, however laudable, in
this transitory world, should never master us; we should guide
them, guide them. I find I am not disagreeably reminded of my
dinner, by hearing my dinner-bell. Perhaps Mr. Crisparkle you
will, before going home, look in on Jasper?"

"Certainly, Mr. Dean. And tell him that you had the kindness to desire to know how he was?"

"Ay; do so, do so. Certainly. Wished to know how he was. By all means. Wished to know how he was."

With a pleasant air of patronage, the Dean as nearly cocks his quaint hat as a Dean in good spirits may, and directs his comely gaiters towards the ruddy dining-room of the snug old red-brick house where he is at present, "in residence" with Mrs. Dean and Miss Dean.

Mr. Crisparkle, Minor Canon, fair and rosy, and perpetually pitching himself head-foremost into all the deep running water in the surrounding country; Mr. Crisparkle, Minor Canon, early riser, musical, classical, cheerful, kind, good-natured, social, contented, and boy-like; Mr. Crisparkle, Minor Canon and good man, lately "Coach" upon the chief Pagan high roads, but since promoted by a patron (grateful for a well-taught son) to his present Christian beat; betakes himself to the gatehouse, on his way home to his early tea.

From THE MYSTERY OF EDWIN DROOD,
by Charles Dickens (1812–70).

77

MR. CHADBAND IS MORTIFIED

MR. CHADBAND is a large yellow man, with a fat smile, and a general appearance of having a good deal of train oil in his system. Mrs. Chadband is a stern, severe-looking, silent woman. Mr. Chadband moves softly and cumbrously, not unlike a bear who has been taught to walk upright. He is very much embarrassed about the arms, as if they were inconvenient to him, and he wanted to grovel; is very much in a perspiration about the head; and never speaks without first putting up his great hand, as delivering a token to his hearers that he is going to edify them.

"My friends," says Mr. Chadband, "Peace be on this house!

On the master thereof, on the mistress thereof, on the young maidens, and on the young men! My friends, why do I wish for peace? What is peace? Is it war? No. Is it strife? No. Is it lovely, and gentle, and beautiful, and pleasant, and serene, and joyful? O yes! Therefore, my friends, I wish for peace, upon you and upon yours."

In consequence of Mrs. Snagsby looking deeply edified, Mr. Snagsby thinks it expedient on the whole to say Amen, which is well received.

"Now, my friends," proceeds Mr. Chadband, "since I am upon this theme——"

Guster presents herself. Mrs. Snagsby, in a spectral bass voice, and without removing her eyes from Chadband, says, with dread distinctness, "Go away!"

"Now, my friends," says Chadband, "since I am upon this theme, and in my lowly path improving it——"

Guster is heard unaccountably to murmur "one thousing seven hundred and eighty-two." The spectral voice repeats more solemnly, "Go away!"

"Now, my friends," says Mr. Chadband, "we will inquire in a spirit of love——"

Still Guster reiterates "one thousing seven hundred and eighty-two."

Mr. Chadband, pausing with the resignation of a man accustomed to be persecuted, and languidly folding up his chin into his fat smile, says, "Let us hear the maiden! Speak, maiden!"

"One thousing seven hundred and eighty-two, if you please, sir. Which he wish to know what the shilling ware for," says Guster, breathless.

"For?" returns Mrs. Chadband. "For his fare!"

Guster replies that "he insistes on one and eightpence, or on summonsizzing the party." Mrs. Snagsby and Mrs. Chadband are proceeding to grow shrill in indignation, when Mr. Chadband quiets the tumult by lifting up his hand.

"My friends," says he, "I remember a duty unfulfilled yesterday. It is right that I should be chastened in some penalty. I ought not to murmur. Rachael, pay the eightpence!"

While Mrs. Snagsby, drawing her breath, looks hard at Mr. Snagsby, as who should say, "You hear this Apostle!" and while Mr. Chadband glows with humility and train oil, Mrs. Chadband pays the money. It is Mr. Chadband's habit—it is the head and front of his pretensions indeed—to keep this sort of debtor and creditor account in the smallest items, and to post it publicly on the most trivial occasions.

"My friends," says Chadband, "eightpence is not much; it might justly have been one and fourpence; it might justly have been half-a-crown. O let us be joyful, joyful! O let us be joyful!"

With which remark, which appears from its sound to be an extract in verse, Mr. Chadband stalks to the table, and, before taking a chair, lifts up his admonitory hand.

"My friends," says he, "what is this which we now behold as being spread before us? Refreshment. Do we need refreshment then, my friends? We do. And why do we need refreshment, my friends? Because we are but mortal, because we are but sinful, because we are but of the earth, because we are not of the air. Can we fly, my friends? We cannot. Why can we not fly, my friends?"

Mr. Snagsby, presuming on the success of his last point, ventures to observe in a cheerful and rather knowing tone, "No wings." But is immediately frowned down by Mrs. Snagsby.

"I say, my friends," pursues Mr. Chadband, utterly rejecting and obliterating Mr. Snagsby's suggestion, "why can we not fly? Is it because we are calculated to walk? It is. Could we walk, my friends, without strength? We could not. What should we do without strength, my friends? Our legs would refuse to bear us, our knees would double up, our ankles would turn over, and we should come to the ground. Then from whence, my friends, in a human point of view, do we derive the strength that is necessary to our limbs? Is it," says Chadband, glancing over the table, "from bread in various forms, from butter which is churned from the milk which is yielded untoe us by the cow, from the eggs which are laid by the fowl, from ham, from tongue, from sausage, and from such like? It is. Then let us partake of the good things which are set before us!"

The persecutors denied that there was any particular gift in

Mr. Chadband's piling verbose flights of stairs, one upon another, after this fashion. But this can only be received as a proof of their determination to persecute, since it must be within everybody's experience, that the Chadband style of oratory is widely received and much admired.

Mr. Chadband, however, having concluded for the present, sits down at Mr. Snagsby's table, and lays about him prodigiously. The conversion of nutriment of any sort into oil of the quality already mentioned, appears to be a process so inseparable from the constitution of this exemplary vessel, that in beginning to eat and drink, he may be described as always becoming a kind of considerable Oil Mills, or other large factory for the production of that article on a wholesale scale. On the present evening of the long vacation, in Cook's Court, Cursitor Street, he does such a powerful stroke of business, that the warehouse appears to be quite full when the works cease.

From BLEAK HOUSE, by
Charles Dickens (1812–70).

78

THE BISHOP'S CHAPLAIN

When Dr. Proudie, newly created Bishop of Barchester set out for his new diocese, he took with him as chaplain the Rev. Obadiah Slope.

MR. SLOPE had been a sizar at Cambridge, and had there conducted himself at any rate successfully, for in due process of time he was an M.A., having university pupils under his care. From thence he was transferred to London, and became preacher at a new district church built on the confines of Baker Street. He was in this position when congenial ideas on religious subjects recommended him to Mrs. Proudie, and the intercourse had become close and confidential.

Having been thus familiarly thrown among the Misses Proudie, it was no more than natural that some softer feeling than friendship should be engendered. There have been some passages of love between him and the eldest hope, Olivia; but they have hitherto resulted in no favourable arrangement. In truth, Mr. Slope having made a declaration of affection, afterwards withdrew it on finding that the doctor had no immediate worldly funds with which to endow his child; and it may easily be conceived that Miss Proudie, after such an announcement on his part, was not readily disposed to receive any further show of affection. On the appointment of Dr. Proudie to the bishopric of Barchester, Mr. Slope's views were in truth somewhat altered. Bishops, even though they be poor, can provide for clerical children, and Mr. Slope began to regret that he had not been more disinterested. He no sooner heard the tidings of the doctor's elevation, than he recommenced his siege, not violently, indeed, but respectfully, and at a distance. Olivia Proudie, however, was a girl of spirit: she had the blood of two peers in her veins, and, better still, she had another lover on her books; so Mr. Slope sighed in vain; and the pair soon found it convenient to establish a mutual bond of inveterate hatred.

It may be thought singular that Mrs. Proudie's friendship for the young clergyman should remain firm after such an affair; but to tell the truth, she had known nothing of it. Though very fond of Mr. Slope herself, she had never conceived the idea that any of her daughters would become so, and remembering their high birth and social advantages, expected for them matches of a different sort. Neither the gentleman nor the lady found it necessary to enlighten her. Olivia's two sisters had each known of the affair, so had all the servants, so had all the people living in the adjoining houses on either side; but Mrs. Proudie had been kept in the dark.

Mr. Slope soon comforted himself with the reflection, that as he had been selected as chaplain to the bishop, it would probably be in his power to get the good things in the bishop's gift, without troubling himself with the bishop's daughter; and he found himself able to endure the pangs of rejected love. As he sat himself down in the railway carriage, confronting the bishop and Mrs. Proudie, as they started on their first journey to Barchester, he began to form in his own mind a plan of his future life. He knew well his patron's strong points, but he knew the weak ones as well. He understood correctly enough to what attempts the new bishop's high spirit would soar, and he rightly guessed that public life would better suit the great man's taste, than the small details of diocesan duty.

He, therefore, he, Mr. Slope, would in effect be Bishop of Barchester. Such was his resolve; and to give Mr. Slope his due, he had both courage and spirit to bear him out in his resolution. He knew that he should have a hard battle to fight, for the power and patronage of the see would be equally coveted by another great mind—Mrs. Proudie would also choose to be Bishop of Barchester. Mr. Slope, however, flattered himself that he could outmanœuvre the lady. She must live much in London, while he would always be on the spot. She would necessarily remain ignorant of much, while he would know everything belonging to the diocese. At first, doubtless, he must flatter and cajole, perhaps yield, in some things; but he did not doubt of ultimate triumph. If all other means failed, he could join the bishop against his wife, inspire courage into the unhappy man, lay an axe to the root of the woman's power, and emancipate the husband.

Such were his thoughts as he sat looking at the sleeping pair in the railway carriage, and Mr. Slope is not the man to trouble himself with such thoughts for nothing. He is possessed of more than average abilities, and is of good courage. Though he can stoop to fawn, and stoop low indeed, if need be, he has still within him the power to assume the tyrant; and with the power he has certainly the wish. His acquirements are not of the highest order, but such as they are they are completely under control, and he knows the use of them. He is gifted with a certain kind of pulpit eloquence, not likely indeed to be persuasive with men, but powerful with the softer sex. In his sermons he deals greatly in denunciations, excites the minds of his weaker hearers with a not unpleasant terror, and leaves an impression on their minds that all mankind are in a perilous state, and all womankind too, except those who attend regularly to the evening lectures in Baker Street. His looks and tones are extremely severe, so much so that one cannot but fancy that he regards the greater part of the world as being infinitely too bad for his care. As he walks through the streets, his very face denotes his horror of the world's wickedness; and there is always an anathema lurking in the corner of his eye.

In doctrine, he, like his patron, is tolerant of dissent, if so strict a mind can be called tolerant of anything. With Wesleyan-Methodists he has something in common, but his soul trembles in agony at the iniquities of the Puseyites. His aversion is carried to things outward as well as inward. His gall rises at a new church with a high-pitched roof; a full-breasted black silk waistcoat is with him a symbol of Satan; and a profane jest-book would not, in his view, more foully desecrate the church seat of a Christian, than a book of prayer printed with red letters, and ornamented with a cross on the back. Most active clergymen have their hobby, and Sunday observances are his. Sunday, however, is a word which never pollutes his mouth—it is always "the Sabbath." The "desecration of the Sabbath," as he delights to call it, is to him meat and drink—he thrives upon that as policemen do on the general evil habits of the community. It is the loved subject of all his evening discourses, the source of all his eloquence, the secret of all his power over the female heart. To him the revelation of God appears only in that one law given for Jewish observance. To him the mercies of our Saviour speak in vain, to him in vain has been preached that sermon which fell from divine lips on the mountain—"Blessed are the meek, for they shall inherit the earth"—"Blessed are the merciful, for they shall obtain mercy." To him the New Testament is comparatively of little moment, for from it can he draw no fresh authority for that dominion which he loves to exercise over at least a seventh part of man's allotted time here below.

Mr. Slope is tall, and not ill made. His feet and hands are large, as has ever been the case with all his family, but he has a broad chest and wide shoulders to carry off these excrescences, and on the whole his figure is good. His countenance, however, is not specially prepossessing. His hair is lank, and of a dull pale reddish hue. It is always formed into three straight lumpy masses, each brushed with admirable precision, and cemented with much grease; two of them adhere closely to the sides of his face, and the other lies at right angles above them. He wears no whiskers, and is always punctiliously shaven. His face is nearly of the same colour as his hair, though perhaps a little redder: it is not unlike beef—beef, however, one would say, of a bad quality. His forehead is capacious and high, but square and heavy, and unpleasantly shining. His mouth is large, though his lips are thin and bloodless; and his big, prominent, pale brown eyes inspire anything but confidence. His nose, however, is his redeeming feature: it is pronounced, straight and well-formed; though I myself should have liked it better did it not possess a somewhat spongy, porous appearance, as though it had been cleverly formed out of a red coloured cork.

I never could endure to shake hands with Mr. Slope. A cold, clammy perspiration always exudes from him, the small drops are ever to be seen standing on his brow, and his friendly grasp is unpleasant.

Such is Mr. Slope—such is the man who has suddenly fallen into the midst of Barchester Close, and is destined there to assume the station which has heretofore been filled by the son of the late bishop. Think, oh, my meditative reader, what an associate we have here for those comfortable prebendaries, those gentlemanlike clerical doctors, those happy, well-used, well-fed minor canons, who have grown into existence at Barchester under the kindly wings of Bishop Grantly!

From BARCHESTER TOWERS, by
Anthony Trollope (1815–82).

79

MR. HARDING MAKES UP HIS MIND

The Wardenship of Hiram's Hospital had long been a pleasant clerical sinecure until a radical newspaper ferreted out the terms of the original bequest. To his infinite distress, the Rev. Septimus Harding, the retiring and kindly Warden, finds himself threatened with a lawsuit for misappropriating public funds. The lawsuit is dropped, but Mr. Harding is not easy about his position. A visit to Sir Abraham Haphazard, his counsel, does nothing to reassure him, and he prepares for once to defy his son-in-law, the forceful Archdeacon Grantly.

"AND you have absolutely been with the attorney-general?" asked the archdeacon.

Mr. Harding signified that he had.

"Good heavens, how unfortunate!" And the archdeacon raised his huge hands in the manner in which his friends are so accustomed to see him express disapprobation and astonishment. "What will Sir Abraham think of it? Did you not know that it is not customary for clients to go direct to their counsel?"

"Isn't it?" asked the warden, innocently. "Well, at any rate, I've done it. Sir Abraham didn't seem to think it so very strange."

The archdeacon gave a sigh that would have moved a man-of-war.

"But, papa, what did you say to Sir Abraham?" asked the lady.

"I asked him, my dear, to explain John Hiram's will to me. He couldn't explain it in the only way which would have satisfied me, and so I resigned the wardenship."

"Resigned it!" said the archdeacon, in a solemn voice, sad and low, but yet sufficiently audible;—a sort of whisper that Macready would have envied, and the galleries have applauded with a couple of rounds. "Resigned it! Good heavens!" And the dignitary of the church sank back horrified into a horse-hair armchair.

"At least I told Sir Abraham that I would resign; and of course I must now do so."

"Not at all," said the archdeacon, catching a ray of hope. "Nothing that you say in such a way to your own counsel can be in any way binding on you. Of course you were there to ask his advice. I'm sure, Sir Abraham did not advise any such step."

Mr. Harding could not say that he had.

"I am sure he disadvised you from it," continued the reverend cross-examiner.

Mr. Harding could not deny this.

"I'm sure Sir Abraham must have advised you to consult your friends."

To this proposition also Mr. Harding was obliged to assent.

"Then your threat of resignation amounts to nothing, and we are just where we were before."

Mr. Harding was now standing on the rug, moving uneasily from one foot to the other. He made no distinct answer to the archdeacon's last proposition, for his mind was chiefly engaged on thinking how he could escape to bed. That his resignation was a thing finally fixed on, a fact all but completed, was not in his mind a matter of any doubt. He knew his own weakness; he knew how prone he was to be led; but he was not weak enough to give way now, to go back from the position to which his conscience had driven him, after having purposely come to London to declare his determination. He did not in the least doubt his resolution, but he greatly doubted his power of defending it against his son-in-law.

"You must be very tired, Susan," said he: "wouldn't you like to go to bed?"

But Susan didn't want to go till her husband went. She had an idea that her papa might be bullied if she were away. She wasn't tired at all, or at least she said so.

The archdeacon was pacing the room, expressing, by certain noddles of his head, his opinion of the utter fatuity of his father-in-law.

"Why," at last he said,—and angels might have blushed at the rebuke expressed in his tone and emphasis,—"Why did you go off from Barchester so suddenly? Why did you take such a step without giving us notice, after what had passed at the palace?"

The warden hung his head, and made no reply. He could not condescend to say that he had not intended to give his son-in-law the slip; and as he had not the courage to avow it, he said nothing.

"Papa has been too much for you," said the lady.

The archdeacon took another turn, and again ejaculated, "Good heavens!" this time in a very low whisper, but still audible.

"I think I'll go to bed," said the warden, taking up a side candle.

"At any rate, you'll promise me to take no further step without consultation," said the archdeacon. Mr. Harding made no answer, but slowly proceeded to light his candle. "Of course," continued the other, "such a declaration as that you made to Sir Abraham means nothing. Come, warden, promise me this. The whole affair, you see, is already settled, and that with very little trouble or expense. Bold has been compelled to abandon his action, and all you have to do is to remain quiet at the hospital." Mr. Harding still made no reply, but looked meekly into his son-in-law's face. The archdeacon thought he knew his father-in-law, but he was mistaken; he thought that he had already talked over a vacillating man to resign his promise. "Come," said he, "promise Susan to give up this idea of resigning the wardenship."

The warden looked at his daughter, thinking probably at the moment that if Eleanor were contented with him, he need not so much regard his other child, and said, "I am sure Susan will not ask me to break my word, or to do what I know to be wrong."

"Papa," said she, "it would be madness in you to throw up your preferment. What are you to live on?"

"God, that feeds the young ravens, will take care of me also," said Mr. Harding, with a smile, as though afraid of giving offence by making his reference to scripture too solemn.

"Pish!" said the archdeacon, turning away rapidly. "If the ravens persisted in refusing the food prepared for them, they wouldn't be fed." A clergyman generally dislikes to be met in argument by any scriptural quotation; he feels as affronted as a doctor does, when recommended by an old woman to take some favourite dose, or as a lawyer when an unprofessional man attempts to put him down by a quibble.

"I shall have the living of Crabtree," modestly suggested the warden.

"Eighty pounds a year!" sneered the archdeacon.

"And the precentorship," said the father-in-law.

"It goes with the wardenship," said the son-in-law. Mr. Harding was prepared to argue this point, and began to do so, but Dr. Grantly stopped him. "My dear warden," said he, "this is all nonsense. Eighty pounds or a hundred and sixty makes very little difference. You can't live on it,—you can't ruin Eleanor's prospects for ever. In point of fact, you can't resign. The bishop wouldn't accept it. The whole thing is settled. What I now want to do is to prevent any inconvenient tittle-tattle,—any more newspaper articles."

"That's what I want, too," said the warden.

"And to prevent that," continued the other, "we mustn't let any talk of resignation get abroad."

"But I shall resign," said the warden, very, very meekly.

"Good heavens! Susan, my dear, what can I say to him?"

"But, papa," said Mrs. Grantly, getting up, and putting her

arm through that of her father, "what is Eleanor to do if you throw away your income?"

A hot tear stood in each of the warden's eyes as he looked round upon his married daughter. Why should one sister who was so rich predict poverty for another? Some such idea as this was on his mind, but he gave no utterance to it. Then he thought of the pelican feeding its young with blood from its own breast, but he gave no utterance to that either;—and then of Eleanor waiting for him at home, waiting to congratulate him on the end of all his trouble.

"Think of Eleanor, papa," said Mrs. Grantly.

"I do think of her," said her father.

"And you will not do this rash thing?" The lady was really moved beyond her usual calm composure.

"It can never be rash to do right," said he. "I shall certainly resign this wardenship."

"Then, Mr. Harding, there is nothing before you but ruin," said the archdeacon, now moved beyond all endurance. "Ruin both for you and Eleanor. How do you mean to pay the monstrous expenses of this action?"

Mrs. Grantly suggested that, as the action was abandoned, the costs would not be heavy.

"Indeed they will, my dear," continued he. "One cannot have the attorney-general up at twelve o'clock at night for nothing. But of course your father has not thought of this."

"I will sell my furniture," said the warden.

"Furniture!" ejaculated the other, with a most powerful sneer.

"Come, archdeacon," said the lady, "we needn't mind that at present. You know you never expected papa to pay the costs."

"Such absurdity is enough to provoke Job," said the archdeacon, marching quickly up and down the room. "Your father is like a child. Eight hundred pounds a year!—Eight hundred and eighty with the house;—with nothing to do. The very place for him. And to throw that up because some scoundrel writes an article in a newspaper! Well;—I have done my duty. If he chooses to ruin his child I cannot help it." And he stood at the fire-place, and looked at himself in a dingy mirror which stood on the chimney-piece.

There was a pause for about a minute, and then the warden, finding that nothing else was coming, lighted his candle, and quietly said, "Good night."

"Good night, papa," said the lady.

And so the warden retired; but, as he closed the door behind him, he heard the well-known ejaculation,—slower, lower, more solemn, more ponderous than ever;—"Good heavens!"

From THE WARDEN, by Anthony Trollope (1815–82).

80

IT IS REALLY TOO MUCH

THERE is, perhaps, no greater hardship at present inflicted on mankind in civilised and free countries, than the necessity of listening to sermons. No one but a preaching clergyman has, in these realms, the power of compelling an audience to sit silent, and be tormented. No one but a preaching clergyman can revel in platitudes, truisms, and untruisms, and yet receive, as his undisputed privilege, the same respectful demeanour as though words of impassioned eloquence, or persuasive logic, fell from his lips. Let a professor of law or physic find his place in a lecture-room, and there pour forth jejune words and useless empty phrases, and he will pour them forth to empty benches. Let a barrister attempt to talk without talking well, and he will talk but seldom. A judge's charge need be listened to perforce by none but the jury, prisoner, and gaoler. A Member of Parliament can be coughed down or counted out. Town-councillors can be tabooed. But no one can rid himself of the preaching clergyman. He is the bore of the age, the old man who we Sinbads cannot shake off, the nightmare that disturbs our Sunday's rest, the incubus that over-loads our religion and makes God's service distasteful. We are not forced into church! No: but we desire more than that. We desire not to be forced to stay away. We desire, nay, we are resolute, to enjoy the comfort of public worship; but we desire also that we may do so without an amount of tedium which ordinary human nature cannot endure with patience; that we may be able to leave the house of God, without that anxious longing for escape, which is the common consequence of common sermons.

With what complacency will a young parson deduce false conclusions from misunderstood texts, and then threaten us with all the penalties of Hades if we neglect to comply with the injunctions he has given us! Yes, my too self-confident juvenile friend, I do believe in those mysteries which are so common in your mouth; I do believe in the unadulterated word which you hold there in your hand; but you must pardon me if, in some things, I doubt your interpretation. The Bible is good, the Prayer-book is good, nay, you yourself would be acceptable, if you would read to me some portion of those time-honoured discourses which our great divines have elaborated in the full maturity of their powers. But you must excuse me, my insufficient young lecturer, if I yawn over your imperfect sentences, your repeated phrases, your false pathos, your drawlings and denouncings, your humming and hawing, your ohing and ahing, your black gloves and your white handkerchief. To me, it all means nothing; and hours are too precious to be so wasted—if one could only avoid it.

And here I must make a protest against the pretence, so often put forward by the working clergy, that they are overburdened by the multitude of sermons to be preached. We are all too fond of our own voices, and a preacher is encouraged in the vanity of making his heard by the privilege of a compelled audience. His sermon is the pleasant morsel of his life, his delicious moment of self-exaltation. "I have preached nine sermons this week," said a young friend to me the other day, with hand languidly raised to his brow, the picture of an overburdened martyr. "Nine this week, seven last week, four the week before. I have preached twenty-three sermons this month. It is really too much." "Too much, indeed," said I, shuddering; "too much for the strength of any one." "Yes," he answered meekly, "indeed it is; I am beginning to feel it painfully." "Would," said I, "you could feel it—would that you could be made to feel it." But he never guessed that my heart was wrung for the poor listeners.

From BARCHESTER TOWERS, by
Anthony Trollope (1815–82).

81

THE BATTLE OF ROYD LANE

The annual tea and sports of the united Sunday schools of the parishes of Whinbury, Nunnely and Briarfield was held on Whit-Monday, and on one notable occasion afforded Establishment the opportunity for a signal victory over Dissent.

AND now, solemn and sombre as to their colour, though bland enough as to their faces, appeared at the dining-room door the three Rectors; they had hitherto been busy in the church, and were now coming to take some little refreshment for the body, ere the march commenced. The large morocco-covered easy-chair had been left vacant for Dr. Boultby; he was put into it, and Caroline, obeying the instigations of Shirley, who had told her now was the time to play the hostess, hastened to hand to her uncle's vast, revered, and, on the whole, worthy friend a glass of wine and a plate of macaroons. Boultby's churchwardens, patrons of the Sunday-school both, as he insisted on their being, were already beside him; Mrs. Sykes and the other ladies of his congregation were on his right hand and on his left, expressing their hopes that he was not fatigued, their fears that the day would be too warm for him. Mrs. Boultby, who held an opinion that when her lord dropped asleep after a good dinner his face became as the face of an angel, was bending over him, tenderly wiping some perspiration, real or imaginary, from his brow. Boultby, in short, was in his glory, and in a round sound "voix de poitrine," he rumbled out thanks for attentions and assurances of his tolerable health. Of Caroline he took no manner of notice as she came near, save to accept what she offered; he did not see her—he never did see her; he hardly knew that such a person existed. He saw the macaroons, however, and, being fond of sweets, possessed himself of a small handful thereof. The wine Mrs. Boultby insisted on mingling with hot water, and qualifying with sugar and nutmeg.

Mr. Hall stood near an open window, breathing the fresh air and scent of flowers, and talking like a brother to Miss Ainley. To him Caroline turned her attention with pleasure. "What should she bring him? He must not help himself—he must be served by her"; and she provided herself with a little salver, that she might offer him variety. Margaret Hall joined them; so did Miss Keeldar. The four ladies stood round their favourite pastor; they also had an idea that they looked on the face of an earthly angel. Cyril Hall was their pope, infallible to them as Dr. Thomas Boultby to his admirers. A throng, too, enclosed the Rector of Briarfield; twenty or more pressed round him, and no parson was ever more potent in a circle than old Helstone. The curates, herding together after their manner, made a constellation of three lesser planets; divers young ladies watched them afar off, but ventured not nigh.

Mr. Helstone produced his watch. "Ten minutes to two," he announced aloud. "Time for all to fall into line. Come." He seized his shovel-hat and marched away; all rose and followed *en masse*.

The twelve hundred children were drawn up in three bodies of four hundred souls each; in the rear of each regiment was stationed a band; between every twenty there was an interval wherein Helstone posted the teachers in pairs; to the van of the armies he summoned:

"Grace Boultby and Mary Sykes lead out Whinbury.

"Margaret Hall and Mary Ann Ainley conduct Nunnely.

"Caroline Helstone and Shirley Keeldar head Briarfield."

Then again he gave command:

"Mr. Donne to Whinbury; Mr. Sweeting to Nunnely; Mr. Malone to Briarfield."

And these gentlemen stepped up before the lady-generals.

The Rectors passed to the full front, the parish clerks fell to the extreme rear; Helstone lifted his shovel-hat; in an instant out clashed the eight bells in the tower, loud swelled the sounding bands, flute spoke and clarion answered, deep rolled the drums, and away they marched.

The broad white road unrolled before the long procession, the sun and sky surveyed it cloudless, the wind tossed the tree-boughs above it, and the twelve hundred children, and one hundred and forty adults, of which it was composed, trod on in time and tune, with gay faces and glad hearts. It was a joyous scene, and a scene to do good; it was a day of happiness for rich and poor: the work, first of God, and then of the clergy. Let England's priests have their due; they are a faulty set in some respects, being only of common flesh and blood, like us all, but the land would be badly off without them: Britain would miss her Church if that Church fell. God save it! God also reform it!

·   ·   ·   ·

Mr. Helstone spoke.

"We shall pass through Royd Lane, to reach Nunnely Common by a short cut," said he.

And into the straits of Royd Lane they accordingly defiled. It was very narrow—so narrow that only two could walk abreast without falling into the ditch which ran along each side. They had gained the middle of it, when excitement became obvious in the clerical commanders; Boultby's spectacles and Helstone's Rehoboam were agitated; the curates nudged each other; Mr. Hall turned to the ladies and smiled.

"What is the matter?" was the demand.

He pointed with his staff to the end of the lane before them. Lo and behold! another, an opposition procession was there entering, headed also by men in black, and followed also, as they could now hear, by music.

"Is it our double?" asked Shirley—"our manifold wraith? Here is a card turned up!"

"If you wanted a battle, you are likely to get one—at least, of looks," whispered Caroline, laughing.

"They shall not pass us!" unanimously cried the curates. "We'll not give way."

"Give way!" retorted Helstone sternly, turning round. "Who

talks of giving way? You boys mind what you are about; the ladies, I know, will be firm—I can trust them. There is not a Church-woman here but will stand her ground against these folks for the honour of the Establishment. What does Miss Keeldar say?"

"She asks 'What is it?' "

"The Dissenting and Methodist schools, the Baptists, Independents and Wesleyans, joined in unholy alliance, and turning purposely into this lane with the intention of obstructing our march and driving us back."

"Bad manners!" said Shirley; "and I hate bad manners. Of course, they must have a lesson."

"A lesson in politeness," suggested Mr. Hall, who was ever for peace; "not an example of rudeness."

Old Helstone moved on. Quickening his step, he marched some yards in advance of his company. He had nearly reached the other sable leaders when he who appeared to act as the hostile commander-in-chief—a large, greasy man, with black hair combed flat on his forehead—called a halt. The procession paused; he drew forth a hymn-book, gave out a verse, set a tune, and they all struck up the most dolorous of canticles.

Helstone signed to his bands: they clashed out with all the power of brass. He desired them to play "Rule Britannia!" and ordered the children to join in vocally, which they did with enthusiastic spirit. The enemy was sung and stormed down, his psalm quelled; as far as noise went, he was conquered.

"Now, follow me!" exclaimed Helstone—"not at a run, but at a firm, smart pace. Be steady, every child and woman of you. Keep together—hold on by each other's skirts, if necessary."

And he strode on with such a determined and deliberate gait, and was, besides, so well seconded by his scholars and teachers—who did exactly as he told them, neither running nor faltering, but marching with cool, solid impetus; the curates, too, being compelled to do the same, as they were between two fires, Helstone and Miss Keeldar, both of whom watched any deviation with lynx-eyed vigilance, and were ready, the one with his cane, the other with her parasol, to rebuke the slightest breach of orders, the least independent or irregular demonstration—that the body of Dissenters were first amazed, then alarmed, then borne down and pressed back, and at last forced to turn tail and leave the outlet from Royd Lane free. Boultby suffered in the onslaught, but Helstone and Malone between them held him up, and brought him through the business, whole in limb, though sorely tried in wind.

The fat Dissenter who had given out the hymn was left sitting in the ditch. He was a spirit merchant by trade, a leader of the Nonconformists, and, it was said, drank more water in that one afternoon than he had swallowed for a twelvemonth before.

From SHIRLEY, by Charlotte Brontë (1816–55).

82

A TALLOW DIP

LOOK at him as he winds through the little churchyard! The silver light that falls aslant on church and tomb, enables you to see his slim black figure, made all the slimmer by tight pantaloons, as it flits past the pale gravestones. He walks with a quick step, and is now rapping with sharp decision at the vicarage door. It is opened without delay by the nurse, cook, and housemaid, all at once—that is to say, by the robust maid-of-all-work, Nanny; and as Mr. Barton hangs up his hat in the passage, you see that a narrow face of no particular complexion—even the small pox that has attacked it seems to have been of a mongrel, indefinite kind—with features of no particular shape, and an eye of no particular expression, is surmounted by a slope of baldness gently rising from brow to crown. You judge him, rightly, to be about forty.

.   .   .   .   .

At eleven o'clock, Mr. Barton walked forth in cape and boa, with the sleet driving in his face, to read prayers at the workhouse, euphuistically called the "College." The College was a huge square stone building, standing on the best apology for an elevation of ground that could be seen for about ten miles round Shepperton. A flat ugly district this; depressing enough to look at even on the brightest days. The roads are black with coal-dust, the brick houses dingy with smoke; and at that time—the time of handloom weavers— every other cottage had a loom at its window, where you might see a pale, sickly-looking man or woman pressing a narrow chest against a board, and doing a sort of tread-mill work with legs and arms. A troublesome district for a clergyman; at least to one who, like Amos Barton, understood the "cure of souls" in something more than an official sense; for over and above the rustic stupidity furnished by the farm-labourers, the miners brought obstreperous animalism, and the weavers an acrid Radicalism and Dissent. Indeed, Mrs. Hackit often observed that the colliers, who many of them earned better wages than Mr. Barton, "passed their time in doing nothing but swilling ale and smoking, like the beasts that perish" (speaking, we may presume, in a remotely analogical sense); and in some of the alehouse corners the drink was flavoured by a dingy kind of infidelity, something like rinsings of Tom Paine in ditch-water. A certain amount of religious excitement created by the popular preaching of Mr. Parry, Amos's predecessor, had nearly died out, and the religious life of Shepperton was falling back towards low-water mark. Here, you perceive, was a terrible stronghold of Satan; and you may well pity the Rev. Amos Barton, who had to stand single-handed and summon it to surrender. We read, indeed, that the walls of Jericho fell down before the sound of trumpets; but we nowhere hear that those trumpets were hoarse and feeble. Doubtless they were trumpets that gave forth clear ringing tones, and sent a mighty vibration through brick and mortar. But the oratory of the Rev. Amos resembled rather a Belgian railway-horn, which shows praiseworthy intentions inadequately fulfilled. He often missed the right note both in public and private exhortation, and got a little angry in consequence. For though Amos thought himself strong, he did not *feel* himself strong. Nature had given him the opinion, but not the sensation. Without that opinion he would probably never have worn cambric bands, but would have been an excellent cabinet-maker and deacon of an Independent church, as his father was before him. . . . He might then have sniffed long and loud in the corner of his pew in Gun Street Chapel; he might have indulged in halting rhetoric at prayer-meetings, and have spoken faulty English in private life; and these little infirmities would not have prevented him, honest faithful man that he was, from being a shining light in the dissenting circle of Bridgeport. A tallow dip, of the long-eight description, is an excellent thing in the kitchen candlestick, and Betty's nose and eye are not sensitive to the difference between it and the finest wax; it is only when you stick it in the silver candlestick, and introduce it into the drawing-room, that it seems plebeian, dim, and ineffectual. Alas for the worthy man who, like that candle, gets himself into the wrong place! It is only the very largest souls who will be able to appreciate and pity him—who will discern and love sincerity of purpose amid all the bungling feebleness of achievement.

From SCENES OF CLERICAL LIFE,
by George Eliot (1819–80).

83

THE ABSENT BROTHER

THIS Thursday, by the by, is the first in the month—the day on which the Clerical Meeting is held at Milby Vicarage; and as the Rev. Amos Barton has reasons for not attending, he will very likely be a subject of conversation amongst his clerical brethren. Suppose we go there, and hear whether Mr. Pilgrim has reported their opinion correctly.

There is not a numerous party to-day, for it is a season of sore throats and catarrhs; so that the exegetical and theological discussions, which are the preliminary of dining, have not been quite so spirited as usual; and although a question relative to the Epistle of Jude has not been quite cleared up, the striking of six by the church clock, and the simultaneous announcement of dinner, are sounds that no one feels to be importunate.

Pleasant (when one is not in the least bilious) to enter a comfortable dining-room, where the closely-drawn red curtains glow with the double light of fire and candle, where glass and silver are glittering on the pure damask, and a soup-tureen gives a hint of the fragrance that will presently rush out to inundate your hungry senses, and prepare them, by the delicate visitation of atoms, for the keen gusto of ampler contact! Especially if you have confidence in the dinner-giving capacity of your host—if you know that he is not a man who entertains grovelling views of eating and drinking as a mere satisfaction of hunger and thirst, and, dead to all the finer influences of the palate, he expects his guest to be brilliant on ill-flavoured gravies and the cheapest Marsala. Mr. Ely was particularly worthy of such confidence, and his virtues as an Amphitryon had probably contributed quite as much as the central situation of Milby to the selection of his house as a clerical rendezvous. He looks particularly graceful at the head of his table, and, indeed, on all occasions where he acts as president or moderator—a man who seems to listen well, and is an excellent amalgam of dissimilar ingredients.

At the other end of the table, as "Vice," sits Mr. Fellowes, rector and magistrate, a man of imposing appearance, with a mellifluous voice and the readiest of tongues. Mr. Fellowes once obtained a living by the persuasive charms of his conversation, and the fluency with which he interpreted the opinions of an obese and stammering baronet, so as to give that elderly gentleman a very pleasing perception of his own wisdom. Mr. Fellowes is a very successful man, and has the highest character everywhere except in his own parish, where, doubtless because his parishioners happen to be quarrelsome people, he is always at fierce feud with a farmer or two, a colliery proprietor, a grocer who was once churchwarden, and a tailor who formerly officiated as clerk.

At Mr. Ely's right hand you see a very small man with a sallow and somewhat puffy face, whose hair is brushed straight up, evidently with the intention of giving him a height somewhat less disproportionate to his sense of his own importance than the measure of five feet three accorded him by an oversight of nature. This is the Rev. Archibald Duke, a very dyspeptic and evangelical man, who takes the gloomiest view of mankind and their prospects, and thinks the immense sale of the *Pickwick Papers*, recently completed, one of the strongest proofs of original sin. Unfortunately, though Mr. Duke was not burdened with a family, his yearly expenditure was apt considerably to exceed his income; and the unpleasant circumstances resulting from this, together with heavy meat breakfasts, may probably have contributed to his desponding views of the world generally.

Next to him is seated Mr. Furness, a tall young man, with blond hair and whiskers, who was plucked at Cambridge entirely owing to his genius; at least I know that he soon afterwards published a volume of poems, which were considered remarkably beautiful by many young ladies of his acquaintance. Mr. Furness preached his own sermons, as any one of tolerable critical acumen might have certified by comparing them with his poems; in both, there was an exuberance of metaphor and simile entirely original, and not in the least borrowed from any resemblance in the things compared.

On Mr. Furness's left you see Mr. Pugh, another young curate, of much less marked characteristics. He had not published any poems; he had not even been plucked; he had neat black whiskers and a pale complexion; read prayers and a sermon twice every Sunday, and might be seen any day sallying forth on his parochial duties in a white tie, a well-brushed hat, a perfect suit of black, and well-polished boots—an equipment which he probably supposed hieroglyphically to represent the spirit of Christianity to the parishioners of Whittlecombe.

Mr. Pugh's *vis-à-vis* is the Rev. Martin Cleves, a man about forty—middle-sized, broad-shouldered, with a negligently-tied cravat, large irregular features, and a large head, thickly covered with lanky brown hair. To a superficial glance, Mr. Cleves is the plainest and the least clerical-looking of the party; yet, strange to say, *there* is the true parish priest, the pastor beloved, consulted, relied on by his flock; a clergyman who is not associated with the undertaker, but thought of as the surest helper under a difficulty, as a monitor who is encouraging rather than severe. Mr. Cleves has the wonderful art of preaching sermons which the wheelwright and the blacksmith can understand; not because he talks condescending twaddle, but because he can call a spade a spade, and knows how to disencumber ideas of their wordy frippery. Look at him more attentively, and you will see that his face is a very interesting one—that there is a great deal of humour and feeling playing in his grey eyes, and about the corners of his roughly-cut mouth:—a man, you observe, who has most likely sprung from the harder-working section of the middle class, and has hereditary sympathies with the checkered life of the people. He gets together the working men in his parish on a Monday evening, and gives them a sort of conversational lecture on useful practical matters, telling them stories, or reading some select passages from an agreeable book, and commenting on them; and if you were to ask the first labourer or artisan in Tripplegate what sort of man the parson was, he would say,—"a uncommon knowin', sensable, free-spoken gentleman; very kind an' good-natur'd too." Yet for all this, he is perhaps the best Grecian of the party, if we except Mr. Baird, the young man on his left.

Mr. Baird has since gained considerable celebrity as an original writer and metropolitan lecturer, but at that time he used to preach in a little church something like a barn, to a congregation consisting of three rich farmers and their servants, about fifteen labourers, and the due proportion of women and children. The rich farmers understood him to be "very high learnt;" but if you had interrogated them for a more precise description, they would have said that he was "a thinnish-faced man, with a sort o' cast in his eye, like."

Seven, altogether: a delightful number for a dinner-party, supposing the units to be delightful, but everything depends on that. During dinner Mr. Fellowes took the lead in the conversation, which set strongly in the direction of mangold-wurzel and the rotation of crops; for Mr. Fellowes and Mr. Cleves cultivated their own glebes. Mr. Ely, too, had some agricultural notions, and even the Rev. Archibald Duke was made alive to that class of mundane subjects by the possession of some potato-ground. The two young curates talked a little aside during these discussions, which had imperfect interest for their unbeneficed minds; and the transcendental and near-sighted Mr. Baird seemed to listen somewhat abstractedly, knowing little more of potatoes and mangold-wurzel than that they were some form of the "Conditioned."

"What a hobby farming is with Lord Watling!" said Mr. Fellowes, when the cloth was being drawn. "I went over his farm at Tetterley with him last summer. It is really a model farm; first-rate dairy, grazing and wheat land, and such splendid farm-buildings! An expensive hobby, though. He sinks a good deal of money there, I fancy. He has a great whim for black cattle, and he sends that drunken old Scotch bailiff of his to Scotland every year, with hundreds in his pocket, to buy these beasts."

"By the by," said Mr. Ely, "do you know who is the man to whom Lord Watling has given the Bramhill living?"

"A man named Sargent. I knew him at Oxford. His brother is a lawyer, and was very useful to Lord Watling in that ugly Brounsell affair. That's why Sargent got the living."

"Sargent," said Mr. Ely. "I know him. Isn't he a showy talkative fellow; has written travels in Mesopotamia, or something of that sort?"

"That's the man."

"He was at Witherington once, as Bagshawe's curate. He got into rather bad odour there, through some scandal about a flirtation, I think."

"Talking of scandal," returned Mr. Fellowes, "have you heard the last story about Barton? Nisbett was telling me the other day that he dines alone with the Countess at six, while Mrs. Barton is in the kitchen acting as cook."

"Rather an apocryphal authority, Nisbett," said Mr. Ely.

"Ah," said Mr. Cleves, with good-natured humour twinkling in his eyes, "depend upon it, that is a corrupt version. The original text is, that they all dined together *with* six—meaning six children—and that Mrs. Barton is an excellent cook."

"I wish dining alone together may be the worst of that sad business," said the Rev. Archibald Duke, in a tone implying that his wish was a strong figure of speech.

"Well," said Mr. Fellowes, filling his glass and looking jocose, "Barton is certainly either the greatest gull in existence, or he has some cunning secret—some philtre or other to make himself charming in the eyes of a fair lady. It isn't all of us that can make conquests when our ugliness is past its bloom."

"The lady seemed to have made a conquest of him at the very outset," said Mr. Ely. "I was immensely amused one night at Granby's when he was telling us her story about her husband's adventures. He said, 'When she told me the tale, I felt I don't know how—I felt it from the crown of my head to the sole of my feet.' "

Mr. Ely gave these words dramatically, imitating the Rev. Amos's fervour and symbolic action, and every one laughed except Mr. Duke, whose after-dinner view of things was not apt to be jovial. He said—

"I think some of us ought to remonstrate with Mr. Barton on the scandal he is causing. He is not only imperilling his own soul, but the souls of his flock."

"Depend upon it," said Mr. Cleves, "there is some simple explanation of the whole affair, if we only happened to know it. Barton has always impressed me as a right-minded man, who has the knack of doing himself injustice by his manner."

"Now *I* never liked Barton," said Mr. Fellowes. "He's not a gentleman. Why, he used to be on terms of intimacy with that canting Prior, who died a little while ago:—a fellow who soaked himself with spirits, and talked of the Gospel through an inflamed nose."

"The Countess has given him more refined tastes, I dare say," said Mr. Ely.

"Well," observed Mr. Cleves, "the poor fellow must have a hard pull to get along, with his small income and large family. Let us hope the Countess does something towards making the pot boil."

"Not she," said Mr. Duke; "there are greater signs of poverty about them than ever."

"Well, come," returned Mr. Cleves, who could be caustic sometimes, and who was not at all fond of his reverend brother, Mr. Duke, "that's something in Barton's favour at all events. He might be poor *without* showing signs of poverty."

Mr. Duke turned rather yellow, which was his way of blushing.

From SCENES OF CLERICAL LIFE,
by George Eliot (1819–80).

84

THE DISAPPOINTING MISSIONARY

Alton Locke, hero of the grim novel in which Charles Kingsley expounded his socialistic views, has a boyish longing to be a missionary —until he meets one. . . .

HE came—and with him the two ministers who often drank tea with my mother; both of whom, as they played some small part in the drama of my after-life, I may as well describe here. The elder was a little, sleek, silver-haired old man, with a blank, weak face, just like a white rabbit. He loved me, and I loved him too, for there were always lollipops in his pocket for me and Susan. Had his head been equal to his heart!—but what has been was to be—and the dissenting clergy, with a few noble exceptions among the Independents, are not the strong men of the day—none knew that better than the workmen. The old man's name was Bowyer. The other, Mr. Wigginton, was a younger man; tall, grim, dark, bilious, with a narrow forehead, retreating suddenly from his eyebrows up to a conical peak of black hair over his ears. He preached "higher doctrine," i.e. more fatalist and antinomian than his gentler colleague,—and, having also a stentorian voice, was much the greater favourite at the chapel. I hated him—and if any man ever deserved hatred, he did.

Well, they came. My heart was in my mouth as I opened the door to them, and sank back again to the very lowest depths of my inner man when my eyes fell on the face and figure of the missionary—a squat, red-faced, pig-eyed, low-browed man, with great soft lips that opened back to his very ears: sensuality, conceit, and cunning marked on every feature—an innate vulgarity, from which the artisan and the child recoil with an instinct as true, perhaps truer, than that of the courtier, showing itself in every tone and motion— I shrank into a corner, so crestfallen that I could not even exert myself to hand round the bread and butter, for which I got duly scolded afterwards. Oh! that man!—how he bawled and contradicted, and laid down the law, and spoke to my mother in a fondling, patronising way, which made me, I knew not why, boil over with jealousy and indignation. How he filled his teacup half full of the white sugar to buy which my mother had curtailed her yesterday's dinner—how he drained the few remaining drops of the three-pennyworth of cream, with which Susan was stealing off to keep it as an unexpected treat for my mother at breakfast the next morning—how he talked of the natives, not as St. Paul might of his converts, but as a planter might of his slaves; overlaying all his unintentional confessions of his own greed and prosperity, with cant, flimsy enough for even a boy to see through, while his eyes were not blinded with the superstition that a man must be pious who sufficiently interlards his speech with a jumble of old English picked out of our translation of the New Testament. Such was the man I saw. I don't deny that all are not like him. I believe there are noble men of all denominations, doing their best according to their light, all over the world; but such was the one I saw—and the men who were sent home to plead the missionary cause, whatever the men may be like who stay behind and work, are, from my small experience, too often such. It appears to me to be the rule that many of those who go abroad as missionaries, go simply because they are men of such inferior powers and attainments that if they stayed in England they would starve.

Three parts of his conversation, after all, was made up of abuse of the missionaries of the Church of England, not for doing nothing, but for being so much more successful than his own sect; accusing them, in the same breath, of being just of the inferior type of which he was himself, and also of being mere University fine gentlemen. Really, I do not wonder, upon his own showing, at the savages preferring them to him; and I was pleased to hear the old white-headed minister gently interpose at the end of one of his tirades—"We must not be jealous, my brother, if the Establishment has discovered what we, I hope, shall find out some day, that it is not wise to draft our missionaries from the offscouring of the ministry, and serve God with that which costs us nothing except the expense of providing for them beyond seas."

From ALTON LOCKE, by
Charles Kingsley (1819–75).

85

A SON'S TRIBUTE

*Matthew Arnold was moved to write his famous tribute to Dr. Arnold
when revisiting Rugby in 1857.*

Fifteen years have gone round
Since thou arosest to tread,
In the summer morning, the road
Of death, at a call unforeseen,
Sudden! For fifteen years
We, who till then in thy shade
Rested as under the boughs
Of a mighty oak, have endured
Sunshine and rain as we might,
Bare, unshaded, alone,
Lacking the shelter of thee!

O strong soul, by what shore
Tarriest thou now? For that force,
Surely, has not been left vain!
Somewhere, surely, afar,
In the sounding labour-house vast
Of being, is practised that strength,
Zealous, beneficent, firm!

Yes, in some far-shining sphere,
Conscious or not of the past,
Still thou performest the word
Of the Spirit in whom thou dost live—
Prompt, unwearied, as here!
Still thou upraisest with zeal
The humble good from the ground,
Sternly repressest the bad!
Still, like a trumpet, dost rouse
Those who with half-open eyes

Tread the borderland dim
'Twixt vice and virtue; reviv'st,
Succourest!—this was thy work,
This was thy life upon earth.

And through thee I believe
In the noble and great who are gone;
Pure souls honour'd and blest
By former ages, who else—
Such, so soulless, so poor
Is the race of men whom I see—
Seem'd but a dream of the heart,
Seem'd but a cry of desire.
Yes! I believe that there lived
Others like thee in the past,
Not like the men of the crowd
Who all round me to-day
Bluster or cringe, and make life
Hideous, and arid, and vile;
But souls temper'd with fire,
Fervent, heroic, and good,
Helpers and friends of mankind.

From RUGBY CHAPEL, by
Matthew Arnold (1822–88).

86

EAST LONDON

'Twas August and the fierce sun overhead
Smote on the squalid streets of Bethnal Green,
And the pale weaver, through his windows seen
In Spitalfields, look'd thrice dispirited.

I met a preacher there I knew, and said:
"Ill and o'erworked, how fare you in this scene?"—
"Bravely!" said he; "for I of late have been
Much cheer'd with thoughts of Christ, *the living bread*."

O human soul! as long as thou canst so
Set up a mark of everlasting light
Above the howling senses' ebb and flow,

To cheer thee, and to light thee if thou roam—
Not with lost toil thou labourest through the night
Thou mak'st the heaven thou hop'st indeed thy home.

By Matthew Arnold (1822–88).

87

DR. MIDDLETON TAKES PORT

DR. MIDDLETON misdoubted the future as well as the past of the man who did not, in becoming gravity, exult to dine. That man he deemed unfit for this world and the next.

An example of the good fruit of temperance, he had a comfortable pride in his digestion, and his political sentiments were attuned by his veneration of the Powers rewarding virtue. We must have a stable world where this is to be done.

The Rev. doctor was a fine old picture; a specimen of art peculiarly English; combining in himself piety and epicurism, learning and gentlemanliness, with good room for each and a seat at one another's table: for the rest, a strong man, an athlete in his youth, a keen reader of facts and no reader of persons, genial, a giant at a task, a steady worker besides, but easily discomposed.

. . . .

He liked Sir Willoughby's tone in ordering the servant at his heels to take up "those two bottles:" it prescribed, without overdoing it, a proper amount of caution, and it named an agreeable number.

Watching the man's hand keenly, he said:

"But here is the misfortune of a thing super-excellent:—not more than one in twenty will do it justice."

Sir Willoughby replied: "Very true, sir, and I think we may pass over the nineteen."

"Women, for example: and most men."

"This wine would be a sealed book to them."

"I believe it would. It would be a grievous waste."

"Vernon is a claret-man: and so is Horace De Craye. They are both below the mark of this wine. They will join the ladies. Perhaps you and I, sir, might remain together."

"With the utmost good will on my part."

"I am anxious for your verdict, sir."

"You shall have it, sir, and not out of harmony with the chorus preceding me, I can predict. Cool, not frigid." Dr. Middleton summed the attributes of the cellar on quitting it: "North side and South. No musty damp. A pure air! Everything requisite. One might lie down oneself and keep sweet here."

Of all our venerable British of the two Isles professing a suckling attachment to an ancient port-wine, lawyer, doctor, squire, rosy admiral, city merchant, the classic scholar is he whose blood is most nuptial to the webbed bottle. The reason must be, that he is full of the old poets. He has their spirit to sing with, and the best that Time has done on earth to feed it. He may also perceive a resemblance in the wine to the studious mind, which is the obverse of our mortality, and throws off acids and crusty particles in the piling of the years, until it is fulgent by clarity. Port hymns to his conservatism. It is magical: at one sip he is off swimming in the purple flood of the ever-youthful antique.

By comparison, then, the enjoyment of others is brutish; they have not the soul for it; but he is worthy of the wine, as are poets of Beauty. In truth, these should be severally apportioned to them, scholar and poet, as his own good thing. Let it be so.

Meanwhile Dr. Middleton sipped.

After the departure of the ladies, Sir Willoughby had practised a studied curtness upon Vernon and Horace.

"You drink claret," he remarked to them, passing it round. "Port, I think, Dr. Middleton? The wine before you may serve for a preface. We shall have *your* wine in five minutes."

The claret jug empty, Sir Willoughby offered to send for more.

De Craye was languid over the question. Vernon rose from the table.

"We have a bottle of Dr. Middleton's Port coming in," Willoughby said to him.

"Mine, you call it?" cried the doctor.

"It's a royal wine, that won't suffer sharing," said Vernon.

"We'll be with you, if you go into the billiard-room, Vernon."

"I shall hurry my drinking of good wine for no man," said the doctor.

"Horace?"

"I'm beneath it, ephemeral, Willoughby. I am going to the ladies."

Vernon and De Craye retired upon the arrival of the wine; and Dr. Middleton sipped. He sipped and looked at the owner of it.

"Some thirty dozen?" he said.

"Fifty."

The doctor nodded humbly.

"I shall remember, sir," his host addressed him, "whenever I have the honour of entertaining you, I am cellarer of that wine."

The Rev. doctor set down his glass. "You have, sir, in some sense, an enviable post. It is a responsible one, if that be a blessing. On you it devolves to retard the day of the last dozen."

"Your opinion of the wine is favourable, sir?"

"I will say this:—shallow souls run to rhapsody:—I will say, that I am consoled for not having lived ninety years back, or at any period but the present, by this one glass of your ancestral wine."

"I am careful of it," Sir Willoughby said modestly; "still its natural destination is to those who can appreciate it. You do, sir."

"Still, my good friend, still! It is a charge: it is a possession, but part in trusteeship. Though we cannot declare it an entailed estate, our consciences are in some sort pledged that it shall be a succession not too considerably diminished."

"You will not object to drink it, sir, to the health of your grandchildren. And may you live to toast them in it on their marriage-day!"

"You colour the idea of a prolonged existence in seductive hues.

214

Ha! It is a wine for Tithonus. This wine would speed him to the rosy Morning—aha!"

"I will undertake to sit you through it up to morning," said Sir Willoughby, innocent of the Bacchic nuptiality of the allusion.

Dr. Middleton eyed the decanter. There is a grief in gladness, for a premonition of our mortal state. The amount of wine in the decanter did not promise to sustain the starry roof of night and greet the dawn. "Old wine, my friend, denies us the full bottle!"

"Another bottle is to follow."

"No!"

"It is ordered."

"I protest."

"It is uncorked."

"I entreat."

"It is decanted."

"I submit. But, mark, it must be honest partnership. You are my worthy host, sir, on that stipulation. Note the superiority of wine over Venus!—I may say, the magnanimity of wine; our jealousy turns on him that will not share! But the corks, Willoughby. The corks excite my amazement."

"The corking is examined at regular intervals. I remember the occurrence in my father's time. I have seen to it once."

"It must be perilous as an operation for tracheotomy; which I should assume it to resemble in surgical skill and firmness of hand, not to mention the imminent gasp of the patient."

A fresh decanter was placed before the doctor.

He said: "I have but a girl to give!" He was melted.

Sir Willoughby replied: "I take her for the highest prize this world affords."

From THE EGOIST, by George Meredith (1828–1909).

88

AT THE DIVINITY SCHOOL

Mark Rutherford was the pen name of William Hale White, a divinity student who left the Congregational ministry when he found he could no longer reconcile the scientific beliefs of his time with the prescribed theological views of his Church.

THE society amongst the students was very poor. Not a single friendship formed then has remained with me. They were mostly young men of no education, who had been taken from the counter, and their spiritual life was not very deep. In many of them it did not even exist, and their whole attention was absorbed upon their chances of getting wealthy congregations or of making desirable matches. It was a time in which the world outside was seething with the ferment which had been cast into it by Germany and by those in England whom Germany had influenced, but not a fragment of it had dropped within our walls. I cannot call to mind a single conversation upon any but the most trivial topics, nor did our talk ever turn even upon our religion, so far as it was a thing affecting the soul, but upon it as something subsidiary to chapels, "causes," deacons, and the like.

The emptiness of some of my colleagues, and their worldliness, too, were almost incredible. There was one who was particularly silly. He was a blond youth with greyish eyes, a mouth not quite shut, and an eternal simper upon his face. He never had an idea in his head, and never read anything except the denominational newspapers and a few well-known aids to sermonising. He was a great man at all tea-meetings, anniversaries, and parties. He was facile in public speaking, and he dwelt much upon the joys of heaven and upon such topics as the possibility of our recognising one another there. I have known him describe for twenty minutes, in a kind of watery rhetoric, the passage of the soul to bliss through death, and its meeting in the next world with those who had gone before.

With all his weakness he was close and mean in money matters, and when he left college, the first thing he did was to marry a widow with a fortune. Before long he became one of the most popular of ministers in a town much visited by sick persons, with whom he was an especial favourite. I disliked him—and specially disliked his unpleasant behaviour to women. If I had been a woman, I should have spurned him for his perpetual insult of inane compliments. He was always dawdling after "the sex," which was one of his sweet phrases, and yet he was not passionate. Passion does not dawdle and compliment, nor is it nasty, as this fellow was. Passion may burn like a devouring flame; and in a few moments, like flame, may bring down a temple to dust and ashes, but it is earnest as flame, and essentially pure.

.   .   .   .   .

An uneasy feeling began to develop itself about me in the minds of the professors, because I did not rest in the "simplicity" of the gospel. To me this meant its unintelligibility.

I remember, for example, discoursing about the death of Christ. There was not a single word which was ordinarily used in the pulpit which I did not use—satisfaction for sin, penalty, redeeming blood, they were all there—but I began by saying that in this world there was no redemption for man but by blood; furthermore, the innocent had everywhere and in all time to suffer for the guilty. It had been objected that it was contrary to our notion of an all-loving Being that He should demand such a sacrifice; but, contrary or not, in this world it was true, quite apart from Jesus, that virtue was martyred every day, unknown and unconsoled, in order that the wicked might somehow be saved. This was part of the scheme of the world, and we might dislike it or not, we could not get rid of it. The consequences of my sin, moreover, are rendered less terrible by virtues not my own. I am literally saved from penalties because another pays the penalty for me. The atonement, and what it accomplished for man, were therefore a sublime summing up as it were of what sublime men have to do for their race; an exemplification, rather than a contradiction, of Nature herself, as we know her in our own experience.

Now, all this was really intended as a defence of the atonement;

but the President heard me that Sunday, and on the Monday he called me into his room. He said that my sermon was marked by considerable ability, but he should have been better satisfied if I had confined myself to setting forth as plainly as I could the "way of salvation" as revealed in Christ Jesus. What I had urged might perhaps have possessed some interest for cultivated people; in fact, he had himself urged pretty much the same thing many years ago, when he was a young man, in a sermon he had preached at the Union meeting; but I must recollect that in all probability my sphere of usefulness would lie amongst humble hearers, perhaps in an agricultural village or a small town, and that he did not think people of this sort would understand me if I talked over their heads as I had done the day before. What they wanted on a Sunday, after all the cares of the week, was not anything to perplex and disturb them; not anything which demanded any exercise of thought; but a repetition of the "old story of which, Mr. Rutherford, you know, we never ought to get weary; an exhibition of our exceeding sinfulness; of our safety in the Rock of Ages, and there only; of the joys of the saints and the sufferings of those who do not believe."

His words fell on me like the hand of a corpse, and I went away much depressed. My sermon had excited me, and the man who of all men ought to have welcomed me, had not a word of warmth or encouragement for me, nothing but the coldest indifference, and even repulse.

From THE AUTOBIOGRAPHY OF MARK RUTHER-
FORD, by William Hale White (1831–1913).

89

THE OLD SCHOLAR-PARSON

I CAN recall several instances of the old scholar-parson, a man chap-ful of quotations. One, a very able classic, and a great naturalist, was rather fond of the bottle. "Mr. West," said a neighbour one day, "I hear you have a wonderfully beautiful spring of water in your glebe." "Beautiful! surpassing! *fons Bandusiæ, splendidior vitro!*—water so good that I never touch it—afraid of drinking too much of it."

Some twenty-five years ago I knew another, a fine scholar, an old bachelor, living in a very large rectory. He was a man of good presence, courteous, old-world manners, and something of old-world infirmities. His sense of his religious responsibilities in the parish was different in quality to that affected nowadays.

He was very old when I knew him, and was often laid up with gout. One day, hearing that he was thus crippled, I paid him a visit, and encountered a party of women descending the staircase from his room. When I entered he said to me, "I suppose you met little Mary-So-and-so, and Janie What's-her-name going out? I've been churching them up here in my bedroom, as I can't go to church."

When a labourer desired to have his child privately baptised, he provided a bottle of rum, a pack of cards, a lemon, and a basin of pure water, then sent for the parson and the farmer for whom he worked. The religious rite over, the basin was removed, the table cleared, cards and rum produced, and sat down to. On such occasions the rector did not return home till late, and the housekeeper left the library window unhasped for the master, but locked the house doors. Under the library window was a violet bed, and it was commonly reported that the rector had on more than one occasion slept in that bed after a christening. Unable to heave up his big body to the sill of the window, he had fallen back among the violets, and there slept off the exertion.

I never had the opportunity of hearing the old fellow preach. His conversation—whether addressing a gentleman, a lady, or one of the lower classes—was garnished with quotations from the classic authors, Greek and Latin, with which his surprising memory was richly stored; and I cannot think that he could resist the temptation of introducing them into his discourse from the pulpit, yet I heard no hint of this in the only sermon of his which was repeated to me by one of his congregation. The occasion of its delivery was this.

He was highly incensed at a long engagement being broken off between some young people in his parish, so next Sunday he preached on "Let love be without dissimulation;" and the sermon, which on this occasion was extempore, was reported by those who heard it to consist of little more than this—"You see, my dearly beloved brethren, what the Apostle says—Let love be without dissimulation. Now I'll tell y' what I think dissimulation is. When a young chap goes out a walking with a girl,—as nice a lass as ever you saw, with an uncommon fresh pair o' cheeks and pretty black eyes too, and not a word against her character, very respectably brought up,—when, I say, my dearly beloved brethren, a young chap goes out walking with such a young woman, after church of a summer evening, seen of every one, and offers her his arm, and they look friendly like at each other, and at times he buys her a present at the fair, a ribbon, or a bit of jewellery—I cannot say I have heard, and I don't say that I have seen,—when, I say, dearly beloved brethren, a young chap like this goes on for more than a year, and lets everybody fancy they are going to be married,—I don't mean to say that at times a young chap may see a nice lass and admire her, and talk to her a bit, and then go away and forget her—there's no dissimulation in that;—but when it goes on for a long time, and he makes her to think he's very sweet upon her, and that he can't live without her, and he gives her ribbons and jewellery that I can't particularise, because I haven't seen them—when a young chap dearly beloved brethren—" and so on, and so on, becoming more and more involved. The parties preached about were in the church, and the young man was just under the pulpit, with the eyes of the whole congregation turned on him. The sermon had its effect—he reverted to his love, and without any dissimulation, we trust, married her.

.   .   .   .   .

A very good story was told of this old parson, which is, I believe, quite true. He was invited to spend a couple of days with a great squire some miles off. He went, stayed his allotted time, and disappeared. Two days later the lady of the house, happening to go into the servants'-hall in the evening, found, to her amazement, her late guest—there. After he had finished his visit upstairs, at the invitation of the butler he spent the same time below. "Like

Persephone, madam," he said,—"half my time above, half in the nether world."

In the matter of personal neatness he left much to be desired. His walled garden was famous for its jargonelle pears. Lady X—, one day coming over, said to him, "Will you come back in my carriage with me, and dine at the Park? You can stay the night, and be driven home to-morrow."

"Thank you, my lady, delighted. I will bring with me some jargonelles. I'll go and fetch them."

Presently he returned with a little open basket and some fine pears in it. Lady X— looked at him, with a troubled expression in her sweet face. The rector was hardly in dining suit; moreover, there was apparent no equipment for the night.

"Dear Mr. M—, will you not *really* want something further? You will dine with us, *and sleep the night.*"

A vacant expression stole over his countenance, as he retired into himself in thought. Presently a flash of intelligence returned, and he said with briskness, "Ah! to be sure; I'll go and fetch two or three more jargonelles."

A kind, good-hearted man the scholar-parson was, always ready to put his hand into his pocket at a tale of distress, but quite incapable of understanding that his parishioners might have spiritual as well as material requirements. I remember a case of a very similar man—a fellow of his college, and professor at Cambridge— to whom a young student ventured to open some difficulties and doubts that tortured him. "Difficulties! doubts!" echoed the old gentleman. "Take a couple of glasses of port. If that don't dispel them, take two more, and continue the dose till you have found ease of mind."

From OLD COUNTRY LIFE, by
S. Baring Gould (1832–1924).

90

ONE WHO LOVED CHILDREN

"That was the light in which God and His ministers were presented to little children," says Dr. Wingfield-Stratford, "objects of fear, the grown-up person in his most terrifying aspect." That all Victorian divines were not grimly inhuman in their dealings with little children, is shown in these delightful letters of Lewis Carroll.

CHRIST CHURCH, OXFORD.
Dec. 9, 1875.

MY DEAR GERTRUDE,—This really will not do, you know, sending one more kiss every time by post: the parcel gets so heavy it is quite expensive. When the postman brought in the last letter, he looked quite grave. "Two pounds to pay, sir!" he said. "Extra weight, sir!" (I think he cheats a little, by the way. He often makes me pay two pounds, when I think it should be pence.) "Oh, if you please, Mr. Postman!" I said, going down gracefully on one knee (I wish you could see me going down gracefully on one knee to a postman—it's a very pretty sight), "do excuse me just this once! It's only from a little girl!"

"Only from a little girl!" he growled. "What are little girls made of?" "Sugar and spice," I began to say, "and all that's ni——" but he interrupted me. "No! I don't mean that. I mean, what's the good of the little girls, when they send such heavy letters?" "Well, they're not much good, certainly," I said, rather sadly.

"Mind you don't get any more such letters," he said, "at least, not from that particular little girl. I know her well, and she's a regular bad one!" That's not true, is it? I don't believe he ever saw you, and you're not a bad one, are you? However, I promised him we would send each other very few more letters—"Only two thousand four hundred and seventy, or so," I said. "Oh!" he said, "a little number like that doesn't signify. What I meant is, you mustn't send many."

So you see we must keep count now, and when we get to two

thousand four hundred and seventy, we mustn't write any more, unless the postman gives us leave.

I sometimes wish I was back on the shore at Sandown; don't you?

Your loving friend,
LEWIS CARROLL.

CHRIST CHURCH, OXFORD.
March 8, 1880.

MY DEAR ADA,—(Isn't that your short name? "Adelaide" is all very well, but you see when one is dreadfully busy one hasn't time to write such long words—particularly when it takes one half an hour to remember how to spell it—and even then one has to go and get a dictionary to see if one has spelt it right, and of course the dictionary is in another room, at the top of a high bookcase—where it has been for months and months, and has got all covered with dust—so one has to get a duster first of all, and nearly choke oneself in dusting it—and when one has made out at last which is dictionary and which is dust, even then, there's a job of remembering which end of the alphabet "A" comes—for one feels pretty certain it isn't in the middle—then one has to go and wash one's hands before turning over the leaves—for they've got so thick with dust one hardly knows them by sight—and, as likely as not, the soap is lost, and the jug is empty, and there's no towel, and one has to spend hours and hours in finding things—and perhaps after all one has to go off to the shop to buy a new cake of soap—so, with all this bother, I hope you won't mind my writing it short and saying, "My Dear Ada.") You said in your last letter you would like a likeness of me: so here it is, and I hope you will like it—I won't forget to call the next time but one I'm in Wallington.

Your very affectionate friend,
LEWIS CARROLL.

From Letters of Lewis Carroll
(Rev. C. L. Dodgson) (1833–90).

91

A KIND OF HUMAN SUNDAY

Fertile in ideas, but with a prickly temper and an impish wit, Samuel Butler put some of his experiences as a child of the Manse into the Way of All Flesh.

THE hymn had engaged my attention; when it was over I had time to take stock of the congregation. They were chiefly farmers—fat, very well-to-do folk, who had come some of them with their wives and children from outlying farms two and three miles away; haters of popery and of anything which any one might choose to say was popish; good, sensible fellows who detested theory of any kind, whose ideal was the maintenance of the *status quo* with perhaps a loving reminiscence of old war times, and a sense of wrong that the weather was not more completely under their control, who desired higher prices and cheaper wages, but otherwise were most contented when things were changing least; tolerators, if not lovers, of all that was familiar, haters of all that was unfamiliar; they would have been equally horrified at hearing the Christian religion doubted, and at seeing it practised.

"What can there be in common between Theobald and his parishioners?" said Christina to me, in the course of the evening, when her husband was for a few moments absent. "Of course one must not complain, but I assure you it grieves me to see a man of Theobald's ability thrown away upon such a place as this. If we had only been at Gaysbury, where there are the A's, the B's, the C's, and Lord D's place, as you know, quite close, I should not then have felt that we were living in such a desert; but I suppose it is for the best," she added more cheerfully; "and then of course the Bishop will come to us whenever he is in the neighbourhood, and if we were at Gaysbury he might have gone to Lord D's."

Perhaps I have now said enough to indicate the kind of place in which Theobald's lines were cast, and the sort of woman he had married. As for his own habits, I see him trudging through muddy lanes and over long sweeps of plover-haunted pastures to visit a cottager's dying wife. He takes her meat and wine from his own table, and that not a little only but liberally. According to his lights also, he administers what he is pleased to call spiritual consolation.

"I am afraid I'm going to Hell, Sir," says the sick woman with a whine. "Oh, Sir, save me, save me, don't let me go there. I couldn't stand it, Sir, I should die with fear, the very thought of it drives me into a cold sweat all over."

"Mrs. Thompson," says Theobald gravely, "you must have faith in the precious blood of your Redeemer; it is He alone who can save you."

"But are you sure, Sir," says she, looking wistfully at him, "that He will forgive me—for I've not been a very good woman, indeed I haven't—and if God would only say 'Yes' outright with His mouth when I ask whether my sins are forgiven me——"

"But they *are* forgiven you, Mrs. Thompson," says Theobald with some sternness, for the same ground has been gone over a good many times already, and he has borne the unhappy woman's misgivings now for a full quarter of an hour. Then he puts a stop to the conversation by repeating prayers taken from the "Visitation of the Sick," and overawes the poor wretch from expressing further anxiety as to her condition.

"Can't you tell me, Sir," she exclaims piteously, as she sees that he is preparing to go away, "can't you tell me that there is no Day of Judgement, and that there is no such place as Hell? I can do without the Heaven, Sir, but I cannot do with the Hell." Theobald is much shocked.

"Mrs. Thompson," he rejoins impressively, "let me implore you to suffer no doubt concerning these two corner-stones of our religion to cross your mind at a moment like the present. If there is one thing more certain than another it is that we shall all appear before the Judgement Seat of Christ, and that the wicked will be consumed in a lake of everlasting fire. Doubt this, Mrs. Thompson, and you are lost."

The poor woman buries her fevered head in the coverlet in a paroxysm of fear which at last finds relief in tears.

"Mrs. Thompson," says Theobald, with his hand on the door,

"compose yourself, be calm; you must please to take my word for it that at the Day of Judgement your sins will be all washed white in the blood of the Lamb, Mrs. Thompson. Yes," he exclaims frantically, "though they be as scarlet, yet shall they be as white as wool," and he makes off as fast as he can from the fetid atmosphere of the cottage to the pure air outside. Oh, how thankful he is when the interview is over!

He returns home, conscious that he has done his duty, and administered the comforts of religion to a dying sinner. His admiring wife awaits him at the Rectory, and assures him that never yet was clergyman so devoted to the welfare of his flock. He believes her; he has a natural tendency to believe everything that is told him, and who should know the facts of the case better than his wife? Poor fellow! He has done his best, but what does a fish's best come to when the fish is out of water? He has left meat and wine—that he can do; he will call again and will leave more meat and wine; day after day he trudges over the same plover-haunted fields, and listens at the end of his walk to the same agony of forebodings, which day after day he silences, but does not remove, till at last a merciful weakness renders the sufferer careless of her future, and Theobald is satisfied that her mind is now peacefully at rest in Jesus.

He does not like this branch of his profession—indeed he hates it—but will not admit it to himself. The habit of not admitting things to himself has become a confirmed one with him. Nevertheless there haunts him an ill-defined sense that life would be pleasanter if there were no sick sinners, or if they would at any rate face an eternity of torture with more indifference. He does not feel that he is in his element. The farmers look as if they were in their element. They are full-bodied, healthy and contented; but between him and them there is a great gulf fixed. A hard and drawn look begins to settle about the corners of his mouth, so that even if he were not in a black coat and white tie a child might know him for a parson.

He knows that he is doing his duty. Every day convinces him of this more firmly; but then there is not much duty for him to do. He is sadly in want of occupation. He has no taste for any of those field sports which were not considered unbecoming for a clergyman forty years ago. He does not ride, nor shoot, nor fish, nor course, nor play cricket. Study, to do him justice, he had never really liked, and what inducement was there for him to study at Battersby? He reads neither old books nor new ones. He does not interest himself in art or science or politics, but he sets his back up with some promptness if any of them show any development unfamiliar to himself. True, he writes his own sermons, but even his wife considers that his *forte* lies rather in the example of his life (which is one long act of self-devotion) than in his utterances from the pulpit.

.   .   .   .

By nature reserved, if he could have found someone to cook his dinner for him, he would rather have lived in a desert island than not. In his heart of hearts he held with Pope that "the greatest nuisance to mankind is man" or words to that effect—only that women, with the exception perhaps of Christina, were worse. Yet for all this when visitors called he put a better face on it than anyone who was behind the scenes would have expected.

He was quick too at introducing the names of any literary celebrities whom he had met at his father's house, and soon established an all-round reputation which satisfied even Christina herself.

Who so *integer vitæ scelerisque purus*, it was asked, as Mr. Pontifex of Battersby? Who so fit to be consulted if any difficulty about parish management should arise? Who such a happy mixture of the sincere uninquiring Christian and of the man of the world? For so people actually called him. They said he was such an admirable man of business. Certainly if he had said he would pay a sum of money at a certain time, the money would be forthcoming on the appointed day, and this is saying a good deal for any man. His constitutional timidity rendered him incapable of an attempt to overreach when there was the remotest chance of opposition or publicity, and his correct bearing and somewhat stern expression were a great protection to him against being overreached. He never talked of money, and invariably changed the subject whenever money was introduced. His expression of unutterable horror at all kinds of meanness was a sufficient guarantee that he was not mean himself. Besides he had no business transactions save of the most ordinary butcher's book and baker's book description. His tastes—if he had any—were, as we have seen, simple; he had £900 a year and a house; the neighbourhood was cheap, and for some time he had no children to be a drag upon him. Who was not to be envied, and if envied why then respected, if Theobald was not enviable?

Yet I imagine that Christina was on the whole happier than her husband. She had not to go and visit sick parishioners, and the management of her house and the keeping of her accounts afforded as much occupation as she desired. Her principal duty was, as she well said, to her husband—to love him, honour him, and keep him in a good temper. To do her justice she fulfilled this duty to the utmost of her power. It would have been better perhaps if she had not so frequently assured her husband that he was the best and wisest of mankind, for no one in his little world ever dreamed of telling him anything else, and it was not long before he ceased to have any doubt upon the matter. As for his temper, which had become very violent at times, she took care to humour it on the slightest sign of an approaching outbreak. She had early found that this was much the easiest plan. The thunder was seldom for herself. Long before her marriage even she had studied his little ways, and knew how to add fuel to the fire as long as the fire seemed to want it, and then to damp it judiciously down, making as little smoke as possible.

．　　．　　．　　．　　．

I have often thought that the Church of Rome does wisely in not allowing her priests to marry. Certainly it is a matter of common observation in England that the sons of clergymen are frequently unsatisfactory. The explanation is very simple, but is so often lost sight of that I may perhaps be pardoned for giving it here.

The clergyman is expected to be a kind of human Sunday. Things must not be done in him which are venial in the week-day classes. He is paid for this business of leading a stricter life than other people. It is his *raison d'être*. If his parishioners feel that he does this, they approve of him, for they look upon him as their own contribution towards what they deem a holy life. This is why the clergyman is so often called a vicar—he being the person whose vicarious goodness is to stand for that of those entrusted to his charge. But his home is his castle as much as that of any other Englishman, and with him, as with others, unnatural tension in public is followed by exhaustion when tension is no longer necessary. His children are the most defenceless things he can reach, and it is on them in nine cases out of ten that he will relieve his mind.

A clergyman, again, can hardly ever allow himself to look facts fairly in the face. It is his profession to support one side; it is impossible, therefore, for him to make an unbiased examination of the other.

We forget that every clergyman with a living or curacy, is as much a paid advocate as the barrister who is trying to persuade a jury to acquit a prisoner. We should listen to him with the same suspense of judgment, the same full consideration of the arguments of the opposing counsel, as a judge does when he is trying a case. Unless we know these, and can state them in a way that our opponents would admit to be a fair representation of their views, we have no right to claim that we have formed an opinion at all. The misfortune is that by the law of the land one side only can be heard.

Theobald and Christina were no exceptions to the general rule. When they came to Battersby they had every desire to fulfil the duties of their position, and to devote themselves to the honour and glory of God. But it was Theobald's duty to see the honour and glory of God through the eyes of a Church which had lived three hundred years without finding reason to change a single one of its opinions.

I should doubt whether he ever got as far as doubting the wisdom of his Church upon any single matter. His scent for possible mischief was tolerably keen; so was Christina's, and it is likely that if either of them detected in him or herself the first faint symptoms of a want of faith they were nipped no less peremptorily in the bud, than signs of self-will in Ernest were—and I should imagine more successfully. Yet Theobald considered himself, and was generally considered to be, and indeed perhaps was, an exceptionally truthful person; indeed he was generally looked upon as an embodiment of all those virtues which make the poor respectable and the rich respected. In the course of time he and his wife became persuaded even to unconsciousness, that no one could even dwell under their roof without deep cause for thankfulness. Their children, their servants, their parishioners must be fortunate *ipso facto* that they were theirs. There was no road to happiness here or hereafter, but the road that they had themselves travelled, no good people who did not think as they did upon every subject, and no reasonable person who had wants the gratification of which would be inconvenient to them—Theobald and Christina.

From THE WAY OF ALL FLESH,
by Samuel Butler (1835–1902).

92

THE REVEREND SIMON MAGUS

A RICH advowson, highly prized,
For private sale was advertised;
And many a parson made a bid;
The REVEREND SIMON MAGUS did.

He sought the agent's: "Agent, I
Have come prepared at once to buy
(If your demand is not too big)
The Cure of Otium-cum-Digge."

"Ah!" said the agent, "*there's* a berth—
The snuggest vicarage on earth;
No sort of duty (so I hear),
And fifteen hundred pounds a year!

"If on the price we should agree,
The living soon will vacant be:
The good incumbent's ninety-five,
And cannot very long survive.

"See—here's his photograph—you see,
He's in his dotage." "Ah, dear me!
Poor soul!" said Simon. "His decease
Would be a merciful release!"

The agent laughed—the agent blinked—
The agent blew his nose and winked
And poked the parson's ribs in play—
It was that agent's vulgar way.

The REVEREND SIMON frowned: "I grieve
This light demeanour to perceive;
It's scarcely *comme il faut*, I think;
Now—pray oblige me—do not wink.

"Don't dig my waistcoat into holes—
Your mission is to sell the souls
Of human sheep and human kids
To that divine who highest bids.

"Do well in this, and on your head
Unnumbered honours will be shed."
The agent said, "Well, truth to tell,
I *have* been doing pretty well."

"You should," said SIMON, "at your age;
But now about the parsonage.
How many rooms does it contain?
Show me the photograph again.

"A poor apostle's humble house
Must not be too luxurious;
No stately halls with oaken floor—
It should be decent and no more.

"No billiard-rooms—no stately trees—
No croquêt-grounds or pineries."
"Ah!" sighed the agent, "very true:
This property won't do for you.

"All these about the house you'll find"—
"Well," said the parson, "never mind;
I'll manage to submit to these
Luxurious superfluities.

"A clergyman who does not shirk
The various calls of Christian work,
Will have no leisure to employ
These 'common forms' of worldly joy.

"To preach three times on Sabbath days—
To wean the lost from wicked ways—
The sick to soothe—the sane to wed—
The poor to feed with meat and bread;

"These are the various wholesome ways
In which I'll spend my nights and days:
My zeal will have no time to cool
At croquêt, archery, or pool."

The agent said, "From what I hear,
This living will not suit, I fear—
There are no poor, no sick at all;
For services there is no call."

The reverend gent looked grave. "Dear me!
Then there is *no* 'society'?—
I mean, of course, no sinners there
Whose souls will be my special care?"

The cunning agent shook his head,
"No, none—except"—(the agent said)—
"The DUKE OF A., the EARL OF B.,
The MARQUIS C., and VISCOUNT D.

"But you will not be quite alone,
For, though they've chaplains of their own,
Of course this noble well-bred clan
Receive the parish clergyman."

"Oh, silence, sir!" said SIMON M.,
"Dukes—earls! What should I care for them?
These worldly ranks I scorn and flout!"
"Of course," the agent said, "no doubt."

"Yet I might show these men of birth
The hollowness of rank on earth."
The agent answered, "Very true—
But I should not, if I were you."

"Who sells this rich advowson, pray?"
The agent winked—it was his way—
"His name is HART; 'twixt me and you,
He is, I'm griev'd to say, a Jew!"

"A Jew?" said SIMON, "happy find!
I purchase this advowson, mind.
My life shall be devoted to
Converting that unhappy Jew!"

From THE BAB BALLADS, by
Sir W. S. Gilbert (1836–1911).

93

THE FALLEN VETERAN

Child of a brilliant Victorian naturalist who sought refuge from the material dogmatism of science in a narrow religious sect, Sir Edmund Gosse recalls many curious associates of his boyhood.

THE Pagets were a retired Baptist minister and his wife, from Exmouth, who had lately settled amongst us, and joined in the breaking of bread. Mr. Paget was a fat old man, whose round pale face was clean-shaven, and who carried a full crop of loose white hair above it; his large lips were always moving, whether he spoke or not. He resembled, as I now perceive, the portraits of S. T. Coleridge in age, but with all the intellect left out of them. He lived in a sort of trance of solemn religious despondency. He had thrown up his cure of souls, because he became convinced that he had committed the Sin against the Holy Ghost. His wife was younger than he, very small, very tight, very active, with black eyes like pin-pricks at the base of an extremely high and narrow forehead, bordered with glossy ringlets. He was very cross to her, and it was murmured that "dear Mrs. Paget had often had to pass through the waters of affliction." They were very poor, but rigidly genteel, and she was careful, so far as she could, to conceal from the world the caprices of her poor lunatic husband.

In our circle, it was never for a moment admitted that Mr. Paget was a lunatic. It was said that he had gravely sinned, and was under the Lord's displeasure; prayers were abundantly offered up that he might be led back into the pathway of light, and that the Smiling Face might be drawn forth for him from behind the Frowning Providence. When the man had an epileptic seizure in the High Street, he was not taken to a hospital, but we repeated to one another, with shaken heads, that Satan, that crookèd Serpent, had been unloosed for a season. Mr. Paget was fond of talking, in private and in public, of his dreadful spiritual condition, and he would drop his voice while he spoke of having committed the Unpardonable Sin, with a sort of shuddering exultation, such as people sometimes feel in the possession of a very unusual disease.

It might be thought that the position held in any community by persons so afflicted and eccentric as the Pagets would be very precarious. But it was not so with us; on the contrary, they took a prominent place at once. Mr. Paget, in spite of his spiritual bankruptcy, was only too anxious to help my Father in his ministrations, and used to beg to be allowed to pray and exhort. In the latter case he took the tone of a wounded veteran, who, though fallen on the bloody field himself, could still encourage younger warriors to march forward to victory. Everybody longed to know what the exact nature had been of that sin against the Holy Ghost which had deprived Mr. Paget of every glimmer of hope for time or for eternity. It was whispered that even my Father himself was not precisely acquainted with the character of it.

This mysterious disability clothed Mr. Paget for us with a kind of romance. We watched him as the women watched Dante in Verona, whispering:

> "Behold him, how Hell's reek
> Has crisped his hair and singed his cheek!"

His person lacked, it is true, something of the dignity of Dante's, for it was his caprice to walk up and down the High Street at noonday with one of those cascades of coloured paper which were known as "ornaments for your fire-place" slung over the back and another over the front of his body. These he manufactured for sale, and he adopted the quaint practice of wearing the exuberant objects as a means for their advertisement.

From FATHER AND SON, by Sir
Edmund Gosse (1849–1928).

94

THE SLEEPING CLERGYMAN

LOOKING up from her sketch of the patent beehive she saw that her husband had fallen asleep, and stayed to gaze at him thoughtfully.

He looked worn, and older than he really was; as if rest or change would do him good; as if he required luxuries and petting. She sighed, and wondered whether the bees would enable her to buy him such things, for though the house was well furnished and apparently surrounded with wealth, they were extremely poor. Yet she did not care for money for their own household use so much as to give him the weight in parish affairs he so sadly needed. She felt that he was pushed aside, treated as a cipher, and that he had little of the influence that properly belonged to him. Her two daughters, their only children, were comfortably, though not grandly, married and settled; there was no family anxiety. But the work, the parish, the people, all seemed to have slipped out of her husband's hands. She could not but acknowledge that he was too quiet and yielding, that he lacked the brazen voice, the personal force that imposes upon men. But surely his good intentions, his way of life, his gentle kindness should carry sway. Instead of which the parish seemed to have quite left the Church, and the parson was outside the real modern life of the village. No matter what he did, even if popular, it soon seemed to pass out of his hands.

It was not for want of effort on his part. Years ago, when first he had come to the parish, it was with determination to improve the lot of those in his care. The edge of the great questions of the day, he declared, had reached the village, and everywhere the clergy must be up and doing. He did not indeed, lift the latch of the cottage or the farm-house door indiscreetly—not unless aware that his presence would not be resented. He was anxious to avoid irritating individual susceptibilities. But wherever people were gathered together, be it for sport or be it in earnest, wherever a man might go in open day, thither he went, and with a set purpose beforehand made it felt that he was there. He did not remain a passive spectator in the background, but came as prominently to the front as was compatible with due courtesy.

When the cloth was cleared at the ordinary in the market town, and the farmers proceeded to the business of their club, or chamber, he appeared in the doorway, and quietly took a seat not far from the chair. If the discussion were purely technical he said nothing; if it touched, as it frequently did, upon social topics, such as those that arose out of education, of the labour question, of the position of the farmer apart from the mere ploughing and sowing, then he delivered his opinion. When the local agricultural exhibition was proceeding and the annual dinner was held he sat at the social board, and presently made his speech. The village benefit club held its *fête*—he was there too, perhaps presiding at the dinner, and addressed the assembled men. He took part in the organisation of the cottage flower show; exerted himself earnestly about the allotments and the winter coal club, and endeavoured to provide the younger people with amusements that did not, in his opinion, lead to evil—supporting cricket and such games as might be played apart from gambling and liquor.

This is but the barest catalogue of his work in those early days; there was nothing that arose, no part of the life of the village and the countryside, to which he did not set his hand. All this was apart from abstract theology. Religion, of course, was in his heart; but he did not carry a list of dogmas in his hand, rather keeping his own peculiar office in the background, knowing that many of those with whom he mingled were members of various sects. He was simply preaching the practical Christianity of brotherhood and goodwill. It was a work that could never be finished, and that was ever extending. His leading idea was not to check the inevitable motion of the age, but to tone it.

He was not permitted to pursue this course unmolested; there were parties in the village that silently opposed his every footstep. Had the battle been open it would have been easier to win it, but it was concealed. The Church is not often denounced from the housetop, but it is certainly denounced under the roof. The poor and ignorant were instructed that the Church was their greatest enemy, the upholder of tyranny, the instrument of their subjection, synonymous with lowered wages and privation, more iniquitous than the landowner. The clergyman was a Protestant Jesuit—a man of deepest guile. The coal club, the cricket, the flower show, the allotments, the village *fête*, everything in which he had a hand was simply an effort to win the good-will of the populace, to keep them quiet, lest they arose and overthrew the property of the Church. The poor man had but a few shillings a week, and the clergyman was the friend of the farmer, who reduced his wages— the Church owned millions and millions sterling. How self-evident, therefore, that the Church was the cottager's enemy!

See, too, how he is beautifying that church, restoring it, making it light and pleasant to those who resort to it; see how he causes sweeter music and singing, and puts new life into the service. This a lesson learnt from the City of the Seven Hills—this is the mark of the Beast. But the ultimate aim may be traced to the same base motive—the preservation of that enormous property.

Another party was for pure secularism. This was not so numerously represented, but had increased of recent years. From political motives both of these silently opposed the parson. Nor were the poor and ignorant alone among the ranks of his foes. There were some tenant-farmers among them, but their attitude was not so coarsely antagonistic. They took no action against, but they did not assist, him. So that, although, as he went about the parish, he was not greeted with hisses, the clergyman was full well aware that his activity was a thorn in the side of many. They reproached him with interfering in matters outside his cloth; and gradually, as the keen edge of his benevolence wore off, he took to the seclusion of the parsonage.

His wife sighed, as she looked at the figure sunken in weary attitude in the sunlight he loved.

. . . . .

Just at present his finances were especially low. The tenants who farmed the glebe land threatened to quit unless their rents were materially reduced, and unless a considerable sum was expended upon improvements. To some very rich men the reduction of rents has made a sensible difference; to the Rev. Francis it meant serious privations. But he had no choice; he had to be satisfied with that or nothing. Then the vicarage house, though substantial and pleasant to look at, was not in a good state within. The rain came through in more places than one, and the ancient woodwork of the roof was rotten. He had already done considerable repairing, and knew that he must soon do more. The nominal income of the living was but moderate; but when the reductions were all made nothing but a cheese-paring seemed left. From this his subscriptions to certain ecclesiastical institutions had to be deducted.

Lastly, he had received a hint that a curate ought to be kept now that his increasing age rendered him less active than before. There was less hope now than ever of anything being done for him in the parish. The landowners complained of rent reductions, of farms idle on their hands, and of increasing expenses. The farmers grumbled about the inclement seasons, their continual losses, and the falling markets. It was not a time when the churlish are almost generous, having such overflowing pockets. There was no testimonial, no address on vellum, no purse with banker's draft for the enfeebled servant of the Church slumbering in the cane chair in the veranda.

Yet the house was exquisitely kept, marvellously kept considering the class of servants they were obliged to put up with. The garden was bright and beautiful with flowers, the lawn smooth; there was an air of refinement everywhere. So the clergyman slept, and the wife turned again to her sketch of the patent hive, hoping that the golden honey might at last bring some metallic gold. The wagon rumbled down the road, and Hodge, lying at full length on the top of the load, could just see over the lowest part of the shrubbery, and thought to himself what a jolly life that parson led, sleeping away the hot hours in the shade.

From HODGE AND HIS MASTERS,
by Richard Jefferies (1849–87).

95

THE PATRIARCH

It was a place in that time like no other: the garden cut into provinces by a great hedge of beech, and overlooked by the church and the terrace of the churchyard, where the tombstones were thick, and after nightfall "spunkies" might be seen to dance at least by children; flower-pots lying warm in sunshine; laurels and the great yew making elsewhere a pleasing horror of shade; the smell of water rising from all round, with an added tang of papermills; the sound of water everywhere, and the sound of mills—the wheel and the dam singing their alternate strain; the birds on every bush and from every corner of the over-hanging woods pealing out their notes until the air throbbed with them; and in the midst of this, the manse. I see it, by the standard of my childish stature, as a great and roomy house. In truth, it was not so large as I supposed, nor yet so convenient, and, standing where it did, it is difficult to suppose that it was healthful. Yet a large family of stalwart sons and tall daughters was housed and reared, and came to man and womanhood in that nest of little chambers; so that the face of the earth was peppered with the children of the manse, and letters with outlandish stamps became familiar to the local postman, and the walls of the little chambers brightened with the wonders of the East. The dullest could see this was a house that had a pair of hands in divers foreign places: a well-beloved house—its image fondly dwelt on by many travellers.

Here lived an ancestor of mine, who was a herd of men. I read him, judging with older criticism the report of childish observation, as a man of singular simplicity of nature; unemotional, and hating the display of what he felt; standing contented on the old ways; a lover of his life and innocent habits to the end. We children admired him: partly for his beautiful face and silver hair, for none more than children are concerned for beauty and, above all, for beauty in the old; partly for the solemn light in which we beheld him once a week, the observed of all observers, in the pulpit. But his strictness and distance, the effect, I now fancy, of old age, slow blood, and settled habit, oppressed us with a kind of terror. When not abroad he sat much alone, writing sermons or letters to his scattered family in a dark and cold room with a library of bloodless books—or so they seemed in those days, although I have some of them now on my own shelves and like well enough to read them; and these lonely hours wrapped him in the greater gloom of our imaginations. But the study had a redeeming grace in many Indian pictures, gaudily coloured and dear to young ·eyes. I cannot depict (for I have no such passions now) the greed with which I beheld them; and when I was once sent in to say a psalm to my grandfather, I went, quaking indeed with fear, but at the same time glowing with hope that, if I said it well, he might reward me with an Indian picture.

> "Thy foot He'll not let slide, nor will
> He slumber that thee keeps,"

it ran: a strange conglomerate of the unpronounceable, a sad model to set in childhood before one who was himself to be a versifier, and a task in recitation that really merited reward. And I must suppose the old man thought so too, and was either touched or amused by the performance; for he took me in his arms with most unwonted tenderness, and kissed me, and gave me a little kindly sermon for my psalm; so that, for that day, we were clerk and parson. I was struck by this reception into so tender a surprise that I forgot my disappointment. And indeed the hope was one of those that childhood forges for a pastime, and with no design upon reality. Nothing was more unlikely than that my grandfather should strip himself of one of those pictures, love-gifts and reminders of his absent sons; nothing more unlikely than that he should bestow it upon me. He had no idea of spoiling children, leaving all that to my aunt; he had fared hard himself, and blubbered under the rod in the last century; and his ways were still Spartan for the young. The last word I heard upon his lips was in this Spartan key. He had overwalked in the teeth of an east wind, and was now near the end of his many days. He sat by the dining-room fire, with his white hair, pale face and bloodshot eyes, a somewhat awful figure; and my aunt had given him a dose of our good old

Scots medicine, Dr. Gregory's powder. Now that remedy, as the work of a near kinsman of Rob Roy himself, may have a savour of romance for the imagination; but it comes uncouthly to the palate. The old gentleman had taken it with a wry face; and that being accomplished, sat with perfect simplicity, like a child's, munching a "barley-sugar kiss." But when my aunt, having the canister open in her hands, proposed to let me share in the sweets, he interfered at once. I had had no Gregory; then I should have no barley-sugar kiss: so he decided with a touch of irritation. And just then the phaeton coming opportunely to the kitchen door—for such was our unlordly fashion—I was taken for the last time from the presence of my grandfather.

From MEMORIES AND PORTRAITS, by
Robert Louis Stevenson (1850–96).

96

ACCUSING JUDGMENT

Stevenson's rage at the disparagement of Father Damien, the Catholic priest who volunteered to live and die with the lepers of Molokai, found expression in his Open Letter to Rev. Dr. Hyde of Honolulu. *He answers Dr. Hyde's indictment point by point; that Damien was coarse, dirty, headstrong, bigoted, and so reaches the most serious charge.*

DAMIEN *was not a pure man in his relations with women, etc.*

How do you know that? Is this the nature of the conversation in that house on Beretania Street which the cabman envied, driving past?—racy details of the misconduct of the poor peasant priest, toiling under the cliffs of Molokai?

Many have visited the station before me; they seem not to have heard the rumour. When I was there I heard many shocking tales, for my informants were men speaking with the plainness of the laity; and I heard plenty of complaints of Damien. Why was this never mentioned? and how came it to you in the retirement of your clerical parlour?

But I must not even seem to deceive you. This scandal, when I read it in your letter, was not new to me. I had heard it once before; and I must tell you how. There came to Samoa a man from Honolulu; he, in a public-house on the beach, volunteered the statement that Damien had "contracted the disease from having connection with the female lepers"; and I find a joy in telling you how the report was welcomed in a public-house. A man sprang to his feet; I am not at liberty to give his name, but from what I heard I doubt if you would care to have him to dinner in Beretania Street. "You miserable little ——" (here is a word I dare not print, it would so shock your ears). "You miserable little ——," he cried, "if the story were a thousand times true, can't you see you are a million times a lower —— for daring to repeat it?" I wish it could be told of you that when the report reached you in your house, perhaps after family worship, you had found in your soul enough holy anger to receive it with the same expressions; ay, even with that one which I dare not print; it would not need to have been blotted away, like Uncle Toby's oath, by the tears of the recording angel; it would have been counted to you for your brightest righteousness. But you have deliberately chosen the part of the man from Honolulu, and you have played it with improvements of your own. The man from Honolulu—miserable, leering creature—communicated the tale to a rude knot of beach-combing drinkers in a public-house, where (I will so far agree with your temperance opinion) man is not always at his noblest; and the man from Honolulu had himself been drinking—drinking, we may charitably fancy, to excess. It was to your "Dear Brother, the Reverend H. B. Gage," that you chose to communicate the sickening story; and the blue ribbon which adorns your portly bosom forbids me to allow you the extenuating plea that you were drunk when it was done. Your "dear brother"—a brother indeed—made haste to deliver up your letter (as a means of grace, perhaps) to the religious papers; where, after many months, I found and read and wondered at it; and whence I have now reproduced it for the wonder of others. And you and your dear brother have, by this cycle of operations, built up a contrast very edifying to examine in detail. The man whom you would not care to have to dinner, on the one side; on the other, the Reverend Dr. Hyde and the Reverend H. B. Gage: the Apia bar-room, the Honolulu manse.

But I fear you scarce appreciate how you appear to your fellow-men; and to bring it home to you, I will suppose your story to be true. I will suppose—and God forgive me for supposing it—that Damien faltered and stumbled in his narrow path of duty; I will suppose that, in the horror of his isolation, perhaps in the fever of incipient disease, he, who was doing so much more than he had sworn, failed in the letter of his priestly oath—he, who was so much a better man than either you or me, who did what we have never dreamed of daring—he too tasted of our common frailty. "O, Iago, the pity of it!" The least tender should be moved to tears; the most incredulous to prayer. And all that you could do was to pen your letter to the Reverend H. B. Gage!

From LAY MORALS, by Robert
Louis Stevenson (1850–94).

97

A MAN FULL OF COMPASSION

WHERE the reader of John Wesley's *Journal* will be shocked is when his attention is called to the public side of the country—to the state of the gaols, to Newgate, to Bethlehem, to the criminal code, to the brutality of so many of the judges and the harshness of the magistrates, to the supineness of the bishops, to the extinction in high places of the missionary spirit—in short, to the heavy slumber of humanity.

Wesley was full of compassion—of a compassion wholly free from hysterics and credulity. In public affairs his was the composed zeal of a Howard. His efforts to penetrate the dark places were long in vain. He says in his dry way: "They won't let me go to

Bedlam because they say I make the inmates mad, or into Newgate because I make them wicked." . . .

If you want to get into the last century, to feel its pulses throb beneath your finger, be content sometimes to leave the letters of Horace Walpole unturned, resist the drowsy temptation to waste your time over the learned triflers who sleep in the seventeen volumes of Nichols—nay, even deny yourself your annual reading of Boswell or your biennial retreat with Sterne, and ride up and down the country with the greatest force of the eighteenth century in England.

No man lived nearer the centre than John Wesley, neither Clive nor Pitt, neither Mansfield nor Johnson. You cannot cut him out of our national life. No single figure influenced so many minds, no single voice touched so many hearts. No other man did such a life's work for England. As a writer he has not achieved distinction. He was no Athanasius, no Augustine. He was ever a preacher and an organiser, a labourer in the service of humanity; but, happily for us, his *Journals* remain, and from them we can learn better than from anywhere else what manner of man he was, and the character of the times during which he lived and moved and had his being.

From MISCELLANIES, by Augustine Birrell (1850–1933).

98

NOTHING TO COMPLAIN OF

The scene is Lady Hunstanton's country house.

THE ARCHDEACON: Lord Illingworth has been most entertaining. I have never enjoyed myself more. (*Sees* MRS. ARBUTHNOT.) Ah, Mrs. Arbuthnot.

LADY HUNSTANTON (*to* DOCTOR DAUBENY): You see I have got Mrs. Arbuthnot to come to me at last.

THE ARCHDEACON: That is a great honour, Lady Hunstanton. Mrs. Daubeny will be quite jealous of you.

LADY HUNSTANTON: Ah, I am so sorry Mrs. Daubeny could not come with you to-night. Headache as usual, I suppose.

THE ARCHDEACON: Yes, Lady Hunstanton; a perfect martyr. But she is happiest alone. She is happiest alone.

.   .   .   .   .

LADY HUNSTANTON: Caroline, shall we all make a move to the music-room? Miss Worsley is going to play. You'll come too, dear Mrs. Arbuthnot, won't you? You don't know what a treat is in store for you. (*To* DOCTOR DAUBENY) I must really take Miss Worsley down some afternoon to the rectory. I should so much like dear Mrs. Daubeny to hear her on the violin. Ah, I forgot. Dear Mrs. Daubeny's hearing is a little defective, is it not?

THE ARCHDEACON: Her deafness is a great privation to her. She can't even hear my sermons now. She reads them at home. But she has many resources in herself, many resources.

LADY HUNSTANTON: She reads a good deal, I suppose?

THE ARCHDEACON: Just the very largest print. The eyesight is rapidly going. But she's never morbid, never morbid.

.   .   .   .   .

MRS. ARBUTHNOT: I am always at work, Lady Hunstanton.

LADY HUNSTANTON: Mrs. Daubeny embroiders a little, too, doesn't she?

THE ARCHDEACON: She was very deft with her needle once, quite a Dorcas. But the gout has crippled her fingers a good deal. She has not touched the tambour frame for nine or ten years. But she has many other amusements. She is very much interested in her own health.

LADY HUNSTANTON: Ah! that is always a nice distraction, is it not? Now, what are you talking about, Lord Illingworth? Do tell us.

.   .   .   .   .

FARQUHAR: Doctor Daubeny's carriage!

LADY HUNSTANTON: My dear Archdeacon! It is only half-past ten.

246

THE ARCHDEACON (*rising*): I am afraid I must go, Lady Hunstanton. Tuesday is always one of Mrs. Daubeny's bad nights.

LADY HUNSTANTON (*rising*): Well, I won't keep you from her. (*Goes with him towards door.*) I have told Farquhar to put a brace of partridge into the carriage. Mrs. Daubeny may fancy them.

THE ARCHDEACON: It is very kind of you, but Mrs. Daubeny never touches solids now. Lives entirely on jellies. But she is wonderfully cheerful, wonderfully cheerful. She has nothing to complain of.

From A WOMAN OF NO IMPORTANCE,
by Oscar Wilde (1854–1900).

99

SPOILED FROM THE CRADLE

CANDIDA: Never mind that just at present. Now I want you to look at this other boy here: my boy! spoiled from his cradle. We go once a fortnight to see his parents. You should come with us, Eugene, to see the pictures of the hero of that household. James as a baby! the most wonderful of all babies. James holding his first school prize, won at the ripe age of eight! James as the captain of his eleven! James in his first frock coat! James under all sorts of glorious circumstances! You know how strong he is (I hope he didn't hurt you): how clever he is: how happy. [*With deepening gravity*] Ask James's mother and his three sisters what it cost to save James the trouble of doing anything but be strong and clever and happy. Ask me what it costs to be James's mother and three sisters and wife and mother to his children all in one. Ask Prossy and Maria how troublesome the house is even when we have no visitors to help us to slice the onions. Ask the tradesmen who want to worry James and spoil his beautiful sermons who it is that puts them off. When there is money to give, he gives it: when there is money to refuse, I refuse it. I build a castle of comfort and indulgence and love for him, and stand sentinel always to keep little vulgar cares out. I make him master here, though he does not know it, and could not tell you a moment ago how it came to be so. [*With sweet irony*] And when he thought I might go away with you, his only anxiety was—what should become of me! And to tempt me to stay he offered me [*leaning forward to stroke his hair caressingly at each phrase*] his strength for my defence! his industry for my livelihood! his dignity for my position! his— [*relenting*] ah, I am mixing up your beautiful cadences and spoiling them, am I not, darling? [*She lays her cheek fondly against his.*]

MORELL [*quite overcome, kneeling beside her chair and embracing her with boyish ingenuousness*]: It's all true, every word. What I am you have made me with the labor of your hands and the love of your heart. You are my wife, my mother, my sisters: you are the sum of all loving care to me.

From CANDIDA, by George
Bernard Shaw (1856–).

100

THE UNREPENTANT VICAR

To me the best thing in or of the village of Coombe was the vicar himself, my put-upon host, a man of so blithe a nature, so human and companionable, that when I, a perfect stranger without an introduction or any excuse for such intrusion, came down like a wolf on his luncheon-table, he received me as if I had been an old friend or one of his own kindred, and freely gave up his time to me for the rest of that day. To count his years he was old: he had been vicar of Coombe for half a century, but he was a young man still and had never had a day's illness in his life—he did not know what a headache was. He smoked with me, and to prove that he was not a total abstainer he drank my health in a glass of port wine—very good wine. It was Coombe that did it—its peaceful life, isolated from a distracting world in that hollow hill, and the marvellous purity of its air. "Sitting there on my lawn," he said, "you are six hundred feet above the sea, although in a hollow four hundred feet deep." It was an ideal open-air room, round and green, with the sky for a roof. In winter it was sometimes very cold, and after a heavy fall of snow the scene was strange and impressive from the tiny village set in its stupendous dazzling white bowl. Not only on those rare arctic days, but at all times it was wonderfully quiet. The shout of a child or the peaceful crow of a cock was the loudest sound you heard. Once a gentleman from London town came down to spend a week at the parsonage. Towards evening on the very first day he grew restless and complained of the abnormal stillness. "I like a quiet place well enough," he exclaimed, "but this tingling silence I can't stand!" And stand it he wouldn't and didn't, for on the very next morning he took himself off. Many years had gone by, but the vicar could not forget the Londoner who had come down to invent a new way of describing the Coombe silence. His tingling phrase was a joy for ever.

He took me to the church—one of the tiniest churches in the country, just the right size for a church in a tiny village, and assured me that he had never once locked the door in his fifty years— day and night it was open to anyone to enter. It was a refuge and shelter from the storm and the tempest, and many a poor homeless wretch had found a dry place to sleep in that church during the last half a century. This man's feeling of pity and tenderness for the very poor, even the outcast and tramp, was a passion. But how strange all this would sound in the ears of many country clergy- men! How many have told me when I have gone to the parsonage to "borrow the key" that it had been found necessary to keep the church door locked, to prevent damage, thefts, etc. "Have *you* never had anything stolen?" I asked him. Yes, once, a great many years ago, the church plate had been taken away in the night. But it was recovered: the thief had taken it to the top of the hill and thrown it into the dew-pond there, no doubt intending to take it out and dispose of it at some more convenient time. But it was found, and had ever since then been kept safe at the vicarage. Nothing of value to tempt a man to steal was kept in the church.

He had never locked it, but once in fifty years it had been locked against him by the churchwardens. This happened in the days of the Joseph Arch agitation, when the agricultural labourer's condition was being hotly discussed throughout the country. The vicar's heart was stirred, for he knew better than most how hard these conditions were at Coombe and in the surrounding parishes. He took up the subject and preached on it in his own pulpit in a way that offended the landowners and alarmed the farmers in the district. The churchwardens, who were farmers, then locked him out of his church, and for two or three weeks there was no public worship in the parish of Coombe. Doubtless their action was applauded by all the substantial men in the neighbourhood; the others who lived in the cottages and were unsubstantial didn't matter. That storm blew over, but its consequences endured, one being that the inflammatory parson continued to be regarded with cold disapproval by the squires and their larger tenants. But the vicar himself was unrepentant and unashamed; on the contrary, he gloried in what he had said and done, and was proud to be able to relate that a quarter of a century later one of the two men who had taken that extreme course said to him, "We locked you out of your own church, but years have brought me to another mind about that question. I see it in a different light now and know that you were right and we were wrong."

From AFOOT IN ENGLAND, by
W. H. Hudson (1841–1922).

101

TO A LITERARY CRITIC

I WOULD not have you scorn archdeaconships,
    Or comfortable deaneries refuse;
Yet should I mourn, did these things quite eclipse
    Your mild and worthy Muse.

Nor shall I watch incurious your career;
    For though your heart on things above be set,
You lack not gifts such as avail us here,
    And may reach Lambeth yet.

From RETROGRESSION, by Sir
William Watson (1858–1935).

102

SOLDIERS OF THE CROSS

BY the way, talking of history, have you read Parkman's works? . . .
A New England man by birth, and writing principally of the early
history of the American Settlements and of French Canada, it is
perhaps excusable that he should have no great vogue in England,
but even among Americans I have found many who have not
read him. . . .

The Jesuits in Canada, is worth a reputation in itself. And how
noble a tribute is this which a man of Puritan blood pays to that
wonderful Order! He shows how in the heyday of their enthusiasm
these brave soldiers of the Cross invaded Canada as they did China
and every other place where danger was to be faced, and a horrible
death to be found. I don't care what faith a man may profess, or
whether he be a Christian at all, but he cannot read these true
records without feeling that the very highest that man has ever
evolved in sanctity and devotion was to be found among these
marvellous men. They were indeed the pioneers of civilisation, for
apart from doctrines they brought among the savages the highest
European culture, and in their own deportment an object-lesson
of how chastely, austerely, and nobly men could live. France has
sent myriads of brave men on to her battlefields, but in all her
long record of glory I do not think that she can point to any courage
so steadfast and so absolutely heroic as that of the men of the
Iroquois Mission.

How nobly they lived makes the body of the book, how serenely
they died forms the end to it. It is a tale which cannot even now be
read without a shudder—a nightmare of horrors. Fanaticism may

brace a man to hurl himself into oblivion, as the Mahdi's hordes did before Khartoum, but one feels that it is at least a higher development of such emotion, where men slowly and in cold blood endure so thankless a life, and welcome so dreadful an end. Every faith can equally boast its martyrs—a painful thought, since it shows how many thousands must have given their blood for error—but in testifying to their faith these brave men have testified to something more important still, to the subjugation of the body and to the absolute supremacy of the dominating spirit.

The story of Father Jogue is but one of many, and yet it is worth recounting, as showing the spirit of the men. He also was on the Iroquois Mission, and was so tortured and mutilated by his sweet parishioners that the very dogs used to howl at his distorted figure. He made his way back to France, not for any reason of personal rest or recuperation, but because he needed a special dispensation to say Mass. The Catholic Church has a regulation that a priest shall not be deformed, so that the savages with their knives had wrought better than they knew. He received his dispensation and was sent for by Louis XIV, who asked him what he could do for him. No doubt the assembled courtiers expected to hear him ask for the next vacant Bishopric. What he did actually ask for, as the highest favour, was to be sent back to the Iroquois Mission, where the savages signalised his arrival by burning him alive.

From THROUGH THE MAGIC DOOR, by
Sir Arthur Conan Doyle (1859–1930).

103

"PAPER WATTS"

EVERY few years, as one might say, the Auld Licht kirk gave way and buried its minister. The congregation turned their empty pockets inside out, and the minister departed in a farmer's cart. The scene was not an amusing one to those who looked on at it. To the Auld Lichts was then the humiliation of seeing their pulpit "supplied" on alternate Sabbaths by itinerant probationers or stickit ministers. When they were not starving themselves to support a pastor the Auld Lichts were saving up for a stipend. They retired with compressed lips to their looms, and weaved and weaved till they weaved another minister. Without the grief of parting with one minister there could not have been the transport of choosing another. To have had a pastor always might have made them vainglorious.

They were seldom longer than twelve months in making a selection, and in their haste they would have passed over Mr. Dishart and mated with a monster. Many years have elapsed since Providence flung Mr. Watts out of the Auld Licht kirk. Mr. Watts was a probationer who was tried before Mr. Dishart, and, though not so young as might have been wished, he found favour in many eyes. "Sluggard in the laft, awake!" he cried to Bell Whamond, who had forgotten herself, and it was felt that there must be good stuff in him. A breeze from Heaven exposed him on Communion Sabbath.

On the evening of this solemn day the door of the Auld Licht kirk was sometimes locked, and the congregation repaired, Bible in hand, to the commonty. They had a right to this common on the Communion Sabbath, but only took advantage of it when it was believed that more persons intended witnessing the evening service than the kirk would hold. On this day the attendance was always very great.

It was the Covenanters come back to life. To the summit of the slope a wooden box was slowly hurled by Hendry Munn and others, and round this the congregation quietly grouped to the tinkle of the cracked Auld Licht bell. With slow majestic tread the session advanced up the steep common with the little minister in their midst. He had the people in his hands now, and the more he squeezed them the better they were pleased. The travelling pulpit consisted of two compartments, the one for the minister and the other for Lang Tammas, but no Auld Licht thought that it looked like a Punch and Judy puppet show. This service on the common was known as the "tent preaching," owing to a tent's being frequently used instead of the box.

253

Mr. Watts was conducting the service on the commonty. It was a fine, still summer evening, and loud above the whisper of the burn from which the common climbs, and the laboured "pechs" of the listeners, rose the preacher's voice. The Auld Lichts in their rusty blacks (they must have been a more artistic sight in the olden days of blue bonnets and knee-breeches) nodded their heads in sharp approval, for though they could swoop down on a heretic like an eagle on carrion, they scented no prey. Even Lang Tammas, on whose nose a drop of water gathered when he was in his greatest fettle, thought that all was fair and above-board. Suddenly a rush of wind tore up the common, and ran straight at the pulpit. It formed in a sieve, and passed over the heads of the congregation, who felt it as a fan, and looked up in awe. Lang Tammas, feeling himself all at once grow clammy, distinctly heard the leaves of the pulpit Bible shiver. Mr. Watts's hands, outstretched to prevent a catastrophe, were blown against his side, and then some twenty sheets of closely-written paper floated into the air. There was a horrible, dead silence. The burn was roaring now. The minister, if such he can be called, shrunk back in his box, and, as if they had seen it printed in letters of fire on the heavens, the congregation realised that Mr. Watts, whom they had been on the point of calling, read his sermon. He wrote it out on pages the exact size of those in the Bible, and did not scruple to fasten these into the Holy Book itself. At theatres a sullen thunder of angry voices behind the scene represents a crowd in a rage, and such a low, long-drawn howl swept the common when Mr. Watts was found out. To follow a pastor who "read" seemed to the Auld Lichts like claiming heaven on false pretences. In ten minutes the session alone, with Lang Tammas and Hendry, were on the common. They were watched by many from afar off, and (when one comes to think of it now) looked a little curious jumping, like trout at flies, at the damning papers still fluttering in the air. The minister was never seen in our parts again, but he is still remembered as "Paper Watts."

Mr. Dishart in the pulpit was the reward of his upbringing. At ten he had entered the university. Before he was in his teens he was practising the art of gesticulation in his father's gallery pew.

From distant congregations people came to marvel at him. He was never more than comparatively young. So long as the pulpit trappings of the kirk at Thrums lasted he could be seen, once he was fairly under weigh with his sermon, but dimly in a cloud of dust. He introduced headaches. In a grand transport of enthusiasm he once flung his arms over the pulpit and caught Lang Tammas on the forehead. Leaning forward, with his chest on the cushions, he would pommel the Evil One with both hands, and then, whirling round to the left, shake his fist at Bell Whamond's neckerchief. With a sudden jump he would fix Pete Todd's youngest boy catching flies at the laft window. Stiffening unexpectedly, he would leap three times in the air, and then gather himself in a corner for a fearsome spring. When he wept he seemed to be laughing, and he laughed in a paroxysm of tears. He tried to tear the devil out of the pulpit rails. When he was not a teetotum he was a windmill. His pump position was the most appalling. Then he glared motionless at his admiring listeners, as if he had fallen into a trance with his arm upraised. The hurricane broke next moment. Nanny Sutie bore up under the shadow of the windmill—which would have been heavier had Auld Licht ministers worn gowns—but the pump affected her to tears. She was stone-deaf.

For the first year or more of his ministry an Auld Licht minister was a mouse among cats. Both in the pulpit and out of it they watched for unsound doctrine, and when he strayed they took him by the neck. Mr. Dishart, however, had been brought up in the true way, and seldom gave his people a chance. In time, it may be said, they grew despondent, and settled in their uncomfortable pews with all suspicion of lurking heresy allayed. It was only on such Sabbaths as Mr. Dishart changed pulpits with another minister that they cocked their ears and leant forward eagerly to snap the preacher up.

From THE AULD LICHT IDYLLS,
by Sir James Barrie (1862–1932).

104

LAST RITES FOR UNCLE PONDEREVO

When the soaring finances he has built up on patent medicine and publicity begin to topple, Uncle Ponderevo escapes to Normandy, but contracts pneumonia in his flight.

THOUGH nothing was said, I could feel that we were no longer regarded as simple, middle-class tourists ; about me, as I went, I perceived almost as though it trailed visibly, the prestige of Finance and a criminal notoriety. Local personages of a plump and prosperous quality appeared in the inn making inquiries, the Luzon priest became helpful, people watched our window, and stared at me as I went to and fro; and then we had a raid from a little English clergyman and his amiable, capable wife in severely Anglican blacks, who swooped down upon us like virtuous but resolute vultures from the adjacent village of Saint Jean de Pollack.

The clergyman was one of those odd types that oscillate between remote country towns in England and the conduct of English Church services on mutual terms in enterprising hotels abroad, a tremulous, obstinate little being with sporadic hairs upon his face, spectacles, a red button nose, and aged black raiment. He was evidently enormously impressed by my uncle's monetary greatness, and by his own inkling of our identity, and he shone and brimmed over with tact and fussy helpfulness. He was eager to share the watching of the bedside with me, he proffered services with both hands, and as I was now getting into touch with affairs in London again, and trying to disentangle the gigantic details of the smash from the papers I had succeeded in getting from Biarritz, I accepted his offers pretty generously, and began the studies in modern finance that lay before me. I had got so out of touch with the old traditions of religion, that I overlooked the manifest possibility of his attacking my poor sinking vestiges of an uncle with theological solicitudes. My attention was called to that, however, very speedily by a polite but urgent quarrel between himself and the Basque landlady as to the necessity of her hanging a cheap crucifix in the shadow over the bed, where it might catch my uncle's eye, where, indeed, I found it had caught his eye.

"Good Lord!" I cried; "is *that* still going on!"

That night the little clergyman watched, and in the small hours he raised a false alarm that my uncle was dying, and made an extraordinary fuss. He raised the house. I shall never forget that scene, I think, which began with a tapping at my bedroom door just after I had fallen asleep, and his voice,—

"If you want to see your uncle before he goes, you must come now."

The stuffy little room was crowded when I reached it, and lit by three flickering candles. I felt I was back in the eighteenth century. There lay my poor uncle amidst indescribably tumbled bedclothes, weary of life beyond measure, weary and rambling, and the little clergyman trying to hold his hand and his attention, and repeating over and over again,—

"Mr. Ponderevo, Mr. Ponderevo, it is all right. It is all right. Only Believe! 'Believe on Me, and ye shall be saved'!"

. . . . .

I replaced the little clergyman on the chair by the bedside, and he hovered about the room.

"I think," he whispered to me mysteriously, as he gave place to me, "I believe—it is well with him."

I heard him trying to render the stock phrases of Low Church piety into French for the benefit of the stolid man in grey alpaca. Then he knocked a glass off the table, and scrabbled for the fragments. From the first I doubted the theory of an immediate death. I consulted the doctor in urgent whispers. I turned round to get champagne, and nearly fell over the clergyman's legs. He was on his knees at the additional chair the Basque landlady had got on my arrival, and he was praying aloud, "Oh, Heavenly Father, have mercy on this thy Child. . . ." I hustled him up and out of the way, and in another minute he was down at another chair praying again, and barring the path of the *religieuse* who had found me the corkscrew. Something put into my head that tremendous blasphemy of Carlyle's about "the last mew of a drowning kitten."

257

He found a third chair vacant presently; it was as if he was playing a game.

"Good Heavens," said I, "we must clear these people out," and with a certain urgency I did.

I had a temporary lapse of memory, and forgot all my French. I drove them out mainly by gesture, and opened the window to the universal horror. I intimated the death scene was postponed, and, as a matter of fact, my uncle did not die until the next night.

I did not let the little clergyman come near him again, and I was watchful for any sign that his mind had been troubled. But he made none. He talked once about "that parson chap."

"Didn't bother you?" I asked.

"Wanted something," he said.

I kept silence, listening keenly to his mutterings. I understood him to say, "they wanted too much." His face puckered like a child's going to cry. "You can't *get* a safe six per cent.," he said. I had for a moment a wild suspicion that those urgent talks had not been altogether spiritual, but that, I think, was a quite unworthy and unjust suspicion. The little clergyman was as simple and honest as the day. My uncle was simply generalising about his class.

From TONO BUNGAY, by
H. G. Wells (1866–1945).

105

BISHOP LIKEMAN EXPOUNDS

In the moral torment of the First World War, the Bishop of Princhester has a vision of the Unknown God. Feeling that he can no longer remain a paid exponent of Anglicanism, he decides to consult his old friend and helper, Bishop Likeman.

SINCE the days when the bishop had been only plain Mr. Scrope, the youngest and most helpful of Likeman's historical band of curates, their friendship had continued. Likeman had been a second father to him; in particular his tact and helpfulness had shone during those days of doubt and anxiety when dear old Queen Victoria, God's representative on earth, had obstinately refused, at the eleventh hour, to make him a bishop. She had those pig-headed fits, and she was touchy about the bishops. She had liked Scrope on account of the excellence of his German pronunciation, but she had been irritated by newspaper paragraphs—nobody could ever find out who wrote them and nobody could ever find out who showed them to the old lady—anticipating his elevation. She had gone very red in the face and stiffened in the Guelphic manner whenever Scrope was mentioned, and so a rich harvest of spiritual life had remained untilled for some months. Likeman had brought her round.

It seemed arguable that Scrope owed some explanation to Likeman before he came to any open breach with the Establishment.

He found Likeman perceptibly older and more shrivelled on account of the war, but still as sweet and lucid and subtle as ever. His voice sounded more than ever like a kind old woman's.

He sat buried in his cushions—for "nowadays I must save every scrap of vitality"—and for a time contented himself with drawing out his visitor's story.

Of course, one does not talk to Likeman of visions or intuitions. "I am disturbed, I find myself getting out of touch"; that was the bishop's tone.

Occasionally Likeman nodded slowly, as a physician might do at the recital of familiar symptoms. "Yes," he said, "I have been through most of this. . . . A little different in the inessentials. . . . How clear you are!

"You leave our stupid old Trinities—as I left them long ago," said old Likeman, with his lean hand feeling and clawing at the arm of his chair.

"*But*——!"

The old man raised his hand and dropped it. "You go away from it all—straight as a line. I did. You take the wings of the morning and fly to the uttermost parts of the earth. And there you find——"

He held up a lean finger, and inclined it to tick off each point.

"Fate—which is God the Father, the Power of the Heart, which is God the Son, and that Light which comes in upon us from the inaccessible Godhead, which is God the Holy Spirit."

"But I know of no God the Holy Spirit, and Fate is not God at all. I saw in my vision one sole God, uncrucified, militant—conquering and to conquer."

Old Likeman stared. "You *saw!*"

The Bishop of Princhester had not meant to go so far. But he stuck to his words. "As if I saw with my eyes. A God of light and courage."

"You have had *visions*, Scrope?"

"I seemed to see."

"No, you have just been dreaming dreams."

"But why should one not see?"

"*See!* The things of the spirit. These symbols as realities! These metaphors as men walking!"

"You talk like an agnostic."

"We are all agnostics. Our creeds are expressions of ourselves and our attitude and relationship to the unknown. The triune God is just the form of our need and disposition. I have always assumed that you took that for granted. Who has ever really seen or heard or felt God? God is neither of the senses nor of the mind; he is of the soul. You are realistic, you are materialistic. . . ."

His voice expostulated.

The Bishop of Princhester reflected. The vision of God was far off among his memories now, and difficult to recall. But he said at last: "I believe there is a God and that he is as real a person as you or I. And he is not the theological God we set out before the world."

"Personification," said Likeman. "In the eighteenth century they used to draw beautiful female figures as Science and Mathematics. Young men have loved Science—and Freedom—as Pygmalion loved Galatea. Have it so if you will. Have a visible person for your Deity. But let me keep up my—spirituality."

"Your spirituality seems as thin as a mist. Do you really believe—anything?"

"*Everything!*" said Likeman emphatically, sitting up with a transitory vigour. "Everything we two have ever professed together.

I believe that the creeds of my church do express all that can possibly be expressed in the relationship of—*That*"—he made a comprehensive gesture with a twist of his hand upon its wrist—"to the human soul. I believe that they express it as well as the human mind can express it. Where they seem to be contradictory or absurd, it is merely that the mystery is paradoxical. I believe that the story of the Fall and of the Redemption is a complete symbol, that to add to it or to subtract from it or to alter it is to diminish its truth; if it seems incredible at this point or that, then simply I admit my own mental defect. And I believe in our Church, Scrope, as the embodied truth of religion, the divine instrument in human affairs. I believe in the security of its tradition, in the complete and entire soundness of its teaching, in its essential authority and divinity."

He paused, and put his head a little on one side and smiled sweetly. "And now can you say I do not believe?"

"But the historical Christ, the man Jesus?"

"A life may be a metaphor. Why not? Yes, I believe it all. All."

The Bishop of Princhester was staggered by this complete acceptance. "I see you believe all you profess," he said, and remained for a moment or so rallying his forces.

"Your vision—if it was a vision—I put it to you, was just some single aspect of divinity," said Likeman. "We make a mistake in supposing that Heresy has no truth in it. Most heresies are only a disproportionate apprehension of some essential truth. Most heretics are men who have suddenly caught a glimpse through the veil of some particular verity. . . . They are dazzled by that aspect. All the rest has vanished. . . . They are obsessed. You are obsessed clearly by this discovery of the militancy of God. God the Son—as Hero. And you want to go out to the simple worship of that one aspect. You want to go out to a Dissenter's tent in the wilderness, instead of staying in the Great Temple of the Ages."

Was that true?

For some moments it sounded true.

The Bishop of Princhester sat frowning and looking at that. Very far away was the vision now of that golden Captain who bade him come. Then at a thought the bishop smiled.

"The Great Temple of the Ages," he repeated. "But do you remember the trouble we had when the little old Queen was so pigheaded?"

"Oh! I remember, I remember," said Likeman, smiling with unshaken confidence. "Why not?"

"For sixty years all we bishops in what you call the Great Temple of the Ages, were appointed and bullied and kept in our places by that pink irascible bit of dignity. . . . I remember how at the time I didn't dare betray my boiling indignation even to you—I scarcely dared admit it to myself. . . ."

He paused.

"It doesn't matter at all," and old Likeman waved it aside.

"Not at all," he confirmed, waving again.

"I spoke of the whole church of Christ on earth," he went on. "These things, these Victorias and Edwards and so on, are temporary accidents—just as the severance of an Anglican from a Roman communion and a Greek orthodox communion are temporary accidents. You will remark that wise men in all ages have been able to surmount the difficulty of these things. Why? Because they knew that in spite of all these splits and irregularities and defacements—like the cracks and crannies and lichens on a cathedral wall—the building held good, that it was shelter and security. There is no other shelter and security. And so I come to your problem. Suppose it is true that you have this incidental vision of the militant aspect of God, and he isn't, as you see him now that is,—he isn't like the Trinity, he isn't like the Creed, he doesn't seem to be related to the Church, then comes the question, are you going out for that?   And whither do you go if you do go out? The Church remains. We alter doctrines not by changing the words but by shifting the accent. We can under-accentuate below the threshold of consciousness."

"But *can* we?"

"We do. Where's Hell now? Eighty years ago it warmed the whole Church. It was—as some atheist or other put it the other day—the central heating of the soul. But never mind that point now. Consider the essential question, the question of breaking with the church. Ask yourself, whither would you go? To become an oddity! A Dissenter. A Negative. Self emasculated. The spirit that denies. You would just go out. You would just cease to serve Religion. That would be all. You wouldn't *do* anything. The Church would go on; everything else would go on. Only you would be lost in the outer wilderness."

"But then——"

Old Likeman leant forward and pointed a bony finger. "Stay in the Church and modify it. Bring this new light of yours to the altar."

There was a little pause.

"No man," the bishop thought aloud, "putteth new wine into old bottles."

Old Likeman began to speak and had a fit of coughing. "Some of these texts—whuff, whuff—like a conjuror's hat—whuff—make 'em—fit anything."

A man-servant appeared and handed a silver box of lozenges into which the old bishop dipped with a trembling hand.

"Tricks of that sort," he said, "won't do, Scrope—among professionals.

"And besides," he was inspired; "true religion is old wine—as old as the soul.

"You are a bishop in the Church of Christ on Earth," he summed it up. "And you want to become a detached and wandering Ancient Mariner from your shipwreck of faith with something to explain—that nobody wants to hear. You are going out—— I suppose you have means?"

The old man awaited the answer to his abrupt enquiry with a handful of lozenges.

"No," said the Bishop of Princhester, "*practically*—I haven't."

"My dear boy!" it was as if they were once more rector and curate. "My dear brother! do you know what the value of an ex-bishop is in the ordinary labour market?"

"I have never thought of that."

"Evidently. You have a wife and children?"

"Five daughters."

"And your wife married you—I remember, she married you soon after you got that living in St. John's Wood. I suppose she took it for granted that you were *fixed* in an ecclesiastical career. That was implicit in the transaction."

"I haven't looked very much at that side of the matter yet," said the Bishop of Princhester.

"It shouldn't be a decisive factor," said Bishop Likeman, "not decisive. But it will weigh. It should weigh. . . ."

The old man opened out fresh aspects of the case. His argument was for delay, for deliberation. He went on to a wider set of considerations. A man who has held the position of a bishop for some years is, he held, no longer a free man in matters of opinion. He has become an official part of a great edifice which supports the faith of multitudes of simple and dependant believers. He has no right to indulge recklessly in intellectual and moral integrities. He may understand, but how is the flock to understand? He may get his own soul clear, but what will happen to them? He will just break away their supports, astonish them, puzzle them, distress them, deprive them of confidence, convince them of nothing.

"Intellectual egotism may be as grave a sin," said Bishop Likeman, "as physical selfishness.

"Assuming even that you are absolutely right," said Bishop Likeman, "aren't you still rather in the position of a man who insists upon Swedish exercises and a strengthening dietary on a raft?"

"I think you have made out a case for delay," said his hearer.

"Three months."

The Bishop of Princhester conceded three months.

"Including every sort of service. Because, after all, even supposing it is damnable to repeat prayers and creeds you do not believe in, and administer sacraments you think superstition, *nobody can be damned but yourself*. On the other hand if you express doubts that are not yet perfectly digested—you experiment with the souls of others. . . ."

From THE SOUL OF A BISHOP,
by H. G. Wells (1866–1945).

106

RELIGIOUS DIFFICULTIES

Queen Victoria has unexpectedly called on the Dean of Windsor to consult him about her religious difficulties. The Dean, who hurried in from a game of tennis, has succeeded in answering Her Majesty's questions about the Book of Jonah.

THE QUEEN: Religion is sometimes very puzzling, is it not?

THE DEAN: It has that quality, Ma'am; but the difficulties have their value. We should not wish them altogether away.

THE QUEEN: Yet I always want to know more—about the next world, I mean.

THE DEAN: That, Ma'am, is understandable—especially under the shadow of such a bereavement as your own. Life is a great mystery.

THE QUEEN: But not so great a mystery as death.

THE DEAN: No, no. Of course to us, here and now, death necessarily seems a terrible and overwhelming event—because life seems to end *with* it. But when we have got beyond it, will it not surely look very different?

THE QUEEN: Yes, very different, no doubt: as one looks *down* a hill, after having come up it.

THE DEAN: Quite so; and therefore, as one looks back, smaller and less important. If one may compare small things to great—a visit to the dentist provides us with a similar comparison. When one goes to have a tooth out, the ordeal beforehand seems great; but when it *is* out, the ordeal is over.

THE QUEEN: Ah, yes! I have only had two teeth out in my life; and that was under gas; so I knew nothing about it.

THE DEAN: Your Majesty has, indeed, been fortunate.

THE QUEEN: And people, when they are dying, *are* generally unconscious, I believe?

THE DEAN: Yes, I suppose that is so. A merciful provision.

THE QUEEN: The Prince was so, during his last hours.

THE DEAN: Ah, indeed? Yes.

THE QUEEN: And that, of course—the added sense of separation while still alive—was a great grief to me.

THE DEAN: But to him a blessing.

THE QUEEN: I wonder how long the unconsciousness lasts?

THE DEAN: After death, Ma'am?

THE QUEEN: Yes. Do we wake up suddenly; or do we sleep for a time?

THE DEAN: That, Ma'am, is one of the mysteries which it is not given us to know.

THE QUEEN: Still, I would *like* to know. The Roman Catholics don't seem to have any doubt about it. Why should *we*?

THE DEAN: The Roman Church, Ma'am, has always pretended to know more than we have any warrant for in Holy Scripture.

THE QUEEN: Oh, yes; of course, I know they are often in many ways superstitious. Still, one would like, about a thing of that sort, to have some assurance. And why shouldn't one? When one goes into the next world—not to meet those who are *waiting* for us, without waste of time, seems such a pity!

THE DEAN: It does, Ma'am, it does! To mere human understanding it must, indeed, seem so. Still, we are bound to believe that, in the other world, everything has been arranged for the best. Indeed, we *must* believe it.

THE QUEEN (*reluctantly*): Yes; I suppose so. . . . Life in the next world, when we really get to it, will be very interesting.

THE DEAN: Very; very.

THE QUEEN: So much to see—and hear—and learn.

THE DEAN: Yes, indeed, Ma'am. Your Majesty has evidently thought deeply on these subjects.

THE QUEEN: I have. Since my beloved Husband was taken from me, naturally my thoughts have followed him a good deal.

THE DEAN: Ah, yes. Has your Majesty a great sense of—nearness, shall I say? As if death were something very slight and unreal?

THE QUEEN: No. It's the separation I feel. I always think of him as he *was*, here with me on earth: so handsome, so thoughtful, so affectionate, so attentive to all my wishes. And taken from me so soon! No one ever knew his true value, his greatness, his goodness, as I did.

THE DEAN: That, Ma'am, is understandable. Who could? It was a terrible bereavement.

THE QUEEN: It would be very disappointing to me to think that death was not going to end it.

THE DEAN: Oh, but it will, Ma'am, of course!

THE QUEEN: *At once*, I mean.

THE DEAN: But however long the unconsciousness may last, it will *seem* at once. When we wake we shall surely be in the presence of those we love.

THE QUEEN: But there will be others, too.

THE DEAN: Undoubtedly.

THE QUEEN: *Many* others—of all ages.

THE DEAN: Yes: parents and children—the old and the young together.

THE QUEEN: I meant—of other ages, in history.

THE DEAN: Ah, yes; and how interesting! To meet all the great characters of history.

THE QUEEN: Yes; the English Kings. I wonder how many of them will be there. Not all, I'm afraid.

THE DEAN: It will be a very interesting encounter for your Majesty; quite an historic event.

THE QUEEN: Yes. I wonder what I shall think of them. Some of them were not what they should have been. Still, they were all my ancestors, or my relatives—quite near relations, some of them.

THE DEAN: But most of them rather distant.

THE QUEEN: Yes, and sometimes distance has its advantages.

THE DEAN: And its interest also. So the further back you go in history, the more interesting it will be:—Julius Cæsar.

THE QUEEN: One hardly thinks of Julius Cæsar as being in Heaven, does one?

THE DEAN: I suppose not, Ma'am. Still, let us hope!

THE QUEEN: Yes; hope is a Christian duty. But I haven't much of it in some directions.

THE DEAN: Still, Ma'am, however far back in history we go, there will always be the great characters of Holy Scripture. Of them, at least, one may be certain: *They* will be there.

THE QUEEN: Yes; that will be very interesting. Moses, and the Prophets; and Elijah—a most interesting character, especially in the way his life on earth ended. And Isaiah, who wrote so beautifully.

THE DEAN: Ah, yes; and the great Psalmist, David. To meet him will indeed be——

THE QUEEN: David? I hope not!

THE DEAN (*astonished*): I beg pardon, your Majesty?

THE QUEEN: I said—"I hope *not*." I do not wish to meet King David anywhere.

THE DEAN: I really fail to know why your Majesty should——

THE QUEEN: He was not the sort of person I could ever wish to know. His conduct about Bathsheba. . . .

THE DEAN: One has to make allowance, Ma'am, for the age in which people lived. Moral standards have changed.

THE QUEEN: He knew he was doing wrong, as well as I do.

THE DEAN: He also repented.

THE QUEEN: I'm not so sure about *that*!

THE DEAN: Oh, but surely!

THE QUEEN: There was Abishag, who came later. He wasn't married to Abishag.

THE DEAN: Well, Ma'am, then what about Solomon?

THE QUEEN: Solomon was a wise King, but he was foolish about women.

THE DEAN: Your Majesty is a shrewd judge of character.

THE QUEEN: I've had a good deal of experience, Mr. Dean: my Uncles—I don't mind telling you.

THE DEAN: Ah, yes, yes. But at your Majesty's Court things have become so different—thanks to your Majesty.

THE QUEEN: The Prince, my dear Husband, set such an example to everybody.

THE DEAN: Ah, yes. Indeed, indeed!

THE QUEEN (*rising*): Well, Mr. Dean, I have taken up quite enough of your valuable time; and now—I must go. But don't play any more tennis. At your age it is too risky.

THE DEAN: I will pay all attention to your Majesty's advice, for which I am duly grateful.

From VICTORIA REGINA, by
Laurence Housman (1865–   ).

107

AN UNWORLDLY CLERIC

CONRAD NOEL, the son of a poet and the grandson of a peer, had all the incalculable elements of the eccentric aristocrat; the sort of eccentric aristocrat who so often figures as a particularly destructive democrat. That great gentleman, Cunninghame Graham, whom I knew more slightly but always respected profoundly, was the same sort of uncompromising rebel; but he had a sort of Scottish seriousness similar to Spanish seriousness; while Noel's humour was half English and half Irish but always mainly humorous. He delighted, of course, in shocking people and taking a rise out of them; I remember how he used to say, shaking his head with an air of brooding concentration: "Ah, how little people know about the work of a clergyman's life; such demands on him! Such distracting and different duties! All the afternoon behind the scenes at the Butterfly Theatre, talking to Poppy Pimpernel; all the evening doing a pub-crawl with Jack Bootle; back to the club after dinner, etc." As a matter of fact, he occupied much of his time with things perhaps equally fantastic but more intellectual. He had a love of nosing out the head-quarters of incredible or insane sects; and wrote an amusing record of them called "Byways of Belief." He had a special affection for an old gentleman with long grey whiskers, living in the suburbs; whose name, it appeared, was King Solomon David Jesus. This prophet was not afraid to protest, as a prophet should, against what he considered the pomps and vanities of this world. He began the interview by coldly rebuking Conrad Noel for having sent in a visiting-card inscribed, "Rev. Conrad Noel"; since all such official titles were abolished in the New Dispensation. Conrad delicately insinuated, in self-defence, that there seemed to be something about calling oneself Solomon David Jesus, which might raise rather grave problems of identity and a somewhat formidable historical comparison. And anyhow, an old gentleman who called himself King could hardly insist on such severe republican simplicity. However, the monarch explained that his title had been given him by an actual voice speaking out of the sky; and the Rev. Conrad admitted that he could not claim that his visiting-card had been thus written at dictation. . . .

It was when I was staying with Conrad Noel, afterwards famous as the parson who flew the Red Flag from his church at Thaxted in Essex, that I happened to be dressing for dinner and made the (it seems to me) very excusable error of mistaking his black clerical trousers for my evening ones. I trust I violated no grave ecclesiastical law, relative to the unlawful assumption of priestly vestments; but Conrad Noel himself was always fairly casual in the matter of costume. The world thought him a very Bohemian sort of clergyman, as it now thinks him a very Bolshevist sort of clergyman. The world would be wiser if it realised that, in spite of this, he was and is a very unworldly sort of clergyman; and much too unworldly to be judged rightly by the world. I did not always agree with his attitude, and I do not now altogether agree with his politics; but I have always known that he glowed with conviction and the simplicity of the fighting spirit. But in those days his external eccentricity was more provocative than is a red rag to a bull or a red flag to a bully. He delighted in making the quaintest combinations of costume made up of the clerical, the artistic and the proletarian. He took great pleasure in appearing in correct clerical clothes, surmounted with a sort of hairy or furry cap, making him look like an æsthetic rat-catcher. I had the pleasure of walking with him, thus attired, right across the vast stretch of South London, starting from Blackfriars Bridge and going on till we saw the green hills beyond Croydon; a very interesting expedition too rarely undertaken by those from the richer side of the river. I also remember one occasion when I was walking away from some meeting with him and with Dr. Percy Dearmer, then chiefly famous as an authority on the history of ritual and vestments. Dr. Dearmer was in the habit of walking about in a cassock and biretta which he had carefully reconstructed as being of exactly the right pattern for an Anglican or Anglo-Catholic priest; and he was humorously grieved when its strictly traditional and national character was misunderstood by the little boys in the street. Somebody would call out, "No Popery," or "To hell with the Pope," or some other sentiment of larger and more liberal religion. And Percy Dearmer would sternly stop them and say, "Are you aware that this is the precise costume in which Latimer went to the stake?"

From AUTOBIOGRAPHY, by G.
K. Chesterton (1874–1936).

108

THEY LOVE NOT LIGHT

Crazed after a night of gross debauchery, Saul Kane, the prize-fighting poacher, leaves "The Lion."

Across the way by almshouse pump
I see old puffing parson stump.
Old parson, red-eyed as a ferret
From nightly wrestlings with the spirit;
I ran across, and barred his path.
His turkey gills went red as wrath

And then he froze, as parsons can.
"The police will deal with you, my man."
"Not yet," said I, "not yet they won't;
And now you'll hear me, like or don't.
The English Church both is and was
A subsidy of Caiaphas.
I don't believe in Prayer nor Bible,
They're lies all through, and you're a libel,
A libel on the Devil's plan
When first he miscreated man.
You mumble through a formal code
To get which martyrs burned and glowed.
I look on martyrs as mistakes,
But still they burned for it at stakes;
Your only fire's the jolly fire
Where you can guzzle port with Squire,
And back and praise his damned opinions
About his temporal dominions.
You let him give the man who digs,
A filthy hut unfit for pigs,
Without a well, without a drain,
With mossy thatch that lets in rain,
Without a 'lotment, 'less he rent it,
And never meat, unless he scent it,
But weekly doles of 'leven shilling
To make a grown man strong and willing
To do the hardest work on earth
And feed his wife when she gives birth,
And feed his little children's bones.
I tell you, man, the Devil groans.
With all your main and all your might
You back what is against what's right.

"You teach the ground-down starving man
That Squire's greed's Jehovah's plan.
You get his learning circumvented
Lest it should make him discontented

(Better a brutal, starving nation
Than men with thoughts above their station),
You let him neither read nor think,
You goad his wretched soul to drink
And then to jail, the drunken boor;
O sad intemperance of the poor.
You starve his soul till it's rapscallion,
Then blame his flesh for being stallion.
You send your wife around to paint
The golden glories of "restraint."
How moral exercise bewild'rin'
Would soon result in fewer children.
You work a day in Squire's fields
And see what sweet restraint it yields;
A woman's day at turnip picking,
Your heart's too fat for plough or ricking."

I said my piece, and when I'd said it,
I'll do old purple parson credit,
He sunk (as sometimes parsons can)
His coat's excuses in the man.
"You think that Squire and I are kings
Who made the existing state of things,
And made it ill. I answer No,
States are not made, nor patched; they grow,
Grow slow through centuries of pain
And grow correctly in the main. . . .
This state is dull and evil, both,
I keep it in the path of growth;
You think the Church an outworn fetter;
Kane, keep it, till you've built a better.
And keep the existing social state;
I quite agree it's out of date,
One does too much, another shirks,
Unjust, I grant; but still . . . it works.
To get the whole world out of bed
And washed, and dressed, and warmed, and fed,

To work, and back to bed again,
Believe me, Saul, costs worlds of pain. . . ."
He took his snuff, and wheezed a greeting,
And waddled off to mothers' meeting;
I hung me head upon my chest,
I give old purple parson best,
For while the Plough tips round the Pole
The trained mind outs the upright soul,
As Jesus said the trained mind might,
Being wiser than the sons of light,
But trained men's minds are spread so thin
They let all sorts of darkness in;
Whatever light man finds they doubt it,
They love not light, but talk about it.

From THE EVERLASTING MERCY,
by John Masefield (1875–   ).

109

A MESSAGE FROM THE LORD

Hazel Woodus, a prey to the hard, remorseless lust of the petty squire of Undern; her marriage to Edward Marston, the minister of God's Little Mountain, in whom almost alone of human creatures she finds tenderness; and the tragic end when she tries to save the tame fox cub from the pitiless human hunters—the progress of Gone to Earth, *as John Buchan says, "is as simple and inevitable as a Greek tragedy."*

BUT upon their love—Edward's dawn of content and Hazel's laughter—broke a loud imperious knocking. Edward went to the door. Outside stood Mr. James, the old man with the elf-locks who shared the honey prizes with Abel, two farmers from the other side of the Mountain, Martha's brother, and the man with the red braces who had won the race when Reddin turned.

They coughed.

"Will you come in?" asked Edward.

They straggled in, very much embarrassed.

Hazel wished them good morning.

"This young woman," Mr. James said, " might, I think, absent herself."

"Would you rather go or stay, Hazel?"

"Stay along of you, Ed'ard."

Hazel had divined that something threatened Edward.

They sat down, very dour. Foxy had retired under the table. The shaggy old man surveyed the bird.

"A nice pet, a bird," he said. "Minds me of a throstle I kep'——"

"Now, now, Thomas! Business!" said Mr. James.

"Yes. Get to the point," said Edward.

James began.

"We've come, minister, six God-fearing men, and me spokesman, being deacon; and we 'ope as good will come of this meeting, and that the Lord'll bless our endeavour. And now, I think, maybe a little prayer?"

"I think not."

"As you will, minister. There are times when folk avoid prayer as the sick avoid medicine."

James had a resonant voice, and it was always pitched on the intoning note. Also, he accented almost every other syllable.

"We bring you the Lord's message, minister. I speak for 'em."

"You are sure?"

"Has not He answered us each and severally with a loud voice in the night-watches?"

"Ah! He 'as! True! Yes, yes!" the crowd murmured.

"And what we are to say," James went on, "is that the adulteress must go. You must put her away at once and publicly; and if she will make open confession of the sin, it will be counted to you for righteousness."

Edward came and stood in front of Hazel.

"Had you," James continued in trumpet tones, "had you, when she played the sinner with Mr. Reddin, Esquire, leading a respectable gentleman into open sin, chastened and corrected her—ay, given her the bread of affliction and the water of affliction and taken counsel with us——"

"Ah! there's wisdom in counsel!" said one of the farmers, a man with crafty eyes.

"Then," James went on, "all would 'a been well. But now to spare would be death."

"Ah, everlasting death!" came the echoes.

"And now" (James' face seemed to Hazel to wear the same expression as when he pocketed the money) "now there is but one cure. She must go to a reformatory. There she'll be disciplined. She'll be made to repent."

He looked as if he would like to be present.

They all leant forward. The younger men were sorry for Edward. None of them were sorry for Hazel. There was a curious likeness, as they leant forward, between them and the questing hounds below.

"And then?" Edward prompted, his face set, tremors running along the nerves under the skin.

"Then we would expect you to make a statement in a sermon, or in any way you chose, that you'd cast your sins from you, that you would never speak or write to this woman again, and that you were at peace with the Lord."

"And then?"

"Then, sir"—Mr. James rose—"we should onst again be proud to take our minister by the 'and, knowing it was but the deceitfulness of youth that got the better of you, and the wickedness of an 'ooman."

Feeling that this was hardly enough to tempt Edward, the man with the crafty eyes said:

"And if in the Lord's wisdom He sees fit to take her, then, sir, you can choose a wife from among us." (He was thinking of his daughter.) He said no more.

Edward was speaking. His voice was low, but not a man ever forgot a word he said.

"Filthy little beasts!" he said, but without acrimony, simply in weariness. "I should like to shoot you; but you rule the world—little pot-bellied gods. There is no other God. Your last suggestion" (he looked at them with a smile of so peculiar a quality and such strange eyes that the old beeman afterwards said "It took you in the stomach") "was worthy of you. It's not enough that unselfish love can't save. It's not enough" (his face quivered horribly) "that love is allowed to torture the loved one; but you must come with your foul minds and eyes to 'view the corpse.' And you know nothing—nothing."

"We know the facts," said James.

"Facts! What are facts? I could flog you naked through the fields, James, for your stupidity alone."

There was a general smile, James being a corpulent man. He shrank. Then his feelings found relief in spite.

"If you don't dismiss the female, I'll appeal to the Presbytery," he said, painfully pulling himself together.

"What for?"

"Notice for you."

"No need. We're going. What d'you suppose I should do here? There's no Lord's Day and no Lord's house, for there's no Lord. For goodness' sake turn the chapel into a cowhouse!"

They blinked. Their minds did not take in his meaning, which was like the upper wind that blows coldly from mountain to mountain and does not touch the plain. They busied themselves with what they could grasp.

"If you take that woman with you, you'll be accurst," said James. "I suppose," he went on, and his tone was, as he afterwards said to his wife with complacency, "very nasty"—"I suppose you dunno what they're all saying, and what I've come to believe, in this shocking meeting, to be God's truth."

"I don't know or care."

"They're saying you've made a tidy bit."

"What d'you mean?"

James hesitated. Filthy thoughts were all very well, but it was awkward to get them into righteous words.

"Well, dear me! they're saying as there was an arrangement betwixt you and 'im—on the gel's account" (the old beeman tried to hush him) "and as cheques signed 'John Reddin' went to your bank. Dear me!"

Slowly the meaning of this dawned on Edward. He sat down and put his hands up before his face. He was broken, not so much by the insult to himself as by the fixed idea that he had exposed Hazel to all this. He traced all her troubles and mistakes back to himself, blaming his own love for them. While he had been fighting for her happiness, he had given her a mortal wound, and none had warned him. That was why he was sure there was no God.

They sat round and looked at their work with some compunction. The old beeman cleared his throat several times.

"O' course," he said, "we know it inna true, minister. Mr. James shouldna ha' taken it on his lips." He looked defiantly at James out of his mild brown eyes.

Edward did not hear what he said. Hazel was puzzling over James' meaning. Why had he made Edward like this? Love gave her a quickness that she did not naturally possess, and at last she understood. It was one of the few insults that could touch her, because it was levelled at her primitive womanhood. Her one instinct was for flight. But there was Edward. She turned her back on the semicircle of eyes, and put a trembling hand on Edward's shoulder. He grasped it.

"Forgive me, dear!" he whispered. "And go, now, go into the woods; they're not as cold as these. When I've done with them we'll go away, far away from hell."

"I dunno mind 'em," said Hazel. "What for should I, my soul?"

Then she saw how dank and livid Edward's face had become, and the anguished rage of the lover against which hurts her darling flamed up in her.

"Curse you!" she said, letting her eyes, dark-rimmed and large with tears, dwell on each man in turn. "Curse you for tormenting my Ed'ard, as is the best man in all the country—and you'm nought, nought at all!"

The everlasting puzzle, why the paltry and the low should have power to torment greatness, was brooding over her mind.

"The best!" said James, avoiding her eyes, as they all did. "A hinfidel!"

"I have become an unbeliever," Edward said, "not because I am unworthy of your God, but because He is unworthy of me. Hazel, wait for me at the edge of the wood."

Hazel crept out of the room. As she went, she heard him say:

278

"The beauty of the world isn't for the beautiful people. It's for beef-witted squires and blear-eyed people like yourselves—brutish, callous. Your God stinks like carrion, James." *Nunc Dimittis*.

From GONE TO EARTH, by
Mary Webb (1883–1927).

110

THE APPOINTMENT TO PYBUS ST. ANTHONY

THE Archdeacon was very sorry for Morrison. He liked him, and was deeply touched by his tragedy; nevertheless one must face facts; it was probable that at any moment now the Chapter would be forced to make a new appointment.

He had been aware—he did not disguise it from himself in the least—for some time now of the way that the appointment must go. There was a young man, the Rev. Rex Forsyth by name, who, in his judgment, could be the only possible man. Young Forsyth was, at the present moment, chaplain to the Bishop of St. Minworth. St. Minworth was only a Suffragan Bishopric, and it could not honestly be said that there was a great deal for Mr. Forsyth to do there. But it was not because the Archdeacon thought that the young man ought to have more to do that he wished to move him to Pybus St. Anthony. Far from it! The Archdeacon, in the deep secrecy of his own heart, could not honestly admit that young Forsyth was a very hard worker—he liked hunting and whist and a good bottle of wine . . . he was that kind of man.

Where, then, were his qualifications as Canon Morrison's successor? Well, quite honestly—and the Archdeacon was one of the honestest men alive—his qualifications belonged more especially to his ancestors rather than to himself. In the Archdeacon's opinion there had been too many *clever* men at Pybus. Time now for a *normal* man. Morrison was normal, and Forsyth would be more normal still.

He was in fact first cousin to young Johnny St. Leath and therefore a very near relation of the Countess herself. His father was the fourth son of the Earl of Trewithen, and, as every one knows, the Trewithens and the St. Leaths are, for all practical purposes, one and the same family, and divide Glebeshire between them. No one ever quite knew what young Rex Forsyth became a parson for. Some people said he did it for a wager; but however true that might be, he was not very happy with dear old Bishop Clematis and very ready for preferment.

Now the Archdeacon was no snob; he believed in men and women who had long and elaborate family-trees simply because he believed in institutions and because it had always seemed to him a quite obvious fact that the longer any one or anything remained in a place, the more chance there was of things being done as they always had been done. It was not in the least because she was a Countess that he thought the old Lady St. Leath a wonderful woman; not wonderful for her looks certainly—no one could call her a beautiful woman—and not wonderful for her intelligence; the Archdeacon had frequently been compelled to admit to himself that she was a little on the stupid side—but wonderful for her capacity for staying where she was like a rock and allowing nothing whatever to move her. In these dangerous days—and what dangerous days they were!—the safety of the country simply depended on a few such figures as the Countess. Queen Victoria was another of them, and for her the Archdeacon had a real and very touching devotion. Thank God he would be able to show a little of it in the prominent part he intended to play in the Polchester Jubilee festivals this year!

Anyone could see then that to have young Rex Forsyth close at hand at Pybus St. Anthony was the very best possible thing for the good of Polchester. Lady St. Leath saw it, Mrs. Combermere saw it, Mrs. Sampson saw it, and young Forsyth himself saw it. The Archdeacon entirely failed to understand how there could be anyone who did not see it. However, he was afraid that there were one or two in Polchester. . . . People said that young Forsyth was stupid! Perhaps he was not very bright; all the easier then to direct him in the way that he should go, and throw his forces into the right direction. People said that he cared more for his hunting and his whist than for his work—well, he was young and, at any rate, there was none of the canting hypocrite about him. The Archdeacon hated canting hypocrites!

There had been signs, once and again, of certain anarchists and devilish fellows, who crept up and down the streets of Polchester spreading their wicked mischief, their lying and disintegrating ideas. The Archdeacon was determined to fight them to the very last breath in his body, even as the Black Bishop before him had fought *his* enemies. And the Archdeacon had no fear of his victory.

Rex Forsyth at Pybus St. Anthony would be a fine step forward. Have one of these irreligious radicals there, and Heaven alone knew what harm he might wreak. No, Polchester must be saved. Let the rest of the world go to pieces, Polchester would be preserved.

On how many earlier occasions had the Archdeacon surveyed the Chapter, considered it in all its details and weighed up judiciously the elements, good and bad, that composed it. How well he knew them all! First the Dean, mild and polite and amiable, his mind generally busy with his beloved flora and fauna, his flowers and his butterflies, very easy indeed to deal with. Then Archdeacon Witheram, most nobly conscientious, a really devout man, taking his work with a seriousness that was simply admirable, but glued to the details of his own half of the diocese, so that broader and larger questions did not concern him very closely. Bentinck-Major next. The Archdeacon flattered himself that he knew Bentinck-Major through and through—his snobbery, his vanity, his childish pleasure in his position and his cook, his vanity in his own smart appearance! It would be difficult to find words adequate for the scorn with which the Archdeacon regarded that elegant little man. Then Ryle, the Precentor. He was, to some extent, an unknown quantity. His chief characteristic perhaps was his hatred of quarrels —he would say or do anything if only he might not be drawn into a "row." "Peace at any price" was his motto, and this, of course, as with the famous Vicar of Bray, involved a good deal of insincerity. The Archdeacon knew that he could not trust him, but a masterful policy of terrorism had always been very successful. Ryle was frankly frightened by the Archdeacon, and a very good thing too! Might he long remain so! Lastly there was Foster, the Diocesan Missioner. Let it be said at once that the Archdeacon hated Foster.

Foster had been a thorn in the Archdeacon's side ever since his arrival in Polchester—a thin, shambly-kneed, untidy, pale-faced prig, that was what Foster was! The Archdeacon hated everything about him—his grey hair, his large protruding ears, the pimple on the end of his nose, the baggy knees to his trousers, his thick heavy hands that never seemed to be properly washed.

Nevertheless beneath that hatred the Archdeacon was compelled to a reluctant admiration. The man was fearless, a fanatic if you please, but devoted to his religion, believing in it with a fervour and sincerity that nothing could shake. An able man too, the best preacher in the diocese, better read in every kind of theology than any clergyman in Glebeshire. It was especially for his open mind about new religious ideas that the Archdeacon mistrusted him. No opinion, however heterodox, shocked him. He welcomed new thought and had himself written a book, *Christ and the Gospels*, that for its learning and broadmindedness had created a considerable stir. But he was a dull dog, never laughed, never even smiled, lived by himself and kept to himself. He had, in the past, opposed every plan of the Archdeacon's, and opposed it relentlessly, but he was always, thanks to the Archdeacon's efforts, in a minority. The other Canons disliked him; the old Bishop, safely tucked away in his Palace at Carpledon, was, except for his satellite Rogers, his only friend in Polchester.

So much for the Chapter. There was now only one unknown element in the situation—Ronder. Ronder's position was important because he was Treasurer to the Cathedral. His predecessor, Hart-Smith, now promoted to the Deanery of Norwich, had been an able man, but one of the old school, a great friend of Brandon's, seeing eye to eye with him in everything. The Archdeacon then had had his finger very closely upon the Cathedral purse, and Hart-Smith's departure had been a very serious blow. The appointment of the new Canon had been in the hands of the Crown, and Brandon had, of course, had nothing to say to it. However, one glance at Ronder—he had seen him and spoken to him at the Dean's a few days after his arrival—had reassured him. Here, surely, was a man whom he need not fear—an easy, good-natured, rather stupid fellow by the look of him. Brandon hoped to have his finger on the Cathedral purse as tightly in a few weeks' time as he had had it before.

And all this was in no sort of fashion for the Archdeacon's personal advancement or ambition. He was contented with Polchester, and quite prepared to live there for the rest of his days and be buried, with proper ceremonies, when his end came. With all his soul he loved the Cathedral, and if he regarded himself as the principal factor in its good governance and order he did so with a sort of divine fatalism—no credit to him that it was so. Let credit be given to the Lord God who had seen fit to make him what he was and to place in his hands that great charge.

His fault in the matter was, perhaps, that he took it all too simply, that he regarded these men and the other figures in Polchester exactly as he saw them, did not believe that they could ever be anything else. As God had created the world, so did Brandon create Polchester as nearly in his own likeness as might be—there they all were and there, please God, they would all be for ever!

From THE CATHEDRAL, by Sir
Hugh Walpole (1884-1941).

III

CHILD OF THE ROMANTIC REVIVAL

IF Newman had never lived, or if his father, when the gig came round on the fatal morning, still undecided between the two Universities, had chanced to turn the horse's head in the direction of Cambridge, who can doubt that the Oxford Movement would have flickered out its little flame unobserved in the Common Room of Oriel? And how different, too, would have been the fate of Newman himself! He was a child of the Romantic Revival, a creature of emotion and of memory, a dreamer whose secret spirit dwelt apart in delectable mountains, an artist whose subtle senses caught, like a shower in the sunshine, the impalpable rainbow of the immaterial world. In other times, under other skies, his days would have been more fortunate. He might have helped to weave the garland of Meleager, or to mix the *lapis lazuli* of Fra Angelico, or to chase the delicate truth in the shade of an Athenian *palæstra*, or his hands might have fashioned those ethereal faces that smile in the niches of Chartres. Even in his own age he might, at Cambridge, whose cloisters have ever been consecrated to poetry and common sense, have followed quietly in Gray's footsteps and brought into flower those seeds of inspiration which now lie embedded amid the faded devotion of the *Lyra Apostolica*. At Oxford, he was doomed. He could not withstand the last enchantment of the Middle Age. It was in vain that he plunged into the pages of Gibbon or communed for long hours with Beethoven over his beloved violin. The air was thick with clerical sanctity, heavy with the odours of tradition and the soft warmth of spiritual authority; his friendship with Hurrell Froude did the rest. All that was weakest in him hurried him onward, and all that was strongest in him too. His curious and vaulting imagination began to construct vast philosophical fabrics out of the writings of ancient monks, and to dally with visions of angelic visitations and the efficacy of the oil of St. Walburga; his emotional nature became absorbed in the partisan passions of a University clique; and his subtle intellect concerned itself more and more exclusively with the dialectical splitting of dogmatical hairs. His future course was marked out for him all too clearly; and yet by a singular chance the true nature of the man was to emerge triumphant in the end. If Newman had died at the age of sixty, to-day he would have been already forgotten, save by a few ecclesiastical historians; but he lived to write his *Apologia*, and to reach immortality, neither as a thinker nor as a theologian, but as an artist who has embalmed the poignant history of an intensely human spirit in the magical spices of words.

From EMINENT VICTORIANS, by
Lytton Strachey (1880–1932).

SECTARIAN BIGOTRY

SECTARIAN bigotry, during the generation that followed Newman's secession, reached a pitch of extraordinary bitterness. Though, as the pages of *Punch* bear witness, no insult was too crude to hurl at the Pope, the principal fury of the Evangelicals was reserved for what they regarded as Romanisers within the Anglican fold, or Ritualists, as the High Churchmen now came to be called.

"We know what Ritualism means," cried a certain Reverend George Chute; "it means the defilement of your daughters, the seduction of your wives, and all the other evils that abound on the Continent." Sometimes invective takes the form of poetry:

> "This wily, crafty Ritualist,
> With cope and incense strong,
> This unctuous and bearded priest,
> With broidered vestments long. . . .

> "Your wives and daughters soon will learn
> On him their hopes to rest,
> And every feeling overturn
> Unless by him expressed."

Sometimes practices that are now part of ordinary ecclesiastical routine are singled out for special denunciation, as in the crusading appeal from which the following is an extract:

> "Let us now make a grand proposition
> To unite in a firm opposition,
>   To do all we can
>   To get rid of a man
> Who favours the Eastward position,"

and ending on the heroic resolve:

> "Though we die in the field,
> We never will yield,
> To this Ritualistic position."

The fact that issues of this sort could excite such passion in clerical minds is significant of the religious outlook of the mid-Victorian decades. With the cessation of *Tracts for the Times*, a great and deceptive calm settled on the Church. Never had she seemed to enjoy such unruffled security. The alarm excited by the Whig triumph had passed away; the few reforms that had been forced upon her had served rather to strengthen her position. Society had become respectable, and the broad-brimmed hat of the parson ranked above the "topper" as a symbol of respectability. . . .

Unfortunately, the stimulus of Tractarian opposition had done nothing to relieve the poverty of thought that had been so fatal an accompaniment of the Evangelical Movement. Of the vast amount of pious prose that was produced under Low Church and Dissenting auspices during the first half of the Queen's reign, practically nothing has stood the test of time. Most of it is of a kind that the modern educated reader would find it difficult to take seriously. Where now can we find a responsible divine to write such a book as *The Church before the Flood* by the Rev. John Cumming, D.D.—over 600 pages in length—which accounts for the acceptance of Abel's sacrifice by the discovery that Abel was a Protestant, and points the subsequent tragedy with the moral:

"Be not deceived; what Romanism has made Spain, Italy and Austria, morally and intellectually, it would make Westminster. The Cain mark is upon it."

Where now would you find a theologian to compose, or a firm to publish, so elephantine a treatise as the *Horæ Apocalypticæ* of the Rev. E. C. Elliott, in which vast labour and considerable erudition are devoted to proving the Book of Revelation to have been an anti-Papal pamphlet? . . .

Particular attention was devoted to the impressionable minds of children, and the output of improving literature for their benefit was enormous. The spirit of Mr. Fairchild was still abroad, though the growing humanitarianism of the age was inclined to lay somewhat less stress upon the inhuman qualities attributed to the Heavenly, even more than to the earthly Father. But a child's nerves must have been tough not to have been permanently affected by the perpetual harping on death-beds, funerals and other

286

accompaniments of mortality, that was supposed to be peculiarly edifying for the young mind. In juvenile literature the moralising tendency of the Victorians had full scope because—since the effective demand was created by the buyer and not by the reader—there was no incentive to aim at being anything but improving.

To give one instance of the sort of fare provided, we will take an incident from a book of Mrs. Carey Brock's, about some children every episode in whose lives is supposed to illustrate one of the journeyings of the Children of Israel. A schoolgirl is just beginning to reover from an attack of scarlet fever, and the doctor has expressly prescribed for her light reading and cheerful talk. But the improving clergyman of the book has gathered from something let fall in her delirium that she has been committing sin—burning a school book—and at all costs he is going to worm it out. Accordingly, no sooner has he got her alone than he produces his Bible, and after having perused it ominously for some little time, asks if he may read to her. The poor child having made the only possible answer, Mr. Somers, the clergyman in question, opens the attack with a chapter of Hosea, "making the cheek yet paler, the uneasy look yet more uneasy."

Having produced these desirable symptoms in the patient, he now proceeds to harrow her feelings with a lurid description of God's wrath and its effects, and having frightened her almost to death, rams home the moral with the words, "it has been thus with you," after which the sick and trembling child has the confession torn out of her.

But Mr. Somers has not done. "Mr. Somers prayed, but before prayer came a thanksgiving, an earnest thanksgiving"; nor does the torture end even here, for the Bible is produced again, and another chapter read, and another sermon preached, "very faithfully, yet with many comforting words," about Moses, and the golden calf, and the quails in the wilderness, and sin, and the consequences of sin, until the triumphant consummation is attained, that little Gertrude, who, we are asked to believe, survived the experience, "abhorred herself and repented in dust and ashes."

That was the light in which God and His ministers were presented to little children, objects of fear, the grown-up person in his most terrifying aspect. Religion was a stern and joyless discipline, and if any element of love entered into it, it was because God would make it exceeding hot for you if you didn't love Him. . . .

On one subject, at least, the Evangelicals were in agreement with the Ritualists, and indeed, with the Catholics. There could be no question of tampering with Hell. The idea that there could be any limit to the implacability of an all-loving Father was too horrible to be entertained for a moment. Even Jesus was not free from complicity with the Devil and his work of eternal torture. This is quite clearly brought out in *Peep of Day*, a book from which countless thousands of children imbibed their first ideas of religion:

"At last Jesus will sit upon a white throne, and everybody will stand round his (the small 'h' is in the original, the capital being doubtless Popish) throne. He will open some books, in which he has written down all the naughty things people have done. God has seen all the naughty things you have done. He can see in the dark as well as in the light, and knows all your naughty thoughts. He will read everything out of his books before the angels that stand round. Yet God will forgive some people, because Christ died upon the cross."

Only some! And these fortunate few would have to accomplish the feat of loving that blend of Peeping Tom and the Marquis de Sade whom pious Evangelists dared to cast for the divine role.

"This is what God will do to those who do not love him. God will bind them in chains and put them in a lake of fire. There they will gnash their teeth and weep and wail for ever. God will put Satan in the same place and all the devils. Satan is the father of the wicked, and he and his children shall be tormented for ever. They shall not have one drop of water to cool their burning tongues."

In view of which prospect, what prudent little child could hesitate for a moment about loving so amiable a Father?

But all these performances are put into the shade by the Catholic Father Furniss—a singularly appropriate name for one whose principal title to fame is to have produced the most super-heated and agonising Hell on imaginative record. His sadistic outpourings were for the special benefit of children—hence his title of the Children's Apostle—and no doubt, with the little boys, he must have achieved considerable popularity as a specialist in torture. Certainly no Red Indians could compete for a moment with Father Furniss's God, Saviour, and Devil, who combine to damn a poor little child to everlasting confinement, screaming, stamping, struggling, in a red-hot oven. This is by no means the only form of torture that the good Father is capable of devising for his little friends—perpetually burning suits of clothes, audibly boiling blood and brains, and one divinely neat practical joke, that of half opening the door of a cell wherein a little girl is agonising in eternal solitude on a red-hot floor, and then shutting it again—for ever. "Oh, that you could hear the horrible, the fearful scream of that girl!" But why horrible?

There was nothing that aroused orthodox divines to a greater pitch of fury than the least attempt to put limits to the divine ferocity. Their attitude was that of the military authorities towards the torture of flogging—take away the stimulus of fear, and it would be impossible to keep the rank and file under authority. But thanks to the sturdy individualism of the age, it was impossible to prevent some of the more earnest and thoughtful spirits from using their brains or following the dictates of their hearts. One of these was Charles Kingsley, who, though in no sense a philosopher, had a fund of John Bullish common sense, and a heart of gold. It was he who pointed out that the use of fire and worms was to set free the elements of decayed and dead matter to enter into other organisms, and that to tax God with perverting it into an instrument of torture was blasphemy. But Kingsley was looked upon as a dangerous firebrand, and his friend, F. D. Maurice, who, though he disclaimed the title of Broad Churchman, held that it was impossible to set limits to God's love, even for defunct sinners, was on that account deprived not only of a professorship of divinity, but one of history, at King's College, London, the Bishop of that diocese having threatened to decline to receive the College certificate as a qualification for examination.

From THE VICTORIAN TRAGEDY, by Dr. Esme Wingfield-Stratford (1882–).

113

THE DEAD PRIEST

THE next morning after breakfast I went down to look at the little house in Great Britain Street. It was an unassuming shop, registered under the vague name of *Drapery*. The drapery consisted mainly of children's bootees and umbrellas; and on ordinary days a notice used to hang in the window, saying: *Umbrellas Re-covered*. No notice was visible now, for the shutters were up. A crape bouquet was tied to the door-knocker with ribbon. Two poor women and a telegram boy were reading the card pinned on the crape. I also approached and read:

July 1st, 1895

The Rev. James Flynn (formerly of S. Catherine's Church, Meath Street), aged sixty-five years.

R.I.P.

The reading of the card persuaded me that he was dead and I was disturbed to find myself at check. Had he not been dead I would have gone into the little dark room behind the shop to find him sitting in his arm-chair by the fire, nearly smothered in his great-coat. Perhaps my aunt would have given me a packet of High Toast for him, and this present would have roused him from his stupefied doze. It was always I who emptied the packet into his black snuff-box, for his hands trembled too much to allow him to do this without spilling half the snuff about the floor. Even as he raised his large trembling hand to his nose little clouds of smoke dribbled through his fingers over the front of his coat. It may have been these constant showers of snuff which gave his ancient priestly garments their green faded look, for the red handkerchief, blackened, as it always was, with the snuff-stains of a week, with which he tried to brush away the fallen grains, was quite inefficacious.

I wished to go in and look at him, but I had not the courage to knock. I walked away slowly along the sunny side of the street, reading all the theatrical advertisements in the shop-windows as

I went. I found it strange that neither I nor the day seemed in a mourning mood and I felt even annoyed at discovering in myself a sensation of freedom as if I had been freed from something by his death. I wondered at this for, as my uncle had said the night before, he had taught me a great deal. He had studied in the Irish college in Rome and he had taught me to pronounce Latin properly. He had told me stories about the catacombs and about Napoleon Bonaparte, and he had explained to me the meaning of the different ceremonies of the Mass and of the different vestments worn by the priest. Sometimes he had amused himself by putting difficult questions to me, asking me what one should do in certain circumstances or whether such and such sins were mortal or venial or only imperfections. His questions showed me how complex and mysterious were certain institutions of the Church which I had always regarded as the simplest acts. The duties of the priest towards the Eucharist and towards the secrecy of the confessional seemed so grave to me that I wondered how anybody had ever found in himself the courage to undertake them; and I was not surprised when he told me that the fathers of the Church had written books as thick as the *Post Office Directory* and as closely printed as the law notices in the newspaper, elucidating all these intricate questions. Often when I thought of this I could make no answer or only a very foolish and halting one, upon which he used to smile and nod his head twice or thrice. Sometimes he used to put me through the responses of the Mass, which he had made me learn by heart; and, as I pattered, he used to smile pensively and nod his head, now and then pushing huge pinches of snuff up each nostril alternately. When he smiled he used to uncover his big discoloured teeth and let his tongue lie upon his lower lip—a habit which had made me feel uneasy in the beginning of our acquaintance before I knew him well.

From THE DUBLINERS, by
James Joyce (1882–1941).

114

FATHER PENGILLY

IF you had cut Andrew Pengilly to the core, you would have found him white clear through. He was a type of clergyman favoured in pious fiction, yet he actually did exist.

To every congregation he had served these forty years, he had been a shepherd. They had loved him, listened to him, and underpaid him. In 1906, when Frank came to Catawba, Mr. Pengilly was a frail stooped veteran with silver hair, thin silver moustache, and a slow smile which embraced the world.

Andrew Pengilly had gone into the Civil War as a drummer boy, slept blanketless and barefoot and wounded in the frost of Tennessee mountains, and come out still a child, to "clerk in a store" and teach Sunday School. He had been converted at ten, but at twenty-five he was overpowered by the preaching of Osage Joe, the Indian evangelist, became a Methodist preacher, and never afterward doubted the peace of God. He was married at thirty to a passionate, singing girl with kind lips. He loved her so romantically—just to tuck the crazy-quilt about her was poetry, and her cowhide shoes were to him fairy slippers—he loved her so ungrudgingly that when she died, in childbirth, within a year after their marriage, he had nothing left for any other woman. He lived alone, with the undiminished vision of her. Not the most scandalmongering Mother in Zion had ever hinted that Mr. Pengilly looked damply upon the widows in his fold.

Little book-learning had Andrew Pengilly in his youth, and to this day he knew nothing of Biblical criticism, of the origin of religions, of the sociology which was beginning to absorb church-leaders, but his Bible he knew, and believed, word by word, and somehow he had drifted into the reading of ecstatic books of mysticism. He was a mystic, complete; the world of ploughs and pavements and hatred was less to him than the world of angels, whose silver robes seemed to flash in the air about him as he meditated alone in his cottage. He was as ignorant of Modern Sunday School Methods as of single tax or Lithuanian finances, yet few Protestants had read more in the Early Fathers.

On Frank Shallard's first day in Catawba, when he was unpacking his books in his room at the residence of Deacon Halter, the druggist, the Reverend Mr. Pengilly was announced. Frank went down to the parlour (gilded cat-tails and a basket of stereopticon views) and his loneliness was warmed by Mr. Pengilly's enveloping smile, his drawling voice:

"Welcome, Brother! I'm Pengilly, of the Methodist Church. I never was much of a hand at seeing any difference between the denominations, and I hope we'll be able to work together for the glory of God. I do hope so! And I hope you'll go fishing with me. I know," enthusiastically, "a pond where there's some elegant pickerel!"

Many evenings they spent in Mr. Pengilly's cottage, which was less littered and odorous than that of the village atheist, Doc Lem Staples, only because the stalwart ladies of Mr. Pengilly's congregation vied in sweeping for him, dusting for him, disarranging his books and hen-tracked sermon-notes, and bullying him in the matters of rubbers and winter flannels. They would not let him prepare his own meals—they made him endure the several boarding-houses in turn—but sometimes of an evening he would cook scrambled eggs for Frank. He had pride in his cooking. He had never tried anything but scrambled eggs.

His living-room was overpowering with portraits and carbon prints. Though every local official board pled with him about it, he insisted on including madonnas, cinquecento resurrections, St. Francis of Assisi, and even a Sacred Heart, with such Methodist worthies as Leonidas Hamline and the cloaked romantic Francis Asbury. In the bay window was a pyramid of wire shelves filled with geraniums. Mr. Pengilly was an earnest gardener, except during such weeks as he fell into dreams and forgot to weed and water, and through the winter he watched for the geranium leaves to wither enough so that he could pick them off and be able to feel busy.

All over the room were the aged dog and ancient cat, who detested each other, never ceased growling at each other, and at night slept curled together.

.   .   .   .   .

Frank had heard in theological seminary of the "practise of the presence of God" as a papist mystery. Now he encountered it. Mr. Pengilly taught him to kneel, his mind free of all worries, all prides, all hunger, his lips repeating "Be thou visibly present with me"—not as a charm but that his lips might not be soiled with more earthly phrases—and, when he had become strained and weary and exalted, to feel a Something glowing and almost terrifying about him, and to experience thus, he was certain, the actual, loving, proven nearness of the Divinity.

He began to call his mentor Father Pengilly, and the old man chided him only a little . . . presently did not chide him at all.

For all his innocence and his mysticism, Father Pengilly was not a fool nor weak. He spoke up harshly to a loud-mouthed grocer, new come to town, who considered the patriarch a subject for what he called "kidding," and who shouted. "Well, I'm getting tired of waiting for you preachers to pray for rain. Guess you don't believe the stuff much yourselves!" He spoke up to old Miss Udell, the purity specialist of the town, when she came to snuffle that Amy Dove was carrying on with the boys in the twilight. "I know how you like a scandal, Sister," said he. "Maybe, 'tain't Christian to deny you one. But I happen to know all about Amy. Now if you'd go out and help poor old crippled Sister Eckstein do her washing, maybe you'd keep busy enough so's you could get along without your daily scandal."

He had humour, as well, Father Pengilly. He could smile over the cranks in the congregation. And he liked the village atheist, Dr. Lem Staples. He had him at the house, and it healed Frank's spirit to hear with what beatific calm Father Pengilly listened to the Doc's gibes about the penny-pinchers and the sinners in the church.

"Lem," said Father Pengilly, "you'll be surprised at this, but I must tell you that there's two-three sinners in your fold, too. Why, I've heard of even horse-thieves that didn't belong to churches. That must prove something, I guess. Yes, sir, I admire to hear you tell about the kind-hearted atheists, after reading about the cannibals, who are remarkably little plagued with us Methodists and Baptists."

From ELMER GANTRY, by
Sinclair Lewis (1885–   ).

115

PORTRAIT OF ELAM

My school was St. Paul's, and Elam was an unimportant master, a soured little clergyman, who taught us in the lower forms when we were about thirteen. He did everything that was wrong and scandalous in the eyes of theorists. He was slovenly in his dress and dirty in his person; he was violent in temper and would thrash us in hot blood; in sudden brain-storms he would shake a boy as a savage woman shakes a child; his language, when indignation overcame him, though brilliant with wit, malice, vindictiveness and humour, would certainly not have passed muster with the police in Victoria Park; he was grossly unpunctual, wandering on splayed feet up to his class-room door long after other masters had taken their thrones and the corridors were silent. He had no dignity and no system in his conduct of a class, but would quite often go to sleep, with a handkerchief over his face, his chair tilted back, and his feet on his writing-desk; he would vilify the school and not a few of its masters, declaring that their souls had long been destroyed and that his own was moribund, but still, thank God! had spasms of life; he would abuse our parents; he would pour scorn on the High Master; most risky of all, he would tell us his spiritual history, analysing his loss of faith in the Church's creed and his resultant degeneration into "a hungry usher, at a shilling an hour." When, in his later years, to the humorous delight of the whole school, a good woman married him, he would discuss his domestic difficulties with his pupils, dilating on the exacting punctuality and "absurd fastidiousness of this woman I've married"; and, in a word, he was undoubtedly mad.

By all theories such a man was the last person to whom adolescent boys should be trusted. And yet the High Master—the famous F. W. Walker, last of the school of terrifying heads—though he knew perfectly well that Elam, whom he had once called "no gentleman" in a deep-throated rage—and by heaven! which of us, masters or boys, have forgotten the deep-throated roar of Walker in a passion, a roar so like the roar of a lion seeking his meat from

God?—though he knew perfectly well that Elam was in the habit of shouting, "*I* shan't report you to the person calling himself the High Master; if I did, I should only be called 'no gentleman' by a man that I despise above most of God's creatures"—never did he remove the mutineer from his place or interfere with his methods. To be sure, I believe that, though not on speaking terms with the man, he liked him best of his colleagues. I know that once I was in Elam's class-room, and my master was asleep with his feet on his desk and his bandana handkerchief over his eyes, and Walker entered. As that ragged beard and billowing silk gown showed itself round the door, I think we expected the room to totter and its windows to crack. But the High Master only looked round, saw the situation, and walked out quietly so as not to disturb the slumberer.

These things sound incredible, but everything about Elam was incredible—incredible that from such a man I, for one, should have learned nothing but good; learned, in truth, almost everything that has been of value to me since, enabling me not only to earn my bread and butter in the practice of an art, but to live as fully as possible and drink deeply of the glory of life while I have time.

From THROUGH LITERATURE TO LIFE,
by Ernest Raymond (1888–   ).

116

DOGGED WARRIOR

THE REV. ALFRED MEADOWS came from a senior curacy at Rotherhithe. He had fearlessness, bull-dog pertinacity and an inability to condescend toward even the most disreputable poverty—qualities which parish work in the wilds of Victorian London could not fail to develop in a man honest and courageous enough to absorb them.

The Church of St. John the Evangelist, Waterloo Road, designed on classical lines by Bedford in 1824, was a forceful and in an aggressive way a dignified building, but one little enough appreciated in the 'fifties and 'sixties, when parsonical gothic, however ill assorted with its surroundings, was considered the only style worthy of Establishment. But Mr. Meadows—who, when he stood square on his short thick legs and thrust forward the firm line of his jaw overhung by heavy dark moustachios, was not unlike the pillared portico of his church—was indifferent to the beauty, either external or ceremonial, of the place of worship in his charge. His duty, as he considered it, was with the bodies and souls of men; and although it would be too much to say he regarded his church services and sermons as a minor element in his activity, it is certain that the work in which his heart really lay was carried on in the streets and alleys of his parish rather than within the precincts of God's House.

. . . . .

He might deplore the degradation of the people, their turbulence and their squalor; he might observe with a heavy heart, as he passed through Tenison Street or along his section of York Road, the perpetual in-and-out traffic, with drunken men in tow, of painted slatterns of all ages who kept an open door or hired six feet of flock on broken springs, somewhere upstairs behind the grimy frontages.

But he did not condemn. What chance had these folk to be other than squalid or vicious?

Nobody cared for them or helped them. From babyhood boys and girls were turned into the streets, to learn such lessons as the streets could teach and thereafter to feed themselves as best they might. These and other shifts forced on its victims by grinding poverty were obstacles enough in the path of goodwill. But there were worse enemies than they—agencies actively at work to drive the boys to loafing, sneak-thievery or pimping and the girls to sell the only labour they could offer. It was with these agencies that Mr. Meadows was doggedly at war. His ceaseless—at times it seemed his hopeless—battle was against the small landlords who

297

profited by debauching their property; against the Vestry, who in part consisted of such landlords; and against the Overseers, whose duty it was to support him but too often found it to their interest to do the opposite.

From FORLORN SUNSET, by
Michael Sadleir (1888–   ).

117

THE FINISHED ARTICLE

THEO was well aware of the purple beneath the formidable chin, the gaiters on the rounded calves, the cross shining at the end of its chain. He was in no doubt who this was, but pretended a pleased surprise when Adela said: "This is my brother."

They shook hands. "You have done me the honour to write to me, sir," said Theo. "It has been a great help." He added with a smile: "One needs it, you know, in Manchester."

"Some do and some don't," said the bishop. "I imagine Burnside is self-sufficient. Didn't you think so?"

They were making their way out of the station. The question came abruptly, almost as a rebuke. "Well," said Theo, "I suppose he's the stuff saints are made of."

The bishop opened the door of the brougham, saw Adela in, and climbed after her. "Don't you believe it," he said, presenting his well-upholstered posterior to Theo's gaze. "Burnside isn't raw material. He's a finished article."

Theo seated himself and the carriage started. "I didn't know you knew Mr. Burnside," Theo said. "He's never mentioned it."

Adrian permitted himself a smile. "He wouldn't," he said. "I imagine he doesn't altogether approve of me. Nevertheless, we were at Christ Church together. He was in his last year when I went up. We became very friendly." He stopped suddenly and placed an affectionate hand on Adela's arm. "My dear, this all seems a terribly long time ago. To think that you were still a babe in arms when I came down from Christ Church."

"Don't side-track yourself," said Adela. "I can see that Mr. Chrystal is terribly interested in what you were saying about Mr. Burnside."

"There's precious little to say. He took Orders at the earliest possible moment, was a curate in the East End of London and in Salford, and then became Vicar of St. Ninian's in Levenshulme. He's been offered several fine benefices and one deanery, but he wants to stay where he is. That's about all, except that he's the only man I know who refused a fortune."

"Now this is something new," said Adela. "You've told me all the rest before."

"Oh, yes. Burnside's father was immensely rich. A tea-merchant in Mincing Lane. And till he came up to Oxford Burnside knew what to do with money. Knew only too well, from all I heard. Yes—dissipation. During his first year at Oxford he was converted, as surely, absolutely and suddenly as Saul on the road to Damascus. His father died soon after he had taken Orders. Burnside was an only son and came in for something like fifty thousand pounds. He gave it all away—every penny."

The countryside, drowsy with summer, spun past the open windows. Honeysuckle hung upon the hedges. The elms were like great ships becalmed, motionless and mute. The horse's hoofs beat musically upon the white dusty road, and the wheels purred with sleek content. Fifty thousand pounds! Fifty thousand pounds could buy all this. Theo thought of Levenshulme on a summer's day: the burning pavements, the arid houses, the afternoon wilting in the treeless streets. He thought of Mr. Burnside with his window open upon the breathless night, the moths batting into his gas-globe, his cat at his feet. Fifty thousand pounds!

"Yes, we had great arguments about it," the bishop was saying. "A priest can do a lot with fifty thousand pounds. I told him so. I remember his answer well. 'My dear Beckwith, when I was commanded—as I was—to become a fisher of men, nothing was said about golden bait.' I had to leave it at that."

"Do you think he decided wisely, sir?" Theo asked.

"It depends, young man, on what you mean by wisdom," said the bishop. "You hear people talk about worldly wisdom, as though wisdom were something sold in various grades and qualities, to be used for various purposes. If a priest took that view, then obviously he would not decide as Burnside did. Equally obviously, Burnside being what he is, there was no other course open to him than the one he did in fact take. . . . Well, Adela my dear, here you are. You must bring Mr. Chrystal over to tea some day while he's here."

From HARD FACTS, by
Howard Spring (1889–   ).

118

MR. BODIHAM AND THE WAR MEMORIAL

IN the parish church of Crome Mr. Bodiham preached on 1 Kings vi. 18: "And the cedar of the house within was carved with knops"—a sermon of immediate local interest. For the past two years the problem of the War Memorial had exercised the minds of all those in Crome who had enough leisure, or mental energy, or party spirit to think of such things. Henry Wimbush was all for a library—a library of local literature, stocked with county histories, old maps of the district, monographs on the local antiquities, dialect dictionaries, handbooks of the local geology and natural history. He liked to think of the villagers, inspired by such reading, making up parties of a Sunday afternoon to look for fossils and flint arrow-heads. The villagers themselves favoured the idea of a memorial reservoir and water supply. But the busiest and most articulate party followed Mr. Bodiham in demanding something religious in character—a second lich-gate, for example, a stained-glass window, a monument of marble, or, if possible, all three. So far, however, nothing had been done, partly because the memorial committee had never been able to agree, partly for the more cogent reason that too little money had been subscribed to carry out any of the proposed schemes. Every three or four months Mr. Bodiham preached a sermon on the subject. His last had been delivered in March; it was high time that his congregation had a fresh reminder.

"And the cedar of the house within was carved with knops."

Mr. Bodiham touched lightly on Solomon's temple. From thence he passed to temples and churches in general. What were the characteristics of these buildings dedicated to God? Obviously, the fact of their, from a human point of view, complete uselessness. They were unpractical buildings "carved with knops." Solomon might have built a library—indeed, what could be more to the taste of the world's wisest man? He might have dug a reservoir— what more useful in a parched city like Jerusalem? He did neither; he built a house all carved with knops, useless and unpractical. Why? Because he was dedicating the work to God. There had been much talk in Crome about the proposed War Memorial. A War Memorial was, in its very nature, a work dedicated to God. It was a token of thankfulness that the first stage in the culminating world-war had been crowned by the triumph of righteousness; it was at the same time a visibly embodied supplication that God might not long delay the Advent which alone could bring the final peace. A library, a reservoir? Mr. Bodiham scornfully and indignantly condemned the idea. These were works dedicated to man, not to God. As a War Memorial they were totally unsuitable. A lich-gate had been suggested. This was an object which answered perfectly to the definition of a War Memorial: a useless work dedicated to God and carved with knops. One lich-gate, it was true, already existed. But nothing would be easier than to make a second entrance into the churchyard; and a second entrance would need a second gate. Other suggestions had been made. Stained-glass windows, a monument of marble. Both these were admirable, especially the latter. It was high time that the War Memorial was erected. It might soon be too late. At any moment, like a thief in the night, God might come. Meanwhile a difficulty stood in the way. Funds were inadequate. All should subscribe according to their means. Those who had lost relations in the war might reasonably be expected to subscribe a sum equal to that which they would have had to pay in funeral expenses if the relative had died while at home. Further delay was disastrous. The War Memorial must be built at once. He appealed to the patriotism and the Christian sentiments of all his hearers.

Henry Wimbush walked home thinking of the books he would present to the War Memorial Library, if ever it came into existence.

From CROME YELLOW, by
Aldous Huxley (1894—).

119

THE GREAT GAME

APART from his wife—whom he loved very dearly—Septimus Jones lived for two things; his work and cricket.

He was a parson, so his job in life wasn't an easy one. In fact, even in a small country parish where homely folk dwelt, it was difficult. But he slogged away at it; christening the babies, trying to make the children behave themselves, marrying the serious lovers, appeasing the quarrelsome, visiting the sick, and burying the dead.

It was wearying and often disappointing labour; but to it he brought the courage, the optimism, the friendliness, and the unselfishness of an old cricketer. And remember! Cricketers are the salt of the earth!

The Great Game—with all it used to be, still is, and ever should be—meant a tremendous lot to this plump little priest with the round red face, the bald head, the boyish smile, and the enormous hands with long fingers.

Ah, those hands! Forty years ago and more, what wizardry had they not performed with a cricket-ball! The break both ways, the flight in the air, the deceptive delivery, the ball that unexpectedly kept low, the top-spinner, the cleverly-disguised faster one, the immaculate length of them all, *and* his speciality, the "popper": that innocent-looking slow ball which rose sharply—and from any kind of wicket—with off or leg break! He was very proud of it; though he couldn't have told you exactly how he did it.

You played forward quite correctly, the ball jumped up almost straight from the pitch, its break took it to the edge of your bat—and out you went, to a catch that a child could have held, at fine leg or in the slips! It was no good looking angrily for a spot on the wicket. Septimus didn't rely on that!

Yes, those huge hands with the long fingers had done wonderful things in the past. His style was in the best tradition. He attacked a batsman's skill; not his nerves or body. His bowling was as academically cultured as his batting and fielding were pathetic.

But nothing happened as a result of this exceptional ability. No distinction, no Blue, no County Cap came his way, because his parents, though gentlefolk, were poor. Some quite good club cricket—that was as far as he ever went; for there was much study to be done and many examinations to be passed before ordination. Then came a curacy in a slum-parish, and much harder work. Life grew very serious, and he loved his calling.

Before he was thirty, the strain of his endeavours found a weakness. A valve of his heart went wrong. The trouble had a long and ominous medical name. He was told to "go slow"—to take things more easily. A grim injunction indeed at his age! Needless to say, it went unheeded.

Physical cricket ended, but *mental* cricket lived on, more strongly each year; till now, in 1948, the slum-work reluctantly given up a decade ago, and a cure of souls in the West Country his lot, he was very worried. Very worried indeed!

It was those Australians again! The beggars worked at cricket —we played at it! Well, it was our casual way, and he wouldn't change it. But things were serious! Here they were—young, well-fed, disciplined, medically passed for the tour, and trained up to concert-pitch. In his opinion, it was the strongest batting side ever sent over; and, though some of it wasn't of a vintage that appealed to *him*, the bowling was more than good enough to deal with the Old Country—now, alas, weaker than she had ever been!

It was very sad. It was tragic. Sometimes he couldn't sleep for thinking about it. What had we? *Honestly*, what had we? It was a distressing fact that we possessed no bowlers who were really up to Test standard—nobody like Richardson, Rhodes, Blythe, Tate, Farnes, Barnes, Verity, and many others, now elderly men grimly watching the sorry state of things, or else young again and presumably disporting themselves in the Elysian Fields, where

Septimus imagined the turf must always be in very fine condition.

A wicket-keeper? Well, of course, that was a different matter. England without a brilliant wicket-keeper would be too awful to contemplate! Yes, the cheery Evans was a worthy successor to the great ones—Ames, Strudwick & Co. *But,* even here there was a slight snag! Evans was perfect at his job; but Ames used to do more than keep wicket! He was good for a century against the finest bowling. Dash it, even now—his keeping-days over—he was knocking up the runs as gaily as ever for his county. Ah, that Canterbury Festival!

But our batting! *Eheu fugaces!* In the whole of this still fair land, we had just four reliable Test batsmen worthy of the name —and they were hampered in their methods by the knowledge that there was no one to back them up if their wickets fell unexpectedly. The dour and stolid Hutton and Washbrook—so typical of their counties—and the Middlesex Twins! Ah, those Twins! How they loved and lived the game for the game's sake! Why couldn't they be dour too—restraining their knightly daring —and resist touching or "having a go" at the ball which, by all the rubrics of skill, never deserved to get a wicket?

Yes, things were in a bad way with a vengeance! Like all sportsmen worthy of the name, he could take a licking; but to be so weak that Australia's victories could give her little genuine satisfaction, was damnable! Yes, *damnable*—a strong word of course, but justified.

He had thought it all out very thoroughly; and it was getting on his nerves. His wife knew that; and so did his doctor. It was no good telling him not to worry. Not the slightest! Cricket was in his very being. He even preached about it, and had done for years.

"The Christian Life! What is it?" he would ask, almost fiercely, from the pulpit. Then—with a beaming smile of happy conviction —he would tell them that the Christian Life was courage, unselfishness, patience, love of one's fellows, a struggle against odds on a bad wicket, sometimes in poor light, against venomous bowling if the Devil was in the field, and against powerful and merciless batting if he was at the wicket. The Toss was the luck of one's birth—the type of bedroom you were in. The Game was Life. The

304

Close of Play was Death. The Reward? "Ah, the Reward, my friends!" he would say—his little eyes moist and his lips trembling. "*That* passeth all understanding!"

Yes, when Septimus Jones brought cricket into a sermon—well, it got you!

Once in the dim past—1905, to be exact—there had been a game he would never forget. His club was enjoying a very good season; so good that, after a little influential wire-pulling, the M.C.C. consented to send an extra strong side down. But more than this! Oh yes, *much* more! With them came one of the great ones—indeed, one of the greatest! He was at the prime of his career; one of the finest batsmen of all time. Let us call him Ulysses. Did he, Septimus wondered, remember the day when a certain young club-cricketer—very near his ordination—tied him up for an over and a half, and then, with the unexpected faster one, went clean through him; with the result that the bails flew joyfully heavenward and the welkin rang?

Yes, even now he probably remembered it; because that evening, after stumps were drawn, and the shadows of the elms were lengthening across the ground—surely the most serene shadows of all!—Ulysses had taken this young man to the nets and made him bowl at him for twenty minutes. Then he had slapped him on the back and advised him to take up the game seriously. Indeed, he had said more! What never-fading joy those words had given!

"Don't let it go to your head, my boy; but I'll tell you this. On your bowling *today*, I've never faced anything better!"

But alas, nothing came of it! That autumn he was ordained, and went to the slum-parish. The stipend was small—very small—*and* there was a very sweet and winsome young lady on his horizon. The years slipped by—matrimony, work, more and more work, less and less cricket—and then that heart-valve began to give trouble. Perhaps he was not the only potentially world-famous bowler denied the chance of proving his worth in big cricket. It is a sad fact that, unless you make the game your doubtful and modest livelihood, you must be comfortably off to play for your county.

From CLOSE OF PLAY by
Alan Miller (1888–   ).

120

THE FUTURE OF THE PULPIT

Eutychus or The Future of the Pulpit *is a dialogue between Archbishop Fénelon, the seventeenth century ecclesiastic, Anthony a sceptical man about town, and Eutychus, who went to sleep when St. Paul preached, and represents the man in the street.*

EUTYCHUS: Well, we must move with the times, you know. And there's a lot of competition now-a-days. I guess that the sermon will have to get a move on like everything else.

FÉNELON: Pray what exactly do you mean by that?

EUTYCHUS: When I was a kid and we used to play at parsons, we had an old tree called the Pulpit Tree in our back garden. And if one of us wanted to be a parson he would climb up into the tree, and look down on the rest of us on the ground and cry out: "Dearly Beloved Brethren, ya, ya, ya!" or whatever he wanted to say until we were tired of it. Now that's what we thought a sermon was—one man in a pulpit talking to others who sat dumb below. That's what sermons have been for long enough. Now, if you come to think of it, gentlemen, that's a bit monotonous. I mean you can have too much of a good thing.

ANTHONY: And what do you suggest?

EUTYCHUS: Well, take this one-preacher-in-pulpit-congregation-below business. Why? Why not two preachers in the pulpit? Why not a debate like those they had at the London School of Economics for the hospitals? We're all for free play of thought and hearing both sides of a question, aren't we? Why not put 'em both up and let 'em out with it? Then you'ld soon draw a congregation, mark my words.

FÉNELON: Do you, indeed, imagine that the public contradiction of one preacher by another would add to the authority of the Pulpit?

EUTYCHUS: Well, they contradict each other now, all right, don't they? Only it's all criticism behind the other fellow's back now. "My learned friends of the Anglican movement tell me . . ." "The heretics and infidels would say, etc., etc." "The fool hath said in his heart there is no God." Well, let the fool say it in the pulpit too, and have your first-class Christian preacher there to tell him to his face that he's a liar, and see if the Churches don't fill. With sermons, believe me, it isn't what you say; it's how you say it.

FÉNELON: And you believe that the future of the pulpit depends upon open argument?

EUTYCHUS: Oh, that's just one little suggestion. You fellows are far cleverer than I am, but I want you to understand it's just the ordinary man's idea I'm trying to get across to you. You've got to advertise your preachers more. It can be done. Look at Aimée Macpherson in the States. Sister Aimée. Not but what she overdid it a bit, getting kidnapped and found in a bathing-tent and all that. It's no use scaring away the pussyfoots and sober-sides. They'll make the bulk of your congregation if you catch them in the right way. No, a good fine, understanding publicity agent, not too coarse-minded, you understand, who'ld put nice little bits in *Home Gossip* and *The Daily Mirror* and so on—just glimpses of the Home Life of a Favourite Preacher, or "My Ideal Marriage" by a bunch of prime good-looking young reverends. That'ld bring 'em in to the fold. Something homely and domestic for the women and a few good sporting items for the men.

From EUTYCHUS, by Winifred Holtby (1898–1935)

121

THE LEAVE-TAKING

FATHER: Come in, my boy, shut the door . . . sit down, sit down . . . *mind* where you sit, boy.

EDWARD: Oh!

FATHER: Upon my soul, Edward, you might look what you're doing.

EDWARD: I'm sorry, father.

FATHER: You've smudged it, too . . .

EDWARD: What is it, father?

FATHER: What is it? What is it? It's my meteorological chart . . . haven't you any eyes in your head?

EDWARD: I didn't expect to find it in an armchair, father.

FATHER: Oh, well . . . ah-hum . . . I was just writing it up and . . . it was . . . it wasn't . . . er . . . but, sit down, sit down, sit down. I want to talk to ye. Have a cigar.

EDWARD: No, thank you, father.

FATHER: Eh? Oh, very well. Have a cigarette.

EDWARD: No, thanks.

FATHER: What? Ain't you smoking?

EDWARD: Er . . . no . . . you see, father, it's . . . er . . . Lent.

FATHER (*expressively*): Hm! . . . Well, so you're off to Belfast.

EDWARD: Yes, father.

FATHER: When do you go?

EDWARD: Wednesday. . . . I have to go by the early train.

FATHER: But . . . that'll mean starting in the dark.

EDWARD: I know. But, otherwise it means stopping a night on the way.

FATHER: You've made arrangements where to stay . . . in Belfast, I mean?

EDWARD: Well, no . . . at least, yes, in a way. My vicar's going to put me up till I get settled into digs.

FATHER: Hm. . . . I see.

EDWARD: I believe there are plenty of good digs.

FATHER: Well . . . er . . . see here, my boy . . . I know a curate's screw isn't . . . well . . . well, I mean it isn't easy to make ends

meet, and your mother and I would like to feel you weren't . . .
I mean, some of these fellows have perhaps been accustomed to
manage on less than you . . .

EDWARD: Oh, but father, I . . .

FATHER: Will you let me *finish*, boy. . . . What I mean is . . .
well . . . where was I? . . . oh, yes . . . what I mean is, your mother
and I . . . that is I . . . oh, damn it all, here's a cheque to supplement
your pay, and there'll be another at Christmas. Here!

EDWARD: Oh, father, it's most awfully g-g-g-good of you . . . it
is, really . . . most awfully . . . but I . . . well, I'd rather n-not
t-take it.

FATHER: What? Eh? Eh? What's that?

EDWARD: No, father, I'd rather not take it . . . really. I'd rather
manage on what I earn.

FATHER: Pooh! Nonsense, boy, nonsense, take it and don't be a
damned fool.

EDWARD: No, father, it's awfully good of you, and I'd love to
take it, but——

FATHER: Well, take it, then . . . take it, and don't make such a
fuss about it.

EDWARD: No, I can't, father. Thanks, very much. I can't *really*.

FATHER: But, why on earth not?

EDWARD: Well, I don't want to be different from the other
men that are in the Church . . . I mean, most of them aren't . . .
well, their people can't afford to . . .

FATHER: Damme, I know that as well as you . . . but, it's quite
different for them . . . they're used to doing without things that
you . . .

EDWARD: Yes, father, but that's just what I don't like . . . I
want to be on an absolutely equal footing with the others.

FATHER: Hm . . . Socialism.

EDWARD: Yes, if you l-like to c-call it so.

FATHER: In other words, you want to abrogate the status of your
family.

EDWARD: No, father, it's got nothing to do with family.

FATHER: But it *has* . . .

EDWARD: It *hasn't* . . . it's simply a question of m-money.

FATHER: No it *isn't* . . . it's a question of the Fitness of Things. But there it is . . . there it is . . . it's always been the same with you. You're not like one of the family at all.

EDWARD: I'm afraid I'm n-n-not.

FATHER: Now if you'd wanted to go into the army or into the navy even . . . but the Church! However, it's your life, my boy, not mine, thank God . . . you must just do whatever you think best. (*Now very kindly and charmingly*) But I wish you'd take the cheque.

EDWARD: N-no, father . . . but . . . thank you.

FATHER (*blustering because his feelings have been touched*): All right, all right, all right . . . no need to thank me for what you haven't got.

EDWARD: No, father, I'm very sorry. . . .

FATHER: Oh, don't be sorry, my boy, I'm not sorry . . . not at all . . . I'm very glad . . . I can find plenty of use for the money . . . it'll just put a roof on the new lodge at Mullaghmore. But it's late and you've an early start . . . you'd better be getting to bed.

EDWARD: Yes, father, are you c-coming?

FATHER: Well, I suppose it's about time . . . it must be nearly twelve.

EDWARD: I'll light your candle. Did you shut the hall-door?

FATHER: Yes, I shut it when your mother went to bed.

EDWARD: Your candle.

FATHER: Thanks . . . glass is falling.

EDWARD: Is it?

FATHER: Rain to-morrow . . . 'fraid you'll have it wet for starting. . . . You might put out the lamp . . . oh, *blow*, man, *blow* . . . here, I'll do it myself.

EDWARD: Can you see where you're going?

FATHER: Hold your candle *straight*, boy, you'll spill the grease. . . . Oh *damn* that chair. (*In the dark he has stumbled against it.*)

EDWARD: Good night, father.

FATHER: Good night.

EDWARD: And father . . .

FATHER: Eh?

EDWARD: I do hope you're not offended.

FATHER: Offended? . . . ho . . . er . . . why on earth should I be?

EDWARD: At my not t-taking the cheque.

FATHER: No—no—no—Good Lord, no, not at all . . . of course I can't help feeling a bit . . . well . . . sorry that . . . but don't lets talk of it again.

EDWARD: No . . . I wish . . .

FATHER: Well?

EDWARD: I wish I could have been more . . . well, you'd like to have seen me in the Regiment.

FATHER: Oh well . . .

EDWARD: I wish I could have been a more satisfactory sort of son . . . from your point of view.

FATHER: Eh? . . . Ach, away to Hell, son, and don't be morbid . . . and for the love of the Lord *hold that candle straight*.

From THE FLOWERS ARE NOT FOR YOU
TO PICK, by Tyronne Guthrie (1900–).

122

FAVOURITE SERMON

THE vicar climbed, with some effort, into the pulpit. He was an endlerly man who had served in India most of his life. Tony's father had given him the living at the instance of his dentist. He had a noble and sonorous voice and was reckoned the best preacher for many miles around.

His sermons had been composed in his more active days for delivery at the garrison chapel; he had done nothing to adapt them to the changed conditions of his ministry and they mostly concluded with some reference to homes and dear ones far away. The villagers did not find this in any way surprising. Few of the things said in church seemed to have any particular reference to themselves. They enjoyed their vicar's sermons very much and they knew that when he began about their distant homes, it was time to be dusting their knees and feeling for their umbrellas.

". . . And so as we stand here bareheaded at this solemn hour of the week," he read, his powerful old voice swelling up for the peroration, " let us remember our Gracious Queen Empress in whose service we are here, and pray that she may long be spared to send us at her bidding to do our duty in the uttermost parts of the earth; and let us think of our dear ones far away and the homes we have left in her name, and remember that though miles of barren continent and leagues of ocean divide us, we are never so near to them as on these Sunday mornings, united with them across dune and mountain in our loyalty to our sovereign and thanksgiving for her welfare; one with them as proud subjects of her sceptre and crown."

("The Reverend Tendril e do speak uncommon igh of the Queen," a gardener's wife had once remarked to Tony.)

After the choir had filed out, during the last hymn, the congregation crouched silently for a few seconds and then made for the door. There was no sign of recognition until they were outside among the graves; then there was an exchange of greetings, solicitous, cordial, garrulous.

Tony spoke to the vet's wife and Mr. Partridge from the shop; then he was joined by the vicar.

"Lady Brenda is not ill, I hope?"

"No, nothing serious." This was the invariable formula when he appeared at Church without her. "A most interesting sermon, vicar."

"My dear boy, I'm delighted to hear you say so. It is one of my favourites. But have you never heard it before?"

"No, I assure you."

"I haven't used it here lately. When I am asked to supply elsewhere it is the one I invariably choose."

. . . . .

That Christmas the vicar preached his usual Christmas sermon. It was one to which his parishioners were greatly attached.

"How difficult it is for us," he began, blandly surveying his congregation, who coughed into their mufflers and chafed their chilblains under their woollen gloves, "to realise that this is indeed Christmas. Instead of the glowing log fire and windows tight shuttered against the drifting snow, we have only the harsh glare of an alien sun; instead of the happy circle of loved faces, of home and family, we have the uncomprehending stares of the subjugated, though no doubt grateful, heathen. Instead of the placid ox and ass of Bethlehem," said the vicar, slightly losing the thread of his comparisons, "we have for companions the ravening tiger and the exotic camel, the furtive jackal and the ponderous elephant . . ." And so on, through the pages of faded manuscript. The words had temporarily touched the heart of many an obdurate trooper, and hearing them again, as he had heard them year after year since Mr. Tendril had come to the parish, Tony and most of Tony's guests felt that it was an integral part of their Christmas festivities; one with which they would find it very hard to dispense. "The ravening tiger and the exotic camel" had long been bywords in the family, of frequent recurrence in all their games.

From A HANDFUL OF DUST,
by Evelyn Waugh (1903–   ).

123

"JUNGLEMEN OR GENTLEMEN?"

THE exciting week worked up to a climax on the Sunday when all Christian people in Hollywood gathered in church for special ceremonials. Every preacher had announced a sermon on the topic of the hour. Ma insisted on Ed coming to church. She took longer than usual over her toilet, put on every number-one item in her wardrobe and spent ten minutes rubbing the spots off Ed's tie. They were seated in a front pew of the First Methodist Church more than half an hour before the starting time. A few minutes later every place was taken and people were beginning to be turned away at the door. The congregation were all dressed as for Easter or Christmas and wore on their faces a special solemnity. They realised the eyes of the whole world were upon them and they looked to the Pastor to speak for them in no uncertain voice. The topic that had been announced was "Junglemen or Gentlemen?"

The choral and gymnastic preliminaries over, Ma sat in her pew with hands neatly folded in her lap and coughed twice with reverent expectancy. The Pastor began to speak and warmed rapidly to his theme. He used the names of Caligula and Nero to brush in the first strokes of his picture. The Arbuckle party was not art; in a land of clean sunlight, wholesome breezes and God-praising larks, it was leprosy—it was the jungle ... turpitude ... decay ... rotten-ness ... bacchanalian revel ... orgy ... debauchery ... sordid ... lecherous ... besotted, animalistic. "Nothing has ever been done more to discredit the cause of labour unionism than the way they stood by Haywood, the MacNamaras and Mooney. The moving picture world stands at the same crossroads." The Pastor leaned forward in his pulpit, his eyes flashing. Most to blame were people like themselves in that church, who had let the light of ideals flicker. "Do you suppose," he cried, "if men and women really cared for folks that they could find fun in the brazen shame of nearly nude women?" Ma sat quite still, wanted to glance at Ed but restrained herself. A comfortable glow inside her betrayed the Holy Ghost at work, castigating her for her sins, cleansing her for

314

the Lord. The Pastor's words melted together so that she both heard them and did not hear.

There was a brief silence. The Pastor waited for his stormy adjectives to sink in before proceeding to the final message in a lower, graver key.

"A gentleman," he said, "is the finest product of God's universe . . . God's angels are paging the corridors of California for gentlemen to roll back the jungle. Pray God they call our name."

From THE PROMISED LAND, by
Cedric Belfrage (1904–   ).

124
ULTIMATE JUDGMENT

WITHIN the sunny greenness of the close,
Secure, a heavy breathing fell, then rose—
Here undulating chins sway to and fro,
As heavy blossoms do; the cheek's faint glow
Points to post-prandial port. The willow weeps,
Hushed are the birds—in fact—the Bishop sleeps.

Then, suddenly, the wide sky blazes red;
Up from their graves arise the solemn dead,
The world is shaken; buildings fall in twain,
Exulting hills shout loud, then shout again
While, with the thunder of deep rolling drums
The angels sing—— At last Salvation comes.
The weak, the humble, the disdained, the poor
Are judged the first, and climb to Heaven's door.

.   .   .   .   .

The Bishop wakes to see his palace crash
Down on the rocking ground—but in a flash

It dawns upon him. With impressive frown,
He sees his second-housemaid in a crown,
In rainbow robes that glisten like a prism.
"I warned them . . ." said the Bishop—
    "Bolshevism!"

By Sir Osbert Sitwell (1892–   ).

JUDGMENT FROM PARNASSUS

By THE COMPILER.

IT has been said that the parson to-day takes the place that in
medieval times was occupied by the Jew: he is the recognised
butt only needing to trip at his entrance upon the stage to set up
a roar of appreciative laughter. In fact it would be easy to furnish
plenty of examples from the modern theatre (to take the suggestion
literally for a moment) of clerics who are treated seriously both as
human beings and as spiritual teachers. The bishop and his Anglo-
Catholic chaplain in *Getting Married* and the Christian Socialist in
Candida are sincere and gifted clerical types to match the less
amiable portraits from Shaw's galaxy. The country vicar in
Galsworthy's *Escape*, torn between the charity that would shelter
the hunted fugitive and a scrupulous regard for the truth, is anything
but contemptible either as a human being or as a priest. Mr.
St. John Ervine held up more than one cleric for our respect in
Robert's Wife, and Mr. Sutton Vane put the seal of divine as well
as human approval upon his clergyman in *Outward Bound*. Clergymen have been attacked in the twentieth century both for what
they proclaim and for what they evade; but modern writers are
far from representing them all as congenitally feeble like the curate
in *The Private Secretary*. But it is true, I think, that whether
harmless or offensive, curates are seldom treated with much respect.
The fatuous triumvirate in *Shirley* are more characteristic of what
literature has to say about them than the humble tragic figure in

316

Mr. Tyrone Guthrie's radio drama, *The Flowers are not for You to Pick*. The reason is, perhaps, that the parson more than any other man must acquire understanding through experience. The selflessness through which alone the finest spiritual values can be achieved has to be learnt in the hardest of all schools. "South Wales," Mr. Lloyd George once observed, "has given us two things—curates and coals. I leave you to judge which has given us more warmth and light." Substitute "ministers" for "curates," and the gibe would lose much of its sting. The youthful holy man, counselling those immeasurably wiser and more experienced than himself is slightly ridiculous. The absurdity is not quite so sharply felt in the case of the Romish priest, who from the beginning, is trained to be a spiritual counsellor, and is supposed to learn in the seminary a wisdom that the Protestant cleric must acquire slowly from life.

I

A volume would be required to trace the changes in clerical beliefs and habits since the days of Chaucer. Yet some characteristics, if literature is to be trusted, have been very persistent, and common to all denominations. Least attractive, perhaps, is the acrimonious bigotry that has led to the embitterment of theological disputes.

The bitterness of yesterday's sectarian controversy seems almost unbelievable to-day. The passage quoted from Dr. Wingfield Stratford describes it amusingly enough for the second half of the nineteenth century, and Macaulay provides an unconscious witness to the virulence of the sects in the earlier years of the century. He ends his graphic description of the trial of the seven bishops, when opposition to Rome brought a few astonishing days' respite in the violent conflict between Establishment and Dissent, by saying that it was absurd to expect the Churches to show mutual goodwill after the common foe had been defeated; and he was neither condemning nor mocking, but merely expressing the common-sense view of the eighteen-forties when he was writing. For although a childhood surrounded by the fervours of the

Clapham sect had left him so bored by religion that he might be described as an indifferentist rather than an agnostic, Thomas "Babbletongue" was always careful to speak of religion in conventional if evasive terms.

The ethical laxness of the preceding century did little or nothing to weaken clerical intolerance, as the opposition to the Methodists shows. "When I mention religion," says Parson Thwackum in *Tom Jones*, "I mean the Christian religion; and not only the Christian religion, but the Protestant religion; and not only the Protestant religion, but the Church of England. And when I mention honour I mean that mode of divine grace which is not only consistent with, but dependent upon, this religion; and is consistent with and dependent upon no other."

The famous passage from *Hudibras* about the errant saints who—

> "Decide all controversies by
> Infallible artillery,
> And prove their doctrine orthodox
> By apostolic blows and knocks;
> Call fire and sword and desolation
> A godly, thorough Reformation,
> Which always must be carried on
> And still be doing, never done;
> As if religion were intended
> For nothing else but to be mended,"

recalls the tragic violence of the seventeenth-century disputes, while Fox provides a grim if gossipy reminder of the days when to be a Protestant was as risky as being a Romanist, and an easy-going conformity to whatever the court ordained, without discussing particulars, was the only safe course.

It is scarcely necessary to remark that sectarian bitterness is not confined to the clergy, and the mental anguish of the cleric who is more liberal than his parishioners has been a fairly common theme of novelists. But it is a comparatively late development, due to literature reflecting the intellectual torments of post-Darwinian society. The parson in these cases usually acquires greater charity because he has lost faith in the creed he once professed, and can therefore no longer share the narrow complacency of his flock. In the more illiterate centuries, however, the professional exponent of religion must obviously bear much of the responsibility for the hard intolerance characterising the sects. In one of his lighter stories dealing with conditions a little more than a hundred years ago, Hardy describes the large attendance at the Methodist church on those moonless nights when the villagers could pass the vicarage without betraying their purpose.

After the Gorham case in 1863, when Lord Chancellor Westbury "dismissed hell with costs," a good deal of the vigour went out of theological controversy, and when the tension between Anglicans and Dissenters ran to bitterness, it was on predominately social and political rather than theological grounds. But whatever fluctuating importance attaches to theological controversy, literature speaks with no uncertain voice about the conflict between the sects having been exacerbated by clerical jealousy. Professional rivalry expressing itself through thundering anathemas or whispered spite is one of the commonest themes for amusement or indignation, from the broad comedy of the quarrel between Chaucer's pardoner and friar to the cold righteousness of Stevenson's *Open Letter to Dr. Hyde* concerning Father Damien.

The servile readiness of the clergy to flatter the great and to dance attendance upon the wealthy, provokes a good deal of criticism, grave and gay, from Langland's—

"Bishops and bachelors, both masters and doctors,
   Who have cares under Christ and are crowned with the tonsure,
   In sign of their service to shrive the parish,
   To pray and preach and give the poor nourishment,
   Lodge in London in Lent and the long year after.
   Some are counting coins in the King's chamber,
   Or in exchequer and chancery challenging his debts
   From wards and wardnotes, waifs and strays.
   Some serve as servants to lords and ladies
   And sit in the seats of stewards and butlers,"

319

down to the vicar in Masefield's *Everlasting Mercy* who taught—

". . . the ground-down starving man
That squire's greed's Jehovah's plan."

2

A good deal can be said to mitigate the harshness of unfavourable literary comment on the parson. Some of the criticism, indeed, is a witness to clerical honesty. Langland, who was in minor orders, not only damns the greed, sophistry and lechery of friars with great heartiness, but laments his own youthful incontinence. It is Colet the preacher who exclaims "O Jesus Christ, wash for us not our feet only, but our hands and our *head*, or our disordered Church cannot be far from death." Crabbe wrote devastatingly about parsons in the eighteenth century; but it is obviously unfair to quote him against them without remembering that he was a parson himself. Literature in fact shows the power of self-purification as well as the corruption at work in the Church.

It need scarcely be said that professional jealousy, love of power, and a readiness to flatter the rich are not confined to the clergy, but are all too common among men of all classes in every age. Nor is it possible to say to what extent human nature is defamed by the collective witness of literature. While the first duty of the writer is to be honest, the only fault certain to damn him is to be dull, and it is probably easier to be lively and entertaining about the follies than about the virtues of mankind, if for no other reason because much goodness, particularly clerical goodness, is a matter of habit, unostentatious, self-consistent, dependable, but in no way dramatic.

Fiction, although it provides valuable data for the social historian, is under no obligation to tell the whole truth. After the early years of the nineteenth century, when the evangelical discipline had banished the grosser forms of self-indulgence from society and brought at least the form of godliness into the Church, the hard-drinking, fox-hunting parson takes his place in English novels as a disreputable figure. Indeed, both Cowper and Crabbe condemned him very strongly in the eighteenth century. Yet it would be possible to read countless novels from Thackeray onwards without gaining an inkling of the valuable field-work done by innumerable clerical naturalists, to which an extract from White of Selborne serves as a witness in the present anthology.

It is altogether outside the scope of the present discussion to consider the theological importance of their work, but it may be noted in passing that the sympathetic approach to the animal creation has affinities with the universal charity of the mystic. If the spiritual interpretation of reality is true, the naturalist may achieve an insight into the character of living creatures that is hidden from the vivisecting biologist. It is in any case grossly unfair to denounce the parson who hunts the fox and forget the parson who has lovingly observed and chronicled the ways of the badger.

3

Yet there is obviously more significance in the castigation parsons have suffered at the hands of so many writers than can be accounted for by the fact that, in seeking to be entertaining literature like journalism, tends to emphasise the exceptional and sensational. By his very office, the parson is a witness to a standard of values and a way of life that should not merely rebuke the evil society condemns; it should challenge many of the standards society allows and approves. Goodness of this quality is certainly not dull, as more conventional morality is apt to be, but those who display it will often create an opposition to their own worldly advancement. In many eventualities the parson can be true to his own centre only by being eccentric in a worldly sense.

The parson who is successful in gaining ecclesiastical preferment is accordingly seldom held up for our admiration in literature, and especially is pulpit eloquence regarded with mistrust. Like acting, preaching is an art which makes the practitioner immediately aware of the influence he is exerting, and the temptation to self-display, conscious or otherwise, must be very strong. When the preacher is a careerist, gratifying his egotism by the impression he creates, it is all too probable that, like Charles

Honeyman, he will avoid painful topics. The pulpit then becomes a coward's castle, not because the listeners are unable to answer back, but because they have no desire to do so, the sermon being designed to flatter their religious and social prejudices, and only to expose those sins whose condemnation they will approve. This is the marrow of the complaint against parsons, whether it be the Archbishops in Shakespeare's *Henry V* approving the King's desire to go to war, Mr. Collins fawning on his patron when the squirearchy ruled, or Bishop in *Little Dorritt* addressing himself reverentially to a financial wizard of the mid-nineteenth century when commercial power was in the ascendent. Being nowise different from other men, they are not sinners, but traitors. "As a Priest or Interpreter of the Holy, is the noblest and highest of all men," in Carlyle's words, "so is the Sham-priest (Schein-priester) the falsest and basest."

An amusing example of Honeyman's ability to gloss the more disturbing features of Christian ethics is provided by an American exposition of *Lay not up for yourselves treasures on earth where moth and rust do corrupt.* "No sensible American," the ingenious expositor assured his approving auditors, "ever does. Moth and rust do not get at Mr. Rockefeller's oil-wells, and thieves do not break through and steal a railway. What Jesus condemned was hoarding wealth." The Vicar of Bray in Prior's *Dialogues of the Dead* was not more blandly on the side of the reigning powers.

It is quite impossible to form the slightest conception of the number of preachers who have been either egotistical or hypocritical by interrogating literature, or to gauge in any way the value of preaching. The rewards of the popular preacher are no different from those of the successful practitioner of any other art, and he is therefore not a good subject for the literary artist who wishes to show that more than human impulses are at work to keep religion alive. The case is at once altered when immediate danger waits upon the proclamation of sincerely held beliefs, and George Eliot, with her study of Savonarola in *Romola*, and Shorthouse, with his study of Molinos in *John Inglesant*, turned to historical instances of the defiance of threatening powers in seeking to show the pulpit glowing with the fire of a more than human eloquence.

4

There is, however, another and very different kind of fervour that English writers have saluted in the clerical ranks, and in which they have discerned the kindling of a more than human spirit. It is that of the poor parson who, in the midst of a scramble for ecclesiastical place and honour, is content to work in ill-paid obscurity, never despising the dull and intractable human material that he must try to shape to a heavenly pattern.

To describe him as the poor parson is inexact, however. Evangelical windbags like Stiggins and Chadband were relatively poor, but compared with the rewards their qualifications could be expected to earn in any other walk of life they were making a comfortable living out of oleaginous humbug. The poor parson whom the imaginative writers call blessed is characterised by learning quite as much as by worldly obscurity and poverty. No doubt integrity without learning is admirable. George Eliot made a deeply-moving study of a parson who has admirable qualities although he is ignorant as well as poor in Amos Barton. But George Eliot's psychological insight and measureless compassion continually prompted her to find the redeeming features in lame dogs and ugly ducklings; and Amos Barton is the exception that proves the rule. It is precisely the learning of the poor cleric that touches his threadbare neediness with nobility. He has gifts that would sell, and instead of selling them, whether in the ecclesiastical market or elsewhere, he dedicates them to the service of the common man, being quite indifferent and often quite innocent of the things that pertain to worldly success.

The prototype of this recurring figure is found, of course, in *The Canterbury Tales*. Although he is devout, patient and benign as well as learned, Chaucer's poor parson is far from being a mere assemblage of virtues. His creator does not forget to breathe into his nostrils the breath of life, and he is as convincingly real as the sleek clerics in whose company he is found at the Tabard Inn. Reluctant to collect his tithes, ever ready to help the poor from his own scanty funds, and visiting the most distant member of his scattered parish "upon his feet" instead of ambling to London after preferment, "he taught the love of Christ, but first followed it himself." Being free from social ambitions he was equally free from inhibitions when the need for plain speaking to his social superiors arose. Chaucer had no more doubt about the revolutionary force of Christian love than John Ball or Conrad Noel.

The second most famous instance is Parson Adams in Fielding's *Joseph Andrews*. There are several other examples in the eighteenth century, including the paragon of *The Deserted Village*; but Parson Adams is of special interest because his creator so obviously set out to scoff and remained to pray. Parson Adams, like Mr. Pickwick, begins by being a mere figure of fun. His tattered cassock hanging below an ancient discoloured coat, his poverty and absent-mindedness, combine to make him a grotesque; and Fielding drags him through one farcical episode after another. Even his learning seems at first to have been intended as a joke; as nothing but a pedantic obsession with the minutiæ of Æschylus. But without losing his childishness, Adams becomes splendidly childlike as the story progresses, as though his creator only slowly came to appreciate his worth. Especially in his indifference to class distinctions in an age when the social code was harsh and rigid, does his magnificent childlikeness appear. The young footman in whose company he is travelling expresses surprise at his honour's condescension. "Child, I should be ashamed of my cloth," he replies, "if I thought a poor man below my notice or familiarity." It is part of the joke, of course, that in a literal sense, Adams had every reason to be ashamed of his cloth, but he has that inner beatitude than can lift a man above all sense of inferiority, no matter how low his outward fortunes may have sunk. "I know not," he continues, "how those who think otherwise can profess themselves followers and servants of Him who made no distinction, unless, peradventure by preferring the poor to the rich." As in the case of Chaucer's poor parson, the unworldliness of Parson Adams makes him bold to rebuke the rich and powerful when occasion demands; and his creator was no less conscious than Chaucer of the social upheaval Christian practice must cause. But an age like our own which has learnt that the dread of inferiority is a great breeder of tyranny, may well regard the inner serenity of Adams as far more significant than his political courage.

Johnson's claim that nowhere were the poor better treated than in England seems astonishingly complacent remembering the distress caused by the Enclosure Acts, though the scale of private charity and conditions in Europe lent some justification to the remark. But the eighteenth century, with all its coarseness and brutality, never knew the stench, degradation, and tortured wretchedness of the slums in the ensuing century. For the parson to descend and share their stifling horrors was a harder test than to endure poverty in the age of Fielding and Smollett. In *East London* Matthew Arnold offers a contemporary tribute to his splendour; and Mr. Michael Sadleir and Mr. Howard Spring in recent years have given arresting character studies of the nineteenth-century slum parson, voluntarily enduring the grey miseries of Manchester and the squalid viciousness of South-East London.

5

Charlotte Brontë's mocking portrayal of the "youthful Levites" in *Shirley* was qualified by her characteristically intense admiration for the Rev. Cyril Hall, "an accomplished scholar" whose practical charity matches his learning. While the rest of the clergy are concerned most about the lawlessness and political menace of the Luddite disturbances, Hall is troubled by the human sufferings that have provoked them, and sets himself unobtrusively to relieve the grim poverty of the workers and to soften their resentment.

Hall is rather too unobtrusive and too comfortably placed however to be in lineal descent from Chaucer's poor parson. He recalls "that class of modest divines" of whom Charles Lamb speaks, "who affect to mix in equal proportions the *gentleman*, the *scholar* and the *Christian*; but, I know not how, the first ingredient is generally found to be the predominating dose in the composition."

Not that there was the slightest affectation about Hall. He was a gentleman in the most praiseworthy sense, displaying a refined considerateness for social inferiors; but he was a gentleman also as the term is used to define social rank, quite apart from ethical attainments, as the poor parson in *The Canterbury Tales* and Parson Adams were not. Neither as priest nor prophet does Hall stand apart from society to challenge or inspire. He is the gentlemanly amateur of Anglicanism who sets a good example within the existing social traditions, but never questions their ethical validity.

Hazlitt's famous description of the Dissenting Minister, written when Charlotte Brontë was in her cradle, presents a startling contrast to Hall's placid acceptance of the social order and the Christian charity that was invoked to relieve poverty, but not to remove injustice. "They were true priests. They set up an image in the mind—it was truth; they worshipped an idol—it was justice. They looked on man as their brother, and only bowed the knee to the Highest. . . . Their sympathy was not with the oppressors but the oppressed. They cherished in their thoughts, and wished to transmit to their posterity, those rights and privileges for asserting which their ancestors had bled on scaffolds, or had pined in dungeons or in foreign climes." Hazlitt, it will be noticed, writes in the past tense. He recognised the worldliness that had set like a hard crust over the fires of Dissent. Sobriety and thriftiness in earlier generations had created powerful vested interests in the treasures of earth. "It is a pity," Hazlitt continued, "that this character has worn itself out; that that pulse of thought and feeling has ceased almost to beat in the heart of the nation." Thirty years later, when *Shirley* appeared, Dr. Jabez Bunting, the President of the Wesleyan Conference, was declaring "Wesleyanism is as much opposed to democracy as to sin." A violent upsurge of ethical protest and social discontent was splitting Methodism and helping to win recognition for the trade unions.

6

This side idolatry, the gentlemanly amateur of Establishment was much admired by Trollope, whose aim in the Barchester novels was to draw parsons "neither better nor worse than they are." He disliked the low Church nominees, like Obadiah Slope, who, after the conversion of Manning and the anti-Romanist scare, were everywhere thrusting their way into Anglican pulpits. He disapproved of absentee pluralists, like Dr. Vesey Stanhope, as much as he disapproved of landlords who neglected their estates. For the rest he was fairly well satisfied with the social and ethical compromises of mid-Victorian England. The Rev. Francis Arabin, a fellow of Lazarus College, Oxford, had almost followed Newman to Rome. "Forty years," Trollope tells us, "had passed over Mr. Arabin's head, and as yet woman's beauty had never given him an uneasy hour." Eleanor Bold gave him many. "A Romish priest," he reflected, "would have escaped all this." His creator sees to it before the end of the book that he has substantial reasons, including a charming wife and a handsome income, to banish all regrets about Rome.

Trollope's clerics have no taste for meddling with the established order of things, or for exploring foundations, theological or economic. Clergymen who denounced Sabbath-breaking as fiercely as Rev. Obadiah Slope wore clothes made by tailors who could only live by working seven days a week, and frequently starved to death even then. About such matters the cloth knew nothing. "Had the question been the investment of a few pounds in speculation," as Kingsley reminded the readers of *Alton Locke*, "these gentlemen would have been careful enough about good security. Ought they to take no security when investing their money in clothes that they are not putting on their backs accursed garments . . . reeking with the sighs of the starving?" The clergy on the whole thought not, and Trollope was disposed to agree with them. St. Paul might rejoice that Christ was preached through faction, but the worst consequences were to be anticipated from social reform advanced in a similar way.

Hence, when John Bold discovers that the rich clerical sinecure established through the increased value of Hiram's charity is wholly false to the founder's bequest, and refuses to suppress the information, the worst sufferers, as Trollope shows in *The Warden*, are the old pensioners on whose behalf John Bold fought. Instead of being gratefully content with their daily pittance, as heretofore, the twelve old men are stirred to greed and envy. Only the well-to-do in Trollope's world can pursue wealth without becoming spiritually poorer. In the poor parson he finds little to admire, though Mr. Quiverful moves him to pity. "The impossible task of bringing up as ladies and gentlemen fourteen children on an income which was insufficient to give them with decency the common necessaries of life, had had an effect upon him not beneficial either to his spirit or his keen sense of honour." Yet in the Rev. Septimus Harding, who renounces the Hiram wardenship because, once the question has been raised, he mistrusts his right to the sinecure, Trollope does after all return to some of the characteristics of the poor parson. But Mr. Harding's sensitive conscience remains entirely untroubled by the dilettante nature of his existence, and he is not left for very long in the ranks of the shabby genteel. If Trollope believed that spiritual power could induce a man to renounce wealth, he had no faith that it could sustain him in poverty with the graces of his character unimpaired.

Admiring though he does the man of sturdy character and good sense who is comfortably adjusted to society and is "careful to stand well with those around him, to shun a breath that might sully his name or a rumour that might affect his honour," Trollope as much as Chaucer and Fielding is driven to acknowledge that the true parson would attack some of the values society approves and not merely the evils it condemns. The conflict is most sharply drawn in *The Vicar of Bullhampton* and the protest the vicar makes against the hard loveless rectitude that persecutes Carry Brattle for her offence against the sexual code. It is difficult to believe that, at the time of publication, the book was regarded as more than a little shocking, but the iconoclastic violence and courage of the vicar of Bullhampton's action can only be realised when that odd fact is given its full weight.

Just because he sought to depict and not to distort, Trollope lights up the disconcerting contradictions involved in assuming an authority that is not of this world, whilst belonging to a profession in which a struggle for place and power is going on in no way distinguished from that in any other worldly guild. The struggle is to some extent forced on the Protestant cleric by family cares; for although, as a follower of Christ, the parson may count the world well lost, it is a nice point of ethics whether he has the right to make a similar renunciation for his wife or children, who may not share his devotional enthusiasm.

The domestic troubles of Bishop Proudie border on farce, while those of Mr. Quiverful verge on tragedy, but comedic and tragic elements alike arise from the fact that the man of God, who is supposed to judge the world, must meekly submit to doing his work by favour of the world; Bishop Proudie in the person of his wife and Mr. Quiverful in the person of his baker.

7

Since the days of Hildebrand the Roman priest has avoided both difficulties. No matter how frugal his living, the unmarried priest can never be harassed by poverty like the parson with a family; and celibacy, by distinguishing the priest from other men, adds force to his claim to belong to a kingdom that is not of this world. If it stimulates his power impulses also (as some psychologists assert), the effect is likely to be felt within the heirarchy, as well as in the Church's struggle for temporal authority. The love of power as the outstanding characteristic of the priest, the fierce battle for ecclesiastical place and authority raging under the cloak of piety, and in distressing or amusing contrast to a profession of meekness, has been a common theme from Heywood to Lytton Strachey.

In the merry play between *Johan Johan the Husband, Tyb His Wife and Sir John the Priest*, the former good humouredly calls attention to a difficulty liable to arise from enforced celibacy, against which good Catholics in Spain are said to insure their families by paying a suitable lady to act as "housekeeper" for the village priest.

The gusto with which English writers from the sixteenth century to the middle of the nineteenth dwelt on the darker aspects of Romanism has not entirely flagged even to-day—witness Mr. H. G. Wells's *Crux Astasia*; but Rome has ceased to be the common enemy helping to create a sense of unity within the nation, and even Wells was unable to arouse any enthusiasm with the cry of "No Popery." Borrow could still write as though the inevitable fate of the Romanist was to be "misgoverned in this world and condemned in the next," and he depicted priests as sinister agents engaged in plotting the overthrow of the country. When Kingsley in the 'sixties accused Newman of bad faith instead of mistaken polemics, the country was still influenced by the scare of the Tractarian apostasy. It had considerably abated when *The Ring and the Book*, with its sympathetic study of a Pope, was published at the beginning of the next decade. That Browning discovered a saint inside the Pope was not very remarkable, however, because Browning was always finding virtue in strange places; it was part of his dramatic technique. But the enormous popularity of Shorthouse's *John Inglesant*, published in 1881, is a social if not a literary portent, for it shows how rapidly intolerance was declining. When at the end of the century Rider Haggard, in *Montezuma's Daughter*, made a dubious reference to the cruelty of the Inquisition, it became "the subject of much public dispute," and the author "expressed his regret that, in all good faith, he should have set down as fact that which has been proved to be a matter of controversy." A. E. W. Mason, returning in the nineteen-thirties to the somewhat faded romance of the struggle between Elizabeth and Philip, neatly drew the sting from the religious conflict by causing his sixteenth-century hero to foresee the reconciliation of warring Christians within the universal embrace of the Cross; and the Romish case for the forcible suppression of religious heresy expounded in a magnificent speech by the Inquisitor in *Saint Joan* was not regarded, like Mr. Shaw's efforts to justify Stalin's inquisitorial methods of dealing with political heretics, as perverse. The intolerance of the seventeenth century, when Burton could quote with mournful approval "the lewdest priests are preferred to be cardinals, and the baddest man among the cardinals is chosen to be Pope," has now almost entirely disappeared.

Much of the decline in bigotry must be traced to a decline in religious conviction of any sort. Toleration is easy in an atmosphere of indifference. One of Chesterton's earliest fantasies, *The Ball and the Cross*, is concerned with the misadventures of a Scotch Catholic who defends the Faith with dogged rationalism, and a Cockney Rationalist who attacks it with mystical passion. It seems entirely reasonable to the disputants that the intellectual battle should be settled with swords—a view with which their creator enthusiastically agrees. Thwarted by the police in their praiseworthy efforts to wipe out religious differences with blood, the sworn enemies have to resist a recurring temptation to amity, to which they are drawn by their mutual hatred of a world that was ceasing to find religious disputes a cause for hatred and violence.

Shared enmity perhaps inspires more goodwill, religious as well as political, than we usually care to admit. While indifference has for the churchless multitudes practically wiped out the old sectarian asperity, the denominations themselves have been drawn closer together by their common fear and dislike of a world that is ceasing to take any religious dogmas or practices seriously. In both ways the cause of tolerance is served.

A more genuine forbearance and goodwill has sprung up between missionaries of rival denominations in distant lands. Not only does it appear scandalous to drag new converts into the festering bitterness of schismatical disputes, not only do the intricacies of such disputes greatly add to the difficulties of expounding a Gospel of love to the adherents of other faiths, but in lonely stations remote from the influence of ecclesiastical boards the disputes themselves are apt to appear somewhat trite and ridiculous. The cordiality marking the encounters of the missionary Catholic priest and the Presbyterian medical missionary in *The Keys of the Kingdom* in no way strains probability; and the greater charity of the mission field has not been without its reflex action upon parent bodies.

But the greatest force exerted to break down the traditional British fear and hatred of Rome in recent years has probably been entirely secular. Numbering his patrons in America and Britain by scores of millions, the film producer no more dares to venture into religious controversy than into the battles over domestic politics. Most cinema audiences, particularly the adolescents who are the most regular patrons, are only very loosely connected or wholly unattached to any religious denomination; and they would be bored by the attempt to discuss theology through the medium of the screen. But Christian sentiment is sufficiently diffused to make an occasional excursion into religious themes worth while, and the competitive demand for novelty has attracted film producers to clerical garb as a fancy dress in which to exhibit the attractions of the male idol of the screen. Hence those Protestant clerics or devoted Catholic priests whose manly piety and conventional charity can be trusted not to offend the nicest susceptibilities, except those of the comparatively small band of sincerely religious believers or militant atheists in the audience. The work of the "understanding publicity agent, not too coarse-minded" of Winifred Holtby's *Eutychus*, who would "bring 'em into the fold" by exhibiting "a bunch of prime, good-looking young reverends," is being done by film producers—and for nothing.

For the sentimental purposes of the screen, the Catholic priest is on the whole a safer bet than the Protestant minister, particularly in America, where there is no State Church and the denominational loyalty of the hero raises perplexities. Moreover, Catholicism encourages a simple faith in miracles and retains an air of mystery lacking from the prosaic moralism of the sects, but very adaptable to the sensationalism and glamour of the screen. The very term "Father" gives the Catholic priest a marked advantage over his Protestant rival; it has a universal appeal, at once tender yet authoritative, that arouses the liveliest emotions. "Reverend," by comparison, is not only difficult to say, but is either emotionally colourless or is liable to arouse feelings of derision. The parson is sometimes the butt of the music-hall stage; the priest seldom or never. And Catholicism, which has had more experience of dealing with illiterates, is probably less sensitive about the debasement of religion by the romanticism of the screen, providing the Church is presented in an attractive light.

The last lingering remnant of the fear and dislike of the papacy which was all that many people retained of their Protestant beliefs, under the assaults of the cinema, has broken down. Since literature does not work in a vacuum, but is strongly influenced by current interests and prejudices, it is not unlikely that the priest will find a larger space and more sympathetic treatment in English novels in the immediate future, quite apart from the work of distinctively Catholic writers.

8

Clerical doubt, sending a thin but steady procession of lonely figures from one ministry to another in search of ghostly comfort, or in despair of finding any to make their way out into a world that seems to have little call for their services, could also provide material for a whole volume. The Goreham case, which, as startlingly as the Prayer Book dispute of 1928, revealed the dependence of Anglican beliefs upon the sanction of a political assembly whose vote was influenced by an admixture of sceptics, Nonconformists and Jews, helped to drive Manning out of the Anglican ministry and to prevent Samuel Butler from entering it. *The Way of All Flesh* was Butler's impish but fervent expression of gratitude for his escape. Like marriage, the ministry is easier to enter than to leave. Exceptional ability can overcome the handicap of making a false start to life in the Church, as the names of Leslie Stephen, John Richard Green, Edward Carpenter, and G. C. Coulton bear impressive witness. But what of the man who has no outstanding natural gifts? His social plight, as *The Autobiography of Mark Rutherford* showed, may be dismal indeed. The longer his break with the Church is delayed the harder does the task of finding suitable employment become; yet the mental turmoil before he can summon up the fortitude to snap his bonds is likely to be prolonged.

It is impossible to guess at the number of clerics who in despair of earning a living outside the Church have smothered their doubts, or, with hidden resentment, have continued to repeat the empty phrases of a creed they no longer believe. Only the self-righteous will condemn them. Except in rare instances those who have yielded to economic pressure are in time likely to become reconciled to their lot, and in not a few cases may recover their faith, either because the emotional cause of its disturbance is removed, or

333

because psychological adjustments follow upon economic necessity, as they did for Theobald Pontifex in *The Way of All Flesh*. In saying that the cleric whose living depends upon it will find no difficulty in believing in the resurrection, Samuel Butler stated the matter too flippantly. Once aroused doubts may prove very difficult to lay: but not impossible. Had Karl Marx asserted that the economic is the most constant factor in history, instead of claiming it as the sole determinant of human conduct, he would, says Mr. Lewis Mumford, "have created a sociological synthesis of the first order." Theobald Pontifex is a searching study of the man whose belief is reared on doubt, and whose sour orthodoxy and hatred of unbelief is a necessary consequence of the effort to repress his fears. The most unpleasant hypocrite is often the man who has managed to convince himself of his own sincerity.

More honourable considerations than the economic hold men to the Church after their theological convictions have begun to slip. Only the most ignorant, conceited, and bigoted mortal imagines that his gropings after the similitude of God represent the last word in theological truth. In its long history, the Church has set its approval upon many and varied doctrines, and the sanction for most theological beliefs can somewhere be found in its teaching. Unless the parson has lost all religious conviction, therefore, he can by selective emphasis preach what he sincerely believes, and ignore the rest. Ought he not to do so? His apostasy may discourage simple believers who have trusted to his guidance. Moreover, it will mean the snapping of social ties, the acceptance of a spiritual exile in which his own faith may wither; and all for the sake of some barren negations made public only to assure himself of his intellectual honesty.

In one of those confidences that men will sometimes make to strangers and hide from friends, a Roman priest once told Donald Hankey that he believed in none of the rites or doctrines of his Church. Because men needed the consolations of religion, however, he found no difficulty in fulfilling his office. In the wisdom of the Church he had perfect confidence. His duty was faithfully to obey its instructions. The Church would judge the opportune moment to make known the final religious mystery that God, no longer

334

needed by mankind, was dead. Presumably the Church, like the State in Marxist theory, would then wither away.

So pragmatic a view of the Church and its ministry must be rare, but the thought that they will be stripped of all effectual spiritual influence upon leaving the Church must have inclined many doubting Thomases to conceal the rents in their faith. In *The Soul of a Bishop*, Mr. H. G. Wells described these more subtle influences that reinforce economic pressure and hold men to the service of a creed they no longer fully believe. The book was written during the brief but colourful burgeoning of Mr. Wells's religious faith, and was propagandist and ephemeral; but the interview of the troubled Bishop of Princhester with his old friend and adviser, Bishop Likeman, rises above journalism. The Bishop of Princhester remains the boring mouthpiece of Mr. Wells's tawdry vision of God, but old Bishop Likeman, with his eclectic beliefs and his elastic terminology, with his soaring ideals and swift descent to the cash nexus, is brilliantly alive.

9

So long as Christian theology provided the generally accepted background for social living, clerical hypocrisy was essentially a matter of practice, of failing to live in accordance with the ethical standards enjoined by the Church; but when the intellectual warrant for Christianity was impugned, the sincerity of clerical belief was laid under suspicion. The tension shows itself most clearly in the literature of two periods: in the eighteenth century, when the general acceptance of the fixed mathematical universe of Newton appeared to rule out the possibility of divine activity within nature; and in the late nineteenth century, when the belief in "the survival of the fittest," popularly interpreted as "the survival of the fiercest," appeared to discredit Christian ethics.

In the eighteenth century, Deism saluted God as the inventor and maker of the universe, but reconciled the gesture with loyalty to a deterministic science by insisting that He was too good a mechanic to have to tinker with the works once the contrivance had been set going. Deism was the modernism of its day. It laid a very wholesome emphasis on ethics, but it assumed that science and not religion held the key to truth, and the parson who questioned its cocksure mechanism was either condemned as a humbug who accepted money to teach something he knew to be untrue, or was despised as a fool incapable of understanding what the truth was; a view to which much clerical ignorance, particularly in the remoter country districts, lent considerable support.

The age of reason ended in the Evangelical Revival, whose influence so permeated society in the next century, that, instead of religion being "set up as a principal subject of mirth and ridicule" and altogether unworthy of serious inquiry, as Bishop Butler had said, it was tacitly agreed that it was altogether beyond inquiry. Indeed the attack on the straight-laced religiosity of the age came first not from the cohorts of science, but from the champions of a more exciting and colourful religion. "The High Churchman of 1850," observed Dickens, "was the dandy of 1820 in another form"; but there were more heady excitements as well as more solid virtues in the Tractarian movement than its vestments supplied. It appealed strongly to the ecclesiastical love of power, but it also broke down the narrow parochialism of the English Creed. While its leaven was transforming pious evangelicals like Frank Fordyce in Charlotte Yonge's *Chantry House* into zealous High Churchmen, an intellectual ferment of a very different kind was coming from Germany.

The undergraduate at Oxford, as Miss Yonge's later novels record, was more likely to have his faith tested by un-Christian arguments than to be compelled to resist a religious intoxication that earlier had caused a dangerous lurch Romewards. Although Miss Yonge only hints at the doubts that were unsettling some of her characters, and their misgivings were relieved with enviable ease, it is clear that the age of scientific optimism and religious scepticism has begun. But the earnest moralism of the Evangelical Revival and the self-denial of Tractarianism had left their mark, and toward the end of the century the parson stood an even chance of being scorned as a humbug for professing to believe in Christianity and denounced as a hypocrite for failing to live according to its demands.

10

To no small extent that remains the case to-day; but the collapse of faith in the inevitability of human progress, the physicist's revolt from the mechanistic view of science, the developments in post-Freudian psychology that are more favourable to religious belief, and the tendency in a time of unprecedented social upheaval to seek guidance from tradition, have all combined to create the feeling that the clergyman does not necessarily surrender his intellectual integrity in taking the doctrines of his Church seriously. As a result, there may be a good deal less of the feeling, strongly reflected in the earlier fiction of the twentieth century, that the clergyman as such is a humbug; that socially in evidence he is intellectually in hiding, as Mr. Wells once said of the bishops, or that he has made of theology "a sort of funk-hole for the mind," as Major Martin Fytche-Fytton says in Mr. J. D. Beresford's *Cleo*. The recrudescence of Catholic theology has had a marked influence on poetry and the literary essay as distinct from more strictly polemical writings, and to discuss Christian doctrines or to profess a belief in theological dogmas no longer seems a curious eccentricity or an amusing pose, as it did when Chesterton began his corybantic defence of the Faith at the beginning of the century.

The ethical challenge remains, however, and is being sharpened by the tension with Communism now assuming world dimensions. Since nobody knows how the Communist tension will be resolved, speculation about the future is somewhat idle, and it must in any case be strongly coloured by subjective prejudices and hopes. The frequency in the present century with which the end of the Church has been announced, or its swift recovery by a new out-burst of religious fervour proclaimed, only goes to show that prophets repeat themselves more monotonously than history. The social influence of the Church continues to decline; but the very willingness of the cleric to remain in a profession from which many social advantages have disappeared may serve to reawaken belief in his sincerity. It would be absurd to pretend that the sufferings of the English clergy to-day are in any way ethically impressive, but at least the Church is not the comfortable refuge it once was.

Whether the result of a declining Church revenue will be to make the Church more subservient to the wealthy supporters who remain, or whether it will liberate it from the fear of poverty, and its bondage to middle-class respectability, who can say? "Poverty," as William James said, "*is* the strenuous life—without brass bands or uniforms or hysteric popular applause or lies or circumlocutions; and when one sees the way in which wealth-getting enters as an ideal into the very bone and marrow of our generation, one wonders whether a revival of the belief that poverty is a worthy religious vocation may not be 'the transformation of military courage' and the spiritual reform of which our time stands most in need of. . . ." In a world in which monopoly capitalism and State control are growing, it is not impossible that the Church may be called upon to endure greater hardships if it is to secure its independence.

Literature at least confirms James to the extent of finding in a willingness to face poverty for Christ's sake a most impressive evidence of moral strength, and of the spiritual reality that has inspired it.

INDEX

The darker figures indicate passages in the Anthology.

340

POCKET CLASSICS

Anthony Trollope
The Vicar of Bullhampton £2.95
The Spotted Dog and Other Stories £1.95
Thomas Hardy
Life's Little Ironies £1.95
A Group of Noble Dames £1.95
Wilkie Collins
The Biter Bit and Other Stories £1.95
Sir Arthur Conan Doyle
The Lost World £1.95
Daniel Defoe
Captain Singleton £2.95
Arnold Bennett
Helen with the High Hand £1.95

SOVEREIGN

The Season of the Year, John Moore £4.95
Come Rain, Come Shine, John Moore £4.95
The Life and Letters of Edward Thomas, John Moore £4.95
Portrait of a Village, Francis Brett Young £4.95
The Lost Villages of England, Maurice Beresford £6.95
Old Farm Implements, Philip Wright £4.95
The Parson in English Literature, Edited by F.E. Christmas £5.95
Journal of a Year's Residence in the United States of America,
    William Cobbett £5.95

Available from all good booksellers.
Prices current at August 1983.